Delinquent-Prone Communities

Despite a century of effort, criminologists do not yet fully understand the relationship between disadvantage and crime. The balance of evidence suggests that economic and social stress increase the risk of involvement in crime by increasing the motivation to offend. But there are a number of empirical anomalies that cannot easily be reconciled with this interpretation of the evidence. Weatherburn and Lind argue that the transmission mechanism linking economic and social stress to crime is not offender motivation but disruption to the parenting process. They put forward an epidemic model of the genesis of delinquent-prone communities and show how this model resolves the empirical anomalies facing conventional interpretations of the disadvantage/crime relationship. This book offers compelling new evidence which will stimulate debate in this area of criminology and will also interest academics, policy makers and practitioners in the field.

DON WEATHERBURN is Director of the New South Wales Bureau of Crime Statistics and Research, Australia.

BRONWYN LIND is Deputy Director of the New South Wales Bureau of Crime Statistics and Research, Australia.

Cambridge Criminology Series

Editors:
Alfred Blumstein, *Carnegie Mellon University*
David Farrington, *University of Cambridge*

This series publishes high quality research monographs of either theoretical or empirical emphasis in all areas of criminology, including measurement of offending, explanations of offending, police, courts, incapacitation, corrections, sentencing, deterrence, rehabilitation, and other related topics. It is intended to be both interdisciplinary and international in scope.

Also in the series:

Delinquent-Prone Communities

Don Weatherburn

and

Bronwyn Lind

New South Wales Bureau of Crime Statistics and Research

CAMBRIDGE
UNIVERSITY PRESS

PUBLISHED BY THE PRESS SYNDICATE OF THE UNIVERSITY OF CAMBRIDGE
The Pitt Building, Trumpington Street, Cambridge United Kingdom

CAMBRIDGE UNIVERSITY PRESS
The Edinburgh Building, Cambridge CB2 2RU, UK   www.cup.cam.ac.uk
40 West 20th Street, New York, NY 10011–4211, USA   www.cup.org
10 Stamford Road, Oakleigh, Melbourne 3166, Australia
Ruiz de Alarcón 13, 28014 Madrid, Spain

© Don Weatherburn and Bronwyn Lind 2001

First published 2001

Printed in the United Kingdom at the University Press, Cambridge

Typeface 10/13pt Baskerville   *System* 3b2   [CE]

A catalogue record for this book is available from the British Library

Library of Congress cataloguing in publication data

Weatherburn, Donald James.
Delinquent-prone communities / Don Weatherburn and Bronwyn Lind.
    p.   cm.
ISBN 0 521 79094 8
1. Juvenile delinquency – Australia – New South Wales. 2. Juvenile delinquency.
3. Crime – Economic aspects. 4. Crime – Social aspects.
5. Juvenile delinquents – Australia – New South Wales – Family relationships.
6. Juvenile delinquents – Family relationships. 7. Community life.
I. Lind, Bronwyn. II. Title.
HV9230.A6 N489 2001
364.36′09944 – dc21   00-036304

ISBN 0 521 79094 8 hardback

Overview

During the 1980s many countries – including Britain, the United States, Australia and New Zealand – experienced a significant growth in income inequality (Saunders, Stott and Hobbes 1991; Levy and Murnane 1992; Saunders 1993; Cowell, Jenkins and Litchfield 1996). In Britain, the United States and Australia this increase was accompanied by a progressive spatial concentration of the poor. Green (1994), for example, found large increases in the spatial concentration of unemployment in large metropolitan areas and traditional mining/manufacturing areas of Wales and in the north of England. In Australia a similar progressive spatial concentration of the unemployed in urban areas of low socioeconomic status has been documented by Gregory and Hunter (1995). In the United States it has been documented by Wilson (1987) and by Massey and Denton (1993). This growth in inequality might be regarded as of little account were it generally matched by a growth in real income but it has not been. The economic position of unskilled men in the United States fell markedly during the 1980s and early 1990s as did the ratio of employment to the population of working age and hours worked per employee across Europe (Freeman 1995). In Australia and New Zealand the growth in inequality occurred largely because of a decline in real household disposable income at the bottom end of the income distribution (Saunders, Stott and Hobbes 1991).

Criminologists have traditionally viewed these sorts of changes with concern. Most classical theories of crime, whether economic or social, predict that crime rates will increase with the level of disadvantage. Many would also lead one to expect spatially concentrated disadvantage to prove more criminogenic than disadvantage which is widely dispersed. Over the years, however, economic and social theories of crime have fallen on hard times. The difficulty facing them is that evidence linking disadvantage and crime is neither consistent or clear. To be sure, cross-sectional studies relying on officially recorded crime data consistently show higher crime rates in areas marked by higher levels of disadvantage. Individual-level studies also consistently show that serious and/or persistent offenders are drawn disproportionately from the ranks of those who are economically disadvantaged. Time series studies, however, often show no relationship between disadvantage and crime at all and sometimes show evidence of a negative relationship. To make matters worse, it has never been entirely clear why material disadvantage would prompt involvement in non-acquisitive crime, yet the relationship between the two is remarkably strong.

The apparent failure of empirical research to confirm the hypothesised link between disadvantage and crime has tended to undermine scholarly faith in the idea that economic and social policy have a significant role to play in preventing crime. This idea has been undermined by other factors as well. Alternative explanations for the spatial distribution of crime have been developed which assign no direct causal role to economic and social disadvantage. The failure to reduce crime through anti-poverty measures – such as the War on Poverty in the United States during the 1970s – led to scepticism about the value of such measures. This scepticism has been fuelled by evidence indicating that the antecedents of individual involvement in crime are to be found well before entry into the labour market and, in many cases, before entry into high school. The discovery that certain kinds of family intervention in early childhood can significantly reduce the subsequent involvement in crime has encouraged a shift in the focus of crime prevention policy from social and economic reform to intervention in micro-social and family environments now thought to trigger offending behaviour.

The irony in this is that the decline of theoretical interest in the role of poverty, inequality and social disadvantage in generating crime-prone communities has coincided with the appearance of a number of individual-level research studies highlighting the existence of indirect pathways between economic stress and individual criminal behaviour. These studies indicate that economic and social stress, under certain conditions, reduce the level of parental supervision of children, weaken the level of parent–child attachment and produce parental discipline which is harsh, erratic and inconsistent. These conditions, in turn, increase the risk of involvement in crime, at least in part because they facilitate or encourage association with delinquent peers. Thus, just as criminological interest in the role of poverty and disadvantage in generating crime began to wane it became possible to argue that economic stress, by a variety of indirect pathways, exerts a causal influence on the spatial distribution of crime.

What remains largely unanswered is how important the indirect pathways from disadvantage to crime are in shaping the aggregate level of and spatial distribution of crime. This is an important issue. Aggregate-level indices of parenting quality are not moving in a very reassuring direction. Britain, the United States and Australia appear to have experienced significant increases over the last decade in levels of child neglect and abuse. Registrations to child protection registers in Britain increased by 44 per cent from 1988 to 1998, rising from 20,900 cases to 30,000 cases (UK Department of Health 1999). In Australia, substantiated cases of child neglect and/or abuse rose by 59 per cent from 1988/89 to 1995/96, rising from 18,816 cases to 29,833 cases (Australian Institute of Health and Welfare 1998). These changes might be thought to reflect just increased willingness to report or increased ability to detect child maltreatment. In the United States, however, where it is possible to estimate the true (as opposed to the reported) level of child abuse and neglect, the estimated number of abused and neglected children grew from 1.4 million in 1986 to over 2.8 million in 1993, an increase of more than 100 per cent (NIS-3 1999).

This book is about the interrelationship between economic and social stress, parental competence and crime-prone communities. We do not, however, put forward a general theory of the role of economic factors in crime, let alone a general theory of crime. Our interest is restricted to the developmental antecedents of crime-prone communities and how these antecedents are influenced by economic and social conditions. Our contention is that economic and social stress create fertile conditions for the development of crime-prone communities, not because they drive otherwise law-abiding people into crime but because they are corrosive of the quality of parenting in a way which renders juveniles more susceptible to delinquent peer influence. An important part of our argument is that this influence creates an autocatalytic effect, in which each increase in the level of delinquency in a neighbourhood lays the foundations for later increases. We use this idea to help explain some of the anomalies surrounding time series analyses of the relationship between economic stress and crime.

Despite the importance we assign to economic and social stress it is not our contention that they alone determine the level and spatial distribution of crime. Factors such as the availability and price of illegal drugs, the supply of criminal opportunities and incentives, the rate of contact between offenders and potential victims and the level and effectiveness of enforcement activity are also important (particularly at very low levels of spatial aggregation) even though we do not discuss them here. They gain their importance, however, only once a community has a supply of motivated offenders. To put the matter another way, the level and distribution of crime may be shaped by a wide range of situational and circumstantial factors but this does not mean that we can take the supply of motivated offenders as a given. There are significant variations across space and time in the number of people willing to participate in crime. We contend, that, at the macro-spatial level, these variations are in large measure attributable to economic and social disadvantage.

Because we argue that economic and social stress exert their effects on crime by disrupting the parenting process, we are led to the conclusion that the kinds of economic and social support required to prevent crime are those directed at fostering better parenting. Economic pressures, changes in family structure, the spatial concentration of poverty and changes in geographical mobility in Western democratic countries over the last twenty or thirty years have combined to place enormous strain on families. An increasing number of parents or caregivers, already struggling on a limited income, must contend without the support of a partner or a close network of friends, neighbours and relatives. They must also often contend with policy makers who are concerned to discourage welfare dependence but do not yet see the importance of childcare as a means of reconciling the competing demands of parenting and work, or the fact that economic growth alone is insufficient to create structural disincentives to involvement in crime. We argue, in the conclusion of this book, that a resolution or amelioration of these problems is central to long-term crime prevention.

The structure of the book is as follows. In Chapter 1 we review theories and evidence bearing on the idea that poverty and unemployment affect crime by increasing the motivation of those affected to offend. In that review we highlight the empirical anomalies which are difficult to reconcile with this thesis. We also attempt to show why efforts to deal with these anomalies have been relatively unsuccessful. In Chapter 2 we review studies examining the effects of economic and social stress on parenting. We argue on the strength of this evidence that economic stress in the absence of social supports reduces the level of parental supervision, weakens the bond between parent and child and increases the risk of parental disciplinary practices which are erratic, harsh and inconsistent. In Chapter 3 we consider the interrelationship between economic stress, incompetent parenting, delinquent peer influence and participation in crime. We make a case for the hypothesis that economic stress, in the absence of social support, exerts its effects on crime by producing parenting practices which render juveniles more susceptible to delinquent peer influence.

In Chapters 4 and 5 we present the results of some individual and aggregate-level research we have conducted which confirm the importance of parenting and peer influence as mediators of the relationship between disadvantage and crime. In Chapter 6 we develop a simple mathematical model based on this hypothesis and attempt to show how it sheds light on the anomalies which have bedevilled previous attempts to explain the relationship between economic stress and crime. In Chapter 7 we compare the model to other explanations for the spatial distribution of crime and assess its ability to explain features of that distribution, such as the concordance between crime-prone neighbourhoods, ethnic heterogeneity, geographical mobility and family dissolution. We also highlight a key difference between the model and criminal opportunity theory in the level at which each explains the spatial distribution of crime. In Chapter 8 we discuss the implications of the preceding chapters for long-term crime prevention.

The ESIOM paradigm and its problems

The ESIOM paradigm

Scholarly interest in the question of how economic stress affects crime has a long pedigree in criminology. Quetelet (1831) and Guerry (1833) both set out to test the belief, widely held in nineteenth-century France, that crime and economic stress were positively related. They found, instead, that crime rates were higher in wealthier areas. Both attributed this result to the fact that wealthier areas provided more opportunities for crime than poorer areas. Guerry and Quetelet's observations about the relationship between crime-prone areas and wealth in nineteenth-century France may not have been mirrored by those taking observations in other countries at later points in time. The balance of evidence now clearly favours the hypothesis that economic stress and crime are highly correlated, at least where serious crime is concerned (Braithwaite 1979; Box 1987; Chiricos 1987; Belknap 1989). But they firmly established the relationship between crime and economic factors as an important observational domain for criminological theory. They also anticipated a debate about the relative importance of offender motivation and offending opportunity which is alive and well today.

The conventional approach to the problem of explaining the relationship between economic stress and crime has been to argue that economic stress – or stress, in one way or another – motivates otherwise law-abiding individuals to offend. For brevity, in what follows we refer to this as the economic stress-induced offender motivation (ESIOM) paradigm. In using this term we do not wish to be taken as suggesting that psychological stress mediates the relationship between economic factors and crime. The term 'economic stress' is used as Fowles and Merva (1996) use it, that is, merely as a shorthand way of denoting the psychological condition or conditions which putatively mediate the link between factors such as unemployment (or poverty) and the individual motivation to offend. We could have followed Sampson and Wilson (1995: 45) in using the term 'materialist theory' to describe theories which maintain that conditions such as unemployment or poverty motivate individuals to offend. We prefer to use the term 'ESIOM paradigm' because some classical theories about the relationship between poverty and crime, while clearly motivational, are not necessarily materialist. Social opportunity theory, for example, is clearly a motivational theory of crime but its explanation for criminal behaviour could not be said to hinge on the assumption that offenders commit crimes for reasons of material gain.

Strain theory (Merton 1968) was the first and remains perhaps the best known of the ESIOM theories. According to this theory all societies define certain material goals as 'worth striving for' and specify certain norms which define the legitimate means available to achieve these goals. Economically disadvantaged persons, however, experience a significant gap or disjunction between their socially inculcated aspirations and the legitimate means available to achieve them. This disjunction, according to strain theory, increases the likelihood of involvement in crime. This explanation makes sense of the association between economic stress and acquisitive crime because such crime can be viewed as a means of fulfilling material aspirations. On the other hand it makes somewhat less sense of evidence linking economic stress to non-acquisitive crime. It also leaves the mechanism by which the hypothesised 'disjunction' achieves its criminogenic effects within an individual entirely unclear. In other words, the theory offers no insight into why some economically disadvantaged individuals become involved in crime while others do not.

A somewhat more wide-ranging treatment of the strain hypothesis is the social opportunity theory put forward by Cloward and Ohlin (1960). They argued that delinquency emerges more as an act of rebellion against blocked social opportunities rather than as a means of achieving culturally approved goals. According to Cloward and Ohlin, structural blockages of social opportunity have the effect of driving youths into delinquent gangs as a means of conferring the social status on themselves unobtainable from conventional society. Mere lack of access to legitimate income-earning activities, however, is not sufficient to produce crime. The theory suggests that access to illegitimate opportunities must also be available. Since participation in any form of illegitimate activity is consonant with the desire to rebel against conventional social values, Cloward and Ohlin's theory gives rise to the possibility that economic stress may have just as strong an effect on non-acquisitive crime as on acquisitive property crime. Like strain theory, however, social opportunity theory says little about why some disadvantaged juveniles become involved in crime while others do not. One might surmise that when disadvantaged individuals do not involve themselves in crime they either have not experienced a blockage of legitimate opportunities and/or do not have access to illegitimate opportunities. But the theory offers no insight into why this occurs and evidence supporting this proposition is nowhere presented.

The theory of crime put forward by Cohen (1955) offers one solution to this problem. Cohen argued that lower-class socialisation equips lower-class boys less adequately than their middle-class counterparts for success in school. The result, according to Cohen, is a sense of personal failure reinforced by stigmatisation at the hands of teachers and more successful students. The rest of Cohen's theory essentially follows the argument pursued by Cloward and Ohlin. The loss of social status engendered by school failure causes juveniles who have done poorly at school to band together. By this means they set up their own social status system, distinguished by the fact of its rejection of conventional social values. The strength of Cohen's theory is that the mechanism by which economic stress achieves its effects – poor school performance – has been explicitly identified. Moreover it is a mechanism whose existence, as Braithwaite (1979) points out, is well-supported by empirical evidence. Juveniles from economically disadvantaged backgrounds are more likely to do poorly at school. Poor school performance is universally found to be highly correlated with juvenile involvement in crime. Since not all economically disadvantaged juveniles do poorly at school, the theory is able to furnish at least some explanation for the fact that not all economically disadvantaged juveniles turn to crime.

Although most theories of the relationship between economic stress and crime appeal to sociological notions there are some notable exceptions. Economic theories of crime offer yet a third perspective on the way in which economic stress motivates individuals to offend. The best known economic theory of crime is that formulated by Becker (1968). He rejected the need for any special set of concepts to explain criminal as opposed to non-criminal forms of human behaviour. Instead, he argued, individuals allocate their time between legitimate and illegitimate activities in proportions which result in equal expected utility. The expected utility of crime is determined by the perceived risks, costs and benefits associated with it. The benefits of crime in Becker's theory can be monetary benefits, benefits in kind or intangible benefits like social status. The costs of crime include not only the penalties imposed on offenders but also opportunity costs, that is, benefits foregone as a result of involvement in crime (e.g. income from legitimate activities). Becker argued, not unreasonably, that the opportunity costs of involvement in crime fall with an individual's income. Thus, although Becker rejected traditional sociological theories of criminal behaviour, he was led to similar conclusions about the relationship between economic stress and crime. As with strain and social opportunity theory, however, the economic theory of crime offers little explanation for the fact that many disadvantaged individuals do not involve themselves in crime. One may attribute this fact to individual differences in the utility assigned to various outcomes associated with legitimate or illegitimate activity, but the theory affords no means of measuring these differences and thereby testing its claims.

There are many other theories of crime which fall within the ESIOM paradigm. As Braithwaite points out in his review of the theoretical literature (Braithwaite 1979) early Marxists argued that capitalism motivates offending because it encourages avarice and disregard for the needs of others. Some psychologists, on the other hand, have ascribed the source of criminal motivation to the fact that disadvantaged individuals experience a higher than average level of frustration and this produces a heightened tendency toward criminality. Despite their ontological differences, the distinctive feature of all these accounts is their appeal to the notion that economic stress increases crime because it motivates individuals affected by that stress to offend. It is a tribute to the influence of this idea that it continues to dominate research and theory on the relationship between economic stress and crime. Strain theory has been revised and extended by Agnew (Agnew 1985; Agnew and White 1992). Elements of social opportunity theory can be found in Braithwaite's theory of reintegrative shaming (Braithwaite 1988). Elements of Becker's economic theory can be found in Wilson and Herrnstein's general theory of crime (Wilson and Herrnstein 1985).

Early challenges to the ESIOM paradigm

The puzzle of all this is that the ESIOM paradigm was placed under theoretical and empirical siege almost from the moment of its inception. Early challenges to the ESIOM paradigm came from two sources. The first source consisted of theoretical, methodological or empirical criticisms of particular ESIOM theories. Strain theory was criticised, for example, on the grounds that there was little evidence to support the proposition that juvenile offenders experienced a more acute disjunction between their aspirations and their expectations than did non-offenders (Vold and Bernard 1986). Indeed delinquents appear to have both low aspirations and low expectations (Kornhauser 1978). Social opportunity theory was criticised by those who argued that, far from being talented but frustrated youths, with a burning sense of injustice, gang members had few social abilities and no strong future aspirations (Nettler 1978). Cohen's theory was criticised on the grounds that it seems to be arguing that delinquents both accept and reject middle-class values (Vold and Bernard 1986). The economic theory of crime, as formulated by Becker, was criticised on the grounds that it involved arbitrary assumptions about the value of key parameters and oversimplified assumptions about the nature of the utility function underpinning the allocation of time to criminal activity (Ehrlich 1973; Block and Heineke 1975; Orsagh and Witte 1980).

These sorts of criticisms are important but they have not generally proved fatal to any of the theories in question. In some cases this is because the theories are so loosely tied to observation that it is easy to modify them in ways which protect them from refutation. Strain theory, for example, is currently enjoying a revival thanks to a reformulation of its theoretical commitments in relation to juvenile aspirations (Agnew 1985). The economic theory of crime has preserved its popularity because its underlying assumptions can easily be modified without abandoning its central notion that criminal activity flows out of rational assessments by offenders of the benefits and costs of involvement in crime (see, for example, Block and Heineke 1975; Buchanan and Hartley 1992). In some cases, however, the early criticisms of particular ESIOM theories failed to make a mark because they only succeeded in targeting assumptions which were essentially peripheral to the theory. One of the more controversial claims made by Cloward and Ohlin, for example, was that delinquent gangs all conform to a particular typology. Although there is little evidence to support this claim, as Vold and Bernard (1986) point out, this is of little consequence because the typology itself does not derive from the notion that delinquency is a consequence of rebellion against blocked social opportunity.

A second and more damaging set of challenges to ESIOM theories came from those who questioned the basic thesis that economic stress increases crime. At first blush the idea that anyone might question the central relationship underpinning at least four major theories of crime might seem somewhat surprising. But even before the emergence of the ESIOM paradigm some theorists rejected the proposition that stress and crime were causally linked. Shaw and McKay (1969), for example, noted the association between stress and crime in their study of delinquency areas of Chicago but rejected the suggestion that the high crime rate areas of Chicago were a direct result of economic stress. They were drawn to this conclusion by the fact that there had been no change in the per capita concentration of delinquents in Chicago despite massive increases in the general level of stress during the Great Depression (Vold and Bernard 1986: 169).

Shaw and McKay were far from the last theorists to question the notion that crime rates increase with the level of economic stress. Doubts were also expressed by Sutherland and Cressey in expounding their theory that criminal behaviour is learned as a result of association with delinquent peers (Sutherland and Cressey 1978). Like Shaw and McKay, they were influenced by the observation that crime rates and unemployment did not always rise and fall together over time. But they also ventured two other reasons for rejecting the view that economic stress and crime were causally linked. First, they suggested that at least some of the spatial association between stress and crime could be attributed to the fact that low socioeconomic status offenders are more likely to be arrested and prosecuted than high socioeconomic status offenders. Second, they suggested that crime rates might be affected by factors associated with economic stress rather than economic stress itself (e.g. early departure from school), arguing that such factors increased the rate of contact between delinquents and non-delinquents.

The emergence of Hirschi's control theory (Hirschi 1969) added a further fillip to the arguments of those who questioned the relevance of economic stress to an understanding of crime. Instead of drawing on official records of juvenile or adult involvement in crime to draw conclusions about the factors which influence crime, Hirschi analysed the relationship between the rate of self-reported delinquency and a variety of factors, including social status, attachment to parents and siblings, and school performance. The results of this analysis indicated that, regardless of race or class and regardless of the delinquency of their friends, boys who were more closely attached to their parents were less likely to report committing delinquent acts than those who were less closely attached. Hirschi also found higher rates of self-reported delinquency among students who did poorly at or disliked school and/or who rejected school authority. On the basis of these observations he concluded that crime is the result of a broken or weakened bond between a juvenile and the persons (e.g. family and friends) and institutions (e.g. school and church) normally involved in fostering or supervising law-abiding behaviour. Moreover, because he found only very weak evidence of an association between the occupational status of a student's father and the likelihood that a student had committed delinquent acts, Hirschi rejected the suggestion that economic stress exerted any significant influence on the likelihood of juvenile participation in crime.[1]

Hirschi's observation that there was no relationship between economic stress and crime was frequently confirmed during the 1960s and 1970s by other studies relying on self-reported measures of offending (Braithwaite 1988: 49). For a time this seemed to secure the proposition that crime is not caused by economic stress and is not more prevalent among those of low socioeconomic status (e.g. Tittle, Villemez and Smith 1978). That proposition was further bolstered by a number of important sociological studies during the 1960s which documented police bias in the handling of juvenile suspects and in the enforcement of legislation against vice and narcotics (Bottomley and Coleman 1981). Such studies seemed to undermine the reliance placed on police statistics by many early studies of crime. Growing interest in labelling theory – the view that criminal justice intervention has the effect of exacerbating rather than ameliorating crime – probably reinforced this trend, as did growing awareness of the importance of white-collar crime. It became commonplace to argue that crime statistics based on reports of crime to police were just 'social constructions' rather than measures of any underlying reality. Indeed, some social theorists went so far as to claim that 'official knowledge' based on crime statistics was little more than an extension of the rhetoric used by those in power to secure political control (Bottomley and Coleman 1981: 1).

These arguments have not held sway with most scholars for reasons which have been comprehensively reviewed by Braithwaite (1979: 23–63) and also by Blumstein et al. (1986: 48). For this reason they will therefore not be rehearsed in detail here. Suffice it to say that most self-reported offending is only relatively minor in nature (Hindelang, Hirschi and Weis 1979) whereas studies relying on officially recorded crime are generally tapping quite serious forms of criminality. Self-report studies examining serious forms of offending do find strong association between economic stress and crime (Elliott and Huizinga 1983; Sampson and Laub 1994). A strong association between stress and crime can also be found for offences such as homicide and vehicle theft which are nearly always reported to and recorded by police (e.g. Devery 1991, 1992; Junankar and Kapuscinski 1992). Furthermore, it is now generally recognised that police resources and police discretion exert a much stronger effect on crimes recorded when police take the initiative in enforcing the law (e.g. drug offences, public order offences) than when crimes are recorded because of action by citizens who report them. In the latter case, the perceived seriousness of an offence has been found to be far more important in shaping the likelihood of it being reported to police than the socioeconomic status of the victim (Gottfredson and Hindelang 1979).[2] Even where socioeconomic status has been found to exert an independent effect on the likelihood of police contact or court referral following commission of an offence, the effect is greatly diminished for serious offences such as assault, robbery, theft and burglary (Sampson 1986). As Gottfredson noted in his review of the United States National Crime Victim Survey (NCS), most of the important social, demographic and spatial/temporal differences shown by the NCS have also repeatedly been found in official data (Gottfredson 1986).

The emergence of more serious anomalies

Interestingly enough, renewed faith in the effect of economic stress on crime has not brought with it a resurgence of confidence in ESIOM theories. There are three reasons for this. First, in the years following the emergence of Hirschi's theory a considerable body of evidence began to accumulate indicating that most individuals commence their involvement in crime long before they enter the labour market and in many instances before they leave school. This phenomenon (which we call the *early onset anomaly*) militated against the view that otherwise law-abiding individuals were tempted into crime by unemployment, a low-paid job or low social status (Tarling 1982). A second reason is that the traditional dominance of motivational explanations for spatial and temporal variation in crime has come under threat from other theories which attribute such variation, at least in part, to changes in the supply of criminal opportunities (Cohen and Felson 1979; Clarke 1983; Cook 1986). A third reason is that, although most studies of the relationship between stress and crime show evidence of a positive relationship, a number of anomalies have emerged which seem inconsistent with the thesis that increases in economic stress uniformly produce increases in crime.

Evidence of the *early onset anomaly* emerged long before the advent of strain theory, social opportunity theory or the economic theory of crime (Glueck and Glueck 1950). Subsequent research using more reliable data has since confirmed the fact that the onset of involvement in crime for most offenders occurs when they are still quite young. In their review of the literature on age of onset for offending Farrington et al. (1990) conclude that the peak age for onset of criminal activity is about age 14. It is possible, however, to predict the onset of involvement in crime long before this. White et al. (1990), for example, were able to predict involvement in criminal activity between the ages of 11–13 from information about child behaviour at age three.[3] In the light of what we now know about the role of developmental factors in the onset of criminal activity, such predictive efficacy may not seem surprising. On current evidence the best independent predictors of early onset of offending are leisure activities rarely spent with the father, troublesome behaviour, parents having authoritarian child-rearing attitudes, and psychomotor impulsivity, with other relatively strong indicators being low family income, low non-verbal intelligence and poor child-rearing behaviour (Farrington and Hawkins 1990). Many of these factors would be expected to exert their effects on family functioning and child behaviour well before entry into school or the labour market. This does not prove that unemployment and economic stress exert no influence on the motivation to offend. But it does run against the grain of theories which contend economic disadvantage is enough to prompt criminal activity in otherwise law-abiding individuals. It has accordingly forced a reappraisal of this assumption even among some contemporary theorists working within the ESIOM tradition (e.g. Paternoster and Mazerolle 1994).

Criminal opportunity theory has also proved a corrosive influence on support for the ESIOM paradigm. The essence of criminal opportunity theory is the view that crime rates are driven by the supply of opportunities and incentives for crime rather than the factors which influence the supply of motivated offenders. While there is still room for doubt about the validity of this thesis (at least when strictly interpreted) the accumulated evidence that situational factors play a very important role in shaping spatial and temporal variation in crime rates is now too strong to be ignored (Clarke 1983; Clarke and Cornish 1985; Clarke 1995; Sutton and Hazlehurst 1996). Research stimulated by criminal opportunity theory has also thrown up phenomena not readily explicable in terms of any theory falling within the ESIOM tradition. To take just two examples, no offender-based explanation has so far been offered for the existence and persistence over time of crime 'hot spots', that is, physical locations which account for a disproportionate amount of reported crime (Sherman, Gartin and Buerger 1989; Sherman 1995). Nor has any offender-based theory been offered for the phenomenon of repeat victimisation (Farrell 1995), that is, the observation that, once victimised, certain locations appear to be at elevated risk of revictimisation for a period.

As with the *early onset anomaly*, the observations pertaining to repeat victimisation and crime 'hot spots' do not so much refute ESIOM theories as erode their claim to offer a satisfactory general framework for explaining criminal behaviour. By contrast, the pattern of anomalies among empirical findings on the relationship between economic stress and crime poses a direct threat to the ESIOM paradigm. The only studies which could be said to provide a consistent pattern of support for the paradigm are those employing social class as a measure of economic stress and measuring crime using official data. In most such studies the relationship between stress and crime is tested by seeing whether individuals occupying low status occupations are more likely to show evidence of involvement in crime. In some studies, however, it is tested by seeing whether low status areas (as measured by the percentage of residents in low status occupations) have higher crime rates. Braithwaite (1979) has conducted what arguably remains the most authoritative review of both types of study. He concluded that the overwhelming weight of evidence supports the view that:

- Lower-class adults commit those types of crime which are handled by police at a higher rate than middle-class adults.
- Adults living in lower-class areas commit those types of crime which are handled by police at a higher rate than adults who live in middle-class areas.
- Lower-class juveniles commit crime at a higher rate than middle-class juveniles.
- Juveniles living in lower-class areas commit crime at a higher rate than juveniles living in middle-class areas.

In some ways, however, social status is arguably the least satisfactory way of measuring the effect of economic stress on crime. Because there is no universally accepted scale of social status it is impossible to compare the magnitude of the social status effects on crime obtained in different studies. The ordinal nature of the social status scale makes it difficult, if not impossible, to examine changes in economic stress and crime over time. Finally, the observation of a relationship between social status and crime gives little clue as to which component of social status (e.g. occupational prestige, income, unemployment) is most important in shaping the likelihood of involvement in crime. These problems have led to a greater focus on more easily measured variables, such as unemployment and income. Studies which measure economic stress through unemployment or income, however, present nowhere near as clear or consistent a picture of the relationship between economic stress and crime as studies examining the relationship between social status and officially recorded rates of offending. Early reviews (Gillespie 1978; Long and Witte 1981) of research on the effects of unemployment have been described as creating a consensus of doubt on the relationship. More recent reviews (Box 1987; Chiricos 1987; Belknap 1989; Allen 1996) claim to have reduced this doubt but a number of puzzling anomalies remain.

Chiricos has conducted the most comprehensive review to date on the relationship between unemployment and crime. He examined the outcome of 288 separate tests for a relationship between unemployment and crime reported in a total of sixty-three published studies. Overall he found that the unemployment–crime relationship was three times more likely to be positive than negative and fifteen times more likely to be significantly positive than significantly negative. Moreover, as might be expected, tests involving property crime were more likely to prove positive and significant than tests involving violent crime. These observations and those we have just reviewed concerning social status provide the main empirical pillars of support for the ESIOM paradigm but even here the paradigm is not without its difficulties. The vast majority of ESIOM theories are materialist in conception, that is, they assume that crime is committed primarily as a means of overcoming some material disadvantage. The fact that a substantial proportion of tests examining the link between unemployment and violent crime proved significant and positive (a finding we call the *non-utilitarian crime anomaly*) remains hard to reconcile with any of these theories. Only social opportunity theory (and its derivatives) avoids this problem because it treats the motivation to offend as an act of rebellion against conventional values rather than as a means of generating income or goods.

The *non-utilitarian crime anomaly* is not the most pressing problem facing the ESIOM paradigm. The most pressing problem lies in the fact that, although the majority of significant test results reviewed by Chiricos supported a positive link between unemployment and crime, overall, the majority of tests for an association failed to produce a significant result either way. In addition, a number of studies have found evidence of a significant inverse association between unemployment and crime (Chiricos 1987: 193). These findings (which we call the *inconsistency problem*) are hard to dismiss as artefacts of measurement error because the pattern of non-significant and negative results does not appear to be either random or attributable to some particular research design problem. The effect of unemployment on aggregate crime rates, for example, appears to depend upon the time period in which the relationship is examined. Cross-sectional tests for an association between unemployment and crime conducted on pre-1970 data were far less likely to find a significant positive association between unemployment and crime than cross-sectional studies conducted on data during the 1970s (Chiricos 1987: 197). These time period anomalies have been found in later studies. Vaughn (1991), for example, found that unemployment was positively related to Japanese crime rates in the period 1926–45 but negatively related thereafter.

The pattern of negative and positive unemployment–crime results also appears to depend upon the methodology employed to examine the unemployment–crime relationship. For example, time series studies appear to have been far more likely than those relying on cross-sectional designs to find a significant negative relationship, particularly where property crime was concerned. No cross-sectional test involving property crime found a significant negative effect of unemployment. By contrast, 14 per cent of the time series tests for property crime found a negative effect of unemployment (Chiricos 1987: 194). The apparent conflict between cross-sectional and time series study results is of particular concern because time series studies arguably provide a stronger test of claims that one variable exerts a causal influence on another than cross-sectional studies (Greenberg 1979: 80; although see also Freeman 1995: 180). It is, after all, much easier to sort out the causal order of events when changes in crime and unemployment are followed over time than when they are only examined at one point in time.

Similar anomalies have also been noted in the literature on income and crime. ESIOM accounts of the relationship between stress and crime would lead one to expect a negative relationship between income and crime. Yet Box (1987) and Belknap (1989) in their reviews cite a number of studies which either fail to find any negative income–crime relationship or which find evidence of a positive relationship. Research conducted since the publication of those reviews has not altered this general picture. Norstrum (1988), for example, found evidence that crime rates in Sweden were positively related to household income in the period 1841–1913 and negatively related to income in the period 1950–84. Field found that property crime rates were positively related and violent crime rates negatively related to consumption growth (which is normally related to income) in post-Second World War England and Wales (Field 1990). Devery (1991) observed a correlation of +0.9 between the percentage of poor families (i.e. income of less than $15,000) in each Local Government Area of Sydney (New South Wales) and the court appearance rate of its residents, over the period 1987–88. Between 1988 and 1991, however, while rates of unemployment in Australia rose by more than 60 per cent (Reserve Bank of Australia 1991) and mortgage interest rates rose by about 13 per cent, rates of break, enter and steal and car theft fell sharply (Weatherburn 1992).

There are three other observations concerning the relationship between economic factors and crime which are common enough to be regarded as anomalous from the vantage point of the ESIOM paradigm. The first (which we call the *income inequality anomaly*) is that income inequality appears more frequently associated with crime than absolute measures of income or unemployment, at least in metropolitan localities. Belknap (1989) cites a number of studies reaching this conclusion. In his review of the literature Box (1987) found that, of the sixteen studies which had examined the association between income inequality and crime, eleven reported significant associations between higher levels of income inequality and crime while five did not. All five studies which failed to find a relationship were concerned with homicide. The studies which supported a positive relationship covered a variety of offences including burglary, larceny, robbery, aggravated assault and rape. Box concluded that the cross-sectional evidence favouring an association between income inequality and crime was much stronger than that concerning the relationship between unemployment and crime. Braithwaite (1978) arrived at much the same conclusion in his review of the evidence. With one exception (Allen 1996) research conducted since these reviews has continued to confirm the importance of income inequality as a predictor of aggregate crime rates although some offences appear to show this result more clearly than others (Patterson 1991; Allen 1996; Fowles and Merva 1996). The importance of income inequality as a predictor of aggregate crime rates is not immediately explicable in terms of most ESIOM theories. Social opportunity theory (Braithwaite 1979) and economic theory (Deutsch, Spiegel and Templeman 1992) can be adapted to the task, at least for property crime, but not without the aid of assumptions drawn from criminal opportunity theory.

The second observation (which we call the *neighbourhood effect anomaly*) is that, at least in Western countries (Matsumoto 1970), the effect of individual-level economic stress on juvenile involvement in crime would appear to be shaped by the level of economic stress in the surrounding neighbourhood. In a reanalysis of data drawn from a study by Reiss and Rhodes (1961), Braithwaite (1979) observed that rates of participation in crime (as measured from court records) among juveniles of low socioeconomic status were much higher when they lived in low socioeconomic status neighbourhoods than when they lived in middle or high socioeconomic status neighbourhoods. Braithwaite repeated the analysis using Australian juvenile court data and obtained the same findings (Braithwaite 1979: 150).

Attempts to confirm the relationship using self-reported crime produced rather more mixed results. In the study referred to above, Braithwaite found that the expected relationship materialised except that juveniles coming from the lowest status families and living in the lowest status areas reported fewer offences than juveniles from middle-class families living in low status areas (Braithwaite 1979: 143). Johnstone (1978), using self-reported arrest frequency, found that the different combinations of neighbourhood and individual economic status exerted different effects for different crime types. In the case of drug offences, for example, lower-class individuals resident in higher-class areas engaged in the most delinquency. Jarjoura and Triplett (1997) examined both self-reported and officially recorded offending among groups of juveniles ranked in terms of neighbourhood and family economic status. However, unlike Braithwaite they found that self-reported offending rates were highest among low-status families resident in middle or upper status neighbourhoods.

The failure of these studies to confirm the original Reiss and Rhodes finding has prompted some to suggest that the alleged 'neighbourhood' economic status effect may be nothing more than a failure to employ adequate controls for all the individual factors which influence involvement in crime (see Gottfredson, McNeil and Gottfredson 1991: 202). This is a difficult claim to assess since neighbourhood effects of any kind must ultimately exert their effects on individual behaviour through some individual characteristic. One cannot therefore test the hypothesis that neighbourhood economic status affects participation in crime by controlling for *all* individual characteristics known to influence such participation. On the other hand, in the absence of a generally accepted theory about how neighbourhood economic status influences individual behaviour, it is difficult to know which individual-level factors ought to be regarded as extraneous influences and which ought to be regarded as factors mediating neighbourhood effects. We will return to this issue in more detail later (see Chapter 3). For now, however, it suffices to observe that the apparent existence of neighbourhood economic status effects on delinquency is a finding not readily explained in terms of most ESIOM accounts of offending.

The third observation (which we call the *individual-level evidence anomaly*) is the fact that direct individual-level evidence that unemployment and income directly affects the probability of involvement in crime is fairly scant. Ethnographic research provides little support for the view that individuals make straightforward choices between employment and crime (McGahey 1986). Indeed, in his discussion of economic conditions, neighbourhood organisation and urban crime, McGahey (1986) concluded on the basis of both survey and ethnographic data that a more important criminogenic effect of persistent unemployment among adults was disruption to the development of stable households. Blumstein et al. (1986) report a Danish experiment which found lower rates of reconviction among a sample of prison releasees given financial and job assistance. The interpretation of this finding is clouded, however, by the fact that releasees were also given a variety of other forms of social support. Rossi, Berk and Lenihan (1980) found that income assistance to prison releasees in the United States reduced their rate of recidivism. However, the study has been sharply criticised by Zeisel (1982) and a subsequent attempt at replicating the finding appears to have failed (Berk, Lenihan and Rossi 1980). The Rand Corporation prison inmate survey found that offenders employed less than half the time in a specified observation period prior to incarceration reported committing property crime at higher rates than offenders employed 50 per cent of the time or more (Blumstein et al. 1986: 75). But this observation might simply mean that offenders with access to lucrative illegitimate sources of income are inclined to spend less time in legitimate forms of income-earning activity.

The most compelling evidence in favour of the hypothesis that economic stress motivates individuals to offend comes from a study by Farrington et al.

(1986). Farrington et al. drew data on individual rates of offending by individuals in the Cambridge Study in Delinquent Development (a prospective longitudinal study of 411 London males followed from the age of eight onwards). The study permitted estimates of individual offending frequency to be obtained during periods in which an individual was employed and compared with estimates obtained from the same individual during periods of unemployment. The differences thus obtained could also be compared for groups of individuals differing in age, occupation status and period of time spent unemployed. Farrington et al. found that estimated rates of offending were significantly higher during periods of unemployment than during periods of employment, even after controls had been introduced for age and the total period of time an individual spent unemployed. The effect of unemployment on crime, however, was confined to offences involving material gain committed by those employed in low-status occupations who had a predisposition to involvement in crime. The study therefore provided no individual-level evidence that unemployment motivates individuals to commit non-acquisitive crime although, as we noted earlier, numerous aggregate-level studies have found a relationship between unemployment and non-acquisitive violent crime.

The observation that suitably disposed individuals were inclined to commit offences involving material gain more frequently during periods of unemployment than during periods of employment might be thought to provide at least some supportive individual-level evidence for the ESIOM paradigm. The support, however, comes at a price. Few ESIOM theories are in a position to provide any explanation for the fact that the unemployment–crime relationship in question appears to be limited to those who have a predisposition to offend. In the Farrington et al. study this predisposition was assessed by reference to low family income, poor housing, large family size, cruel or neglectful parenting, erratic parental discipline and parental conflict because these factors had been shown in past research to be good predictors of future offending. Most traditional ESIOM theories have nothing to say about these factors. Thus, if the study by Farrington et al. is to be taken as a partial vindication of the ESIOM paradigm it is at the cost of having to look elsewhere for a general account of the disposition to involvement in crime. Such an outcome would be of little concern to economists, whose interest in explaining the origins of criminal behaviour is subordinated to the task of why economic factors exert *any* influence on crime (see Buchanan and Hartley 1992: xi). It should, however, be of great concern to sociologists within the ESIOM tradition as they assign economic stress a central role in shaping the individual disposition to involvement in crime.

Grappling with the anomalies

There are three broad ways of responding to the empirical anomalies surrounding the effect of unemployment and income on crime. One possible response is essentially to ignore the empirical anomalies and to rely on the fact that the balance of evidence does show a positive association between economic stress and crime. A second possible response is to abandon the idea that aggregate crime rates are driven solely by the supply of motivated offenders and to try to bolster the ESIOM paradigm with some other assumption or set of assumptions. A third response is to abandon the ESIOM paradigm and search for some other pathway or set of pathways linking economic stress to individual offending behaviour in the hope that this will provide a better foundation for explaining the aggregate-level association between economic stress and crime.

The first of these three types of response was the course taken by Chiricos (1987) and has tended to characterise those whose work remains strongly influenced by social opportunity theory or strain theory (e.g. Agnew 1985; Elliott, Huizinga and Ageton 1985; Braithwaite 1988). Braithwaite (1988), to be fair, acknowledges that the putative association between social status and crime has been the subject of some debate but treats that debate as essentially settled by the discovery that self-report studies only tap minor forms of criminality (Braithwaite 1988: 49). While we have no difficulty with Chiricos's summary of the research evidence regarding unemployment and crime, that summary cannot be regarded as a vindication of theories within the ESIOM paradigm. The anomalies we have discussed cannot reasonably be dismissed as artefacts of measurement error or research design. Indeed, few would be prepared to argue that they are. In our view they suggest that past attempts to characterise the way in which economic variables influence crime are either incomplete or misconceived. An adequate theory of the relationship between economic stress and crime might not be expected to account for every recalcitrant empirical observation on the subject of unemployment or income and crime. We would argue, however, that an adequate theory should at least shed some light on the inconsistency problem. Ideally it should also help resolve the other anomalies we have mentioned (i.e. the *early onset, non-utilitarian crime, income inequality, neighbourhood effect* and *individual-level evidence* anomalies).

The theory integration response

Two notable attempts have been made to bolster the ESIOM paradigm in order to deal with the anomalies we have discussed. Both draw on the notion of criminal opportunity. Braithwaite (1979) developed the social opportunity theory notion that crime requires both a blockage of legitimate activities and access to illegitimate activities.[4] Cantor and Land (1985) developed a model of crime rate variation which combines some features of economic theory, criminal opportunity theory and conventional motivation theory.

We turn first to Braithwaite's (1979) adaptation of social opportunity theory. It is important to begin by pointing out that in adapting the theory Braithwaite was not motivated by a desire to explain or resolve the inconsistencies then emerging among studies examining the association between economic stress and crime. Furthermore, although the focus of Braithwaite's (1979) analysis was on the effect of inequality on crime, he did not set out to explain why the level of income inequality in a community was a better marker of its crime problems than the average level of income. Instead, he took this fact for granted and sought to use it to explain other features of crime, such as delinquency among middle-class adolescents (Braithwaite 1979: 203). He was, however, concerned to replicate and explain the *neighbourhood effect anomaly*. Braithwaite's argument was that this finding could be explained in terms of social opportunity theory if one assumed that disadvantaged individuals living in disadvantaged areas had access to a greater range of illegitimate opportunities. The illegitimate activities appealed to by Braithwaite, however, were not those contemplated by criminal opportunity theorists (e.g. unlocked cars, unguarded households). Instead they were 'criminal role models, criminal learning structures, the social support of delinquent gangs, weak community control etc.' (Braithwaite 1979: 108). In other words, the source of criminal opportunities appealed to by Braithwaite was none other than that championed by differential association theory, that is, delinquent peer influence.

The notion that the effects of economic stress might be mediated by delinquent peer influence does indeed provide an explanation for the observation that individual and area economic status interact in shaping rates of delinquency. As we shall see later, there is abundant evidence that association with delinquent peers increases the likelihood of involvement in crime. Delinquent peer influence would therefore be expected to magnify any effects on crime generated by economic stress. One significant problem with Braithwaite's adaptation of social opportunity theory, however, is that it shares the principal weakness of that theory. He offers no basis on which one can determine a priori which groups of disadvantaged individuals will offend and which will not. One is left to assume that an economically deprived individual who does not engage in crime has either somehow found a means of access to legitimate opportunities or, alternatively, failed to find a means of access to illegitimate opportunities. This is a useful conjecture if operational criteria are laid down which allow some a priori judgement about which of the two possibilities applies to which groups of cases and in what circumstances, but no such criteria are provided. Furthermore, although Braithwaite goes to great pains to deal with evidence inimical to the claim that social class and crime are related, his treatment of this issue does nothing to resolve the inconsistencies apparent among studies examining the effect of unemployment or income on crime. Nor does it do anything to resolve the other anomalies we have discussed.

Unlike Braithwaite (1979), Cantor and Land (1985) were expressly preoccupied with solving what we have called the *inconsistency problem*. Their approach to this problem was both imaginative and resourceful. They combined the traditional notion that unemployment motivates individuals to offend with the insight that economic factors affect the supply of criminal opportunities. Their central claim was that the criminogenic effects of unemployment are offset by the reduction in the supply of opportunities for involvement in crime which accompanies the economic contractions that produce unemployment. Although it was developed in the context of unemployment, the theory can easily be extended to findings on the income–crime relationship. Increases in personal income would be expected to decrease the motivation to offend but increase the supply of opportunities for involvement in crime. The theory can thus be used to explain evidence of a positive income–crime relationship as well as evidence of a negative unemployment–crime relationship.

Although Cantor and Land only apply their argument to time series data it could in fact be seen as offering some insight into why cross-sectional studies examining the relationship between crime and unemployment or income sometimes fail to obtain evidence of a significant positive association between economic stress and crime. It has been known for some time, for example, that there is some divergence between the spatial distribution of offenders and the spatial distribution of offences (Herbert 1980: 31). This observation suggests that motivated offenders do not necessarily commit all their offences in their own neighbourhood and, therefore, that neighbourhoods with larger numbers of motivated offenders will not always have higher crime rates. It follows that cross-sectional studies seeking to tap the effect of economic stress on offender motivation may in many cases have failed to observe such an effect simply because they wrongly assumed that areas with high levels of economic stress will inevitably have higher crime rates.

Unfortunately, the explanatory strength of the theory is in some ways one of its major weaknesses. A negative unemployment–crime relationship can be explained by saying that the effect of unemployment dominates its effect on criminal opportunity. A positive unemployment–crime relationship can be explained by simply putting the argument into reverse. The failure to find any effect of unemployment on crime, on the other hand, can be read as indicating that the positive and negative effects of unemployment have cancelled each other out. As a general explanation for the relationship between stress and crime, then, the theory is impossible to test, at least with aggregate-level crime data.

Cantor and Land dealt with this problem in the context of unemployment by making a special assumption. They suggested that the opportunity effect is immediate but the motivational effect is delayed because social security and family support temporarily 'cushions' the effect of unemployment. Note that this assumption is only tenable in countries such as the United States where unemployment benefits are only provided as a temporary measure. Nevertheless, as long as the assumption is accepted, the theory implies that the initial effect of a rise in unemployment should be to reduce crime while the lagged effect should be to increase it. Cantor and Land endeavoured to test the implication by analysing the impact of unemployment on time series trends in seven offences in post-Second World War United States. The results provided some support for the theory. The expected combination of a negative contemporaneous and lagged positive effect showed up for some property offences but only one of the seven offences they examined exhibited both significant negative and significant positive effects. The study was later criticised on various technical grounds by Hale and Sabbagh (1991) and Hale (1991). Land, Cantor and Russell (1995) repeated the analysis using additional data and a different form of analysis, and they obtained similar results. There remain, nonetheless, a number of troubling questions, both about the assumptions underlying Cantor and Land's theory and about its capacity to make sense of the general relationship between economic stress and crime.

First it must be observed that, although the general assumption that crime rates are influenced by the supply of opportunities is an entirely reasonable one, no direct evidence was offered by Cantor and Land to support the much stronger claim that economic contractions always reduce the supply of opportunities for involvement in all forms of crime. This is an issue of some significance, first because at least one attempt to test this part of Cantor and Land's thesis study has failed to find strong confirming evidence (Allan and Steffensmeier 1989) and, second because a priori arguments can be mounted both for and against the claim. For example, economic contractions might increase the opportunities for property offences involving the resale of stolen goods. But by the same token they should also increase the incentives for cash-generating offences such as robbery. They might reduce the opportunities for conflict between strangers if people respond to a drop in income by going out less frequently to hotels and entertainment venues. But by the same token they should increase the opportunities for domestic assault. They might reduce the opportunities for employee theft if there are fewer people in work. But they should then also increase the opportunities and incentives for social security and insurance fraud. None of this would matter if it were possible to determine from Cantor and Land's theory when the net effects of criminal opportunity and criminal motivation should be positive, negative or zero. It is the fact that this determination cannot be made a priori which makes the absence of independent evidence for the assumed effects of economic growth on criminal opportunity a significant problem.

The theory faces more serious difficulties in relation to its claims about the effect of unemployment on criminal motivation. It brings to light no evidence which would resolve the *individual-level evidence anomaly*. In any event, even if unemployment did motivate individuals to commit offences involving material gain, as we have already noted, the theory offers no explanation for the *non-utilitarian crime anomaly*. Yet both Cantor and Land (1985) and Land, Cantor and Russell (1995) treat unemployment as a factor which increases the motivation to commit offences such as rape, homicide and assault. The theory also offers no explanation for the other anomalies we have mentioned, although to criticise it for failing to do so would be somewhat unfair. Neither Cantor and Land (1985) nor Land, Cantor and Russell (1995) set out to offer a general theory of crime. This said, it must be acknowledged that, even on its chosen ground, the theory is not without its problems. In our view these problems stem not from the basic thesis that aggregate crime rates are determined both by the supply of motivated offenders and the supply of criminal opportunities. They stem from the assumption that the effect of unemployment on aggregate crime rates is mediated by the effect of unemployment on the motivation to offend.

Abandoning the ESIOM paradigm

In our view the anomalies we have discussed are serious enough to warrant abandonment of the ESIOM paradigm, at least as a framework for understanding the aggregate-level spatial relationship between economic stress and crime. We are not the first to suggest that the ESIOM paradigm has outlived its explanatory utility. In one of the more insightful analyses of the crime–unemployment relationship yet published, Hagan (1993) has suggested that, rather than unemployment causing crime, there are compelling reasons for believing that crime, or involvement in crime, can in some circumstances cause unemployment. Hagan makes the point (and provides evidence to support it) that juveniles embedded in a criminal subculture are likely to be cut off from access to information about employment yet have detailed information about illegitimate alternatives to employment as a means of raising income.

There is much in Hagan's argument we find appealing, and we return to it again in Chapter 8. It suffices to observe at this point that there is no need to choose between the thesis that crime causes unemployment and the thesis that unemployment causes crime. Both may be true. In the next two chapters of this book we review theory and evidence suggesting that factors such as unemployment do produce crime but not in the way conventionally assumed. The central thrust of our argument will be that economic stress sets in train two interrelated processes which, over time, have the effect of rendering communities 'offender-prone'. The first of these processes involves a disruption of the parenting process. The second involves an interaction between parenting and association with delinquent peers. In the next chapter we discuss the first of these processes.

Summary and conclusion

The ESIOM paradigm attempts to make sense of the fact that crime rates appear higher in areas of economic stress by assuming that such stress, in one way or another, motivates individuals affected by it to offend. Such an assumption is no less integral to traditional sociological theories, such as strain theory, as it is to economic theories of crime. The evidence and arguments we have reviewed suggest that the ESIOM paradigm provides an inadequate framework for handling what we know about the relationship between stress and crime. The paradigm faces at least five major anomalies. These are:

1. The fact that there is limited and somewhat ambiguous evidence available to support the claim that economic adversity increases individual offending rates (the *individual-level evidence anomaly*).
2. The fact that aggregate rates of non-utilitarian violent crime are strongly affected by economic stress (the *non-utilitarian crime anomaly*).
3. The fact that many of the processes which shape involvement in crime substantially precede entry into the labour market and, in some cases, precede entry into school (the *early onset anomaly*).
4. The fact that studies examining the relationship between economic stress and crime have frequently produced non-significant and occasionally negative results (the *inconsistency problem*).

5. The fact that the effect of economic stress on rates of juvenile offending appears to be influenced by the level of economic stress in the surrounding neighbourhood (the *neighbourhood effect anomaly*).
6. The fact that income inequality appears to be a better predictor of area crime rates than absolute levels of income (the *income inequality anomaly*).

In addition to these problems, only social opportunity theory (within the ESIOM paradigm) has any explanation to offer for the *non-utilitarian crime anomaly*, that is the fact that economic stress appears to exert a strong effect on aggregate rates of violent crime even if that effect appears somewhat weaker than the effect of economic stress on property crime.

There seems little reason to believe that the problems surrounding the ESIOM paradigm can be resolved simply by integrating ESIOM theories with some form of criminal opportunity theory. The weaknesses in any such proposed merger stem not so much from the criminal opportunity side of the ledger but from the notion that economic stress affects crime solely by motivating those affected by it to offend. Braithwaite's (1979) analysis of social opportunity highlighted the important fact that the effects of economic stress on crime are likely to be mediated by peer influence. This provides at least some explanation for the neighbourhood anomaly. However, he did not adequately address himself to the other anomalies we have mentioned.

Cantor and Land's (1985) integration of offender motivation and criminal opportunity theories offers one solution to the *inconsistency problem*. But it does not (and was not intended to) shed much light on any of the other anomalies we have mentioned. Furthermore, although the general thesis that aggregate crime rates are driven both by the supply of motivated offenders and by the supply of criminal opportunities is well supported by empirical evidence, the specific assumption that unemployment reduces the supply of criminal opportunities lacks independent supporting evidence, as does the assumption that unemployment motivates individuals to commit both utilitarian and non-utilitarian forms of crime.

The insidious effects of economic and social stress on parenting

Aggregate-level studies of the effect of economic stress on child maltreatment

If the aggregate level association between economic stress and crime is ambiguous, the association between economic stress and official reports of child maltreatment is far less so. Aggregate-level studies almost universally show a strong positive association between measures of economic stress and reported rates of child maltreatment (Garbarino and Sherman 1980; Spearly and Lauderdale 1983; US Department of Health and Human Services 1988; Young and Gately 1988; Coulton and Pandey 1992; Garbarino and Kostelny 1992; Durkin et al. 1994; Coulton et al. 1995; Krishnan and Morrison 1995; Kotch et al. 1995; Chaffin, Kelleher and Hollenberg 1996). Although Australian research examining the relationship between economic stress and child maltreatment is far more limited than overseas research, cross-sectional analyses of the relationship between socioeconomic status and official reports of child maltreatment in Australia show exactly the same pattern (Young, Baker and Monnone 1989).

Most studies of the effect of economic stress on child maltreatment do not separately examine its effects on neglect and abuse, let alone on the various subcategories of these problems, such as emotional versus physical neglect or physical versus sexual abuse (Ney, Fung and Wickett 1994). The strength of the aggregate-level association between economic stress and child maltreatment (broadly defined) suggests that economic stress probably increases the risk of both child neglect and child abuse. This conclusion is further supported by the few extant studies which have separately examined the risk factors for child neglect and child abuse. Temporary financial problems were a characteristic feature of four of the five types of maltreatment examined by Martin and Walters (1982), including physical and sexual abuse. Spearly and Lauderdale (1983) found that the percentage of families earning less than $15,000 per annum was a good predictor of both reported rates of abuse and neglect in Texas. Durkin et al. (1994) found that the percentage of low-income families was a good predictor of the incidence of severe paediatric injury in New York City.

There is some evidence, however, that indices of economic stress are more strongly correlated with child neglect than with physical abuse. Giovannoni (1971) found that abusive families were more likely than neglectful families to have more members in higher status positions, higher incomes, independent sources of income and male heads who had gone beyond high-school education. Martin and Walters (1982) cite data from a study conducted by the American Humane Association of 16,040 cases of abuse and neglect. 'Insufficient income' was found to be a factor in 25.2 per cent of abusive families and 48.0 per cent of neglectful families. In an analysis of 489 case reports of substantiated child maltreatment in Georgia, USA, Martin and Walters (1982) found that abandonment, neglect and sexual abuse were the strongest discriminators among families grouped according to whether they had temporary financial problems or not. Watters et al. (1986) compared the characteristics of families reported only for abuse, only for neglect or reported for both abuse and neglect. They found that, in families reported only for neglect, male partners were more likely to be in receipt of Government assistance and less likely to be employed than were families reported only for abuse. Chaffin, Kelleher and Hollenberg (1996) also found that family socioeconomic status was significantly associated with self-reported child neglect but not with self-reported child abuse. Similar findings have been obtained by Jones and McCurdy (1992).

The surveillance hypothesis

In some ways it is hardly surprising to observe that there is a close relationship between economic stress and child maltreatment. Disputes over money are among the most frequently cited sources of disputation between parents with dependent children (Andrew Brion Research 1995). Despite the weight of aggregate-level evidence showing an association between economic stress and child neglect and abuse, doubts continue to be expressed from time to time about whether the association should be regarded as a causal one (Tomison 1996a). These doubts have their origin in what might be called the surveillance hypothesis. This is the thesis that reported rates of child neglect and abuse are only higher in poorer areas because the poor are subjected to greater official scrutiny (National Research Council 1993). In fact only one study has been reported which provides evidence in support of the surveillance hypothesis. Hampton and Newberger (1985) compared official reports of maltreatment with maltreatment reported to researchers working for the first national (US) study of the incidence and prevalence of child abuse. They found income affected the likelihood of child abuse being reported to protection authorities. They did not find, however, that the association between economic stress and child maltreatment could be explained away by the association between socioeconomic status and the likelihood of child abuse being officially reported.

As Baumrind (1994) has pointed out, there is general consensus within the scholarly literature that the relationship between economic stress and child maltreatment is not entirely artefactual. Three lines of evidence can be adduced to support this conclusion. First, the effects of economic stress on parents are consistent with the expectation that it would increase the risk of child maltreatment. Second, a relationship between economic stress and child maltreatment can be found even among very low-income families. Third, a relationship between economic stress and the level of nurturance toward children can be found among studies which rely on self-report or direct observation of families for information about parental behaviour rather than on official records.

The effects of economic stress are certainly consistent with the expectation that it would increase the risk of child maltreatment. It does not take much imagination to understand how depressing poverty can be, especially in the absence of social support from a spouse or friends and especially in societies such as ours which assiduously cultivate high expectations concerning the ownership and consumption of material goods. Research confirms this. Single parenthood and low income have been found greatly to increase the risk of depression in women (Dore 1993). Depression among parents with dependent children has been shown, in turn, to lead to lowered tolerance for child misbehaviour and the use of highly authoritarian, overcontrolling responses (Lahey et al. 1984). Rates of substance abuse are also generally much higher among low socioeconomic groups than among middle or upper socio-economic groups (Robins and Regier 1991). Drug abuse has been also been shown to increase the risk of child neglect and abuse (Davis 1990; Kelley 1992; Dore, Doris and Wright 1995; Jaudes, Ekwo and Van Voorhis 1995; Tomison 1996b; Chaffin, Kelleher and Hollenberg 1996).

The credibility of the surveillance hypothesis as an explanation for the association between economic stress and child maltreatment is further weakened by the fact that the association holds up even within the poorest communities. Giovannoni and Billingsley (1970) compared rates of neglect among two populations of low-income families. One group was drawn from the caseloads of public health nurses and the other was drawn from the caseloads the Protective Services Units at the San Francisco office of the Department of Social Services. The second group constituted the sample of neglecting families. Public health nurses rated the families from their caseloads on six areas of family functioning. Those families rated as having no problem in any of the six areas constituting the sample of 'adequate' families. Those rated as having problems in all six areas were grouped together as 'potentially neglectful'. For the purposes of assessing the effect of income on child neglect, Giovannoni and Billingsley then split each of the three groups into those earning less than $2,000 per year and those earning between $2,000 and $4,000 per year. Proceeding in this way they found a significant association between extreme economic stress and neglect. Sixty-three per cent of the 'adequate' mothers were in extreme economic stress, while 84 per cent of the 'potentially neglectful' and 88 per cent of the neglectful mothers could be so described. Similar results in relation to physical abuse have been obtained in Australia by Vinson, Berreen and McArthur (1989). They found that reported rates of child physical abuse were 2.5 times higher in the bottom 4 per cent of postcodes, ranked in terms of socioeconomic status, than in the 6 per cent of postcodes ranked immediately above.

The most compelling evidence against the surveillance hypothesis, however, comes from studies which have found evidence of a relationship between economic stress and neglectful or abusive parenting without relying on official records. At least eight such studies have been conducted. Given the importance of these studies to the arguments we develop in later chapters we will examine them in some detail here. It should be noted in passing that the parental behaviours examined by these studies would not necessarily be classified as child neglect or abuse if they came to official notice. It will become obvious, however, that they are just milder forms of those same behaviours. As we will show later, problems such as weak parental supervision do not have to amount to child neglect (as welfare authorities would typically understand that term) to increase the risk of juvenile involvement in crime. Studies examining the relationship between delinquency and weak parental supervision, nagging, harsh and inconsistent discipline or lack of a strong bond between parent and child are therefore relevant to our examination of the relationship between economic stress and crime regardless of whether or not these conditions would typically be regarded as manifestations of child neglect and abuse.

Elder, Van Nguyen and Caspi (1985) examined the effects of income loss during the Great Depression on parenting behaviour using data from the Oakland Growth Study, a longitudinal study of 167 California children born between 1920 and 1921. Economic loss was measured by splitting the group into two: those whose families had lost at least 35 per cent of their income during the Great Depression and those whose families lost nothing or less than 35 per cent of their income. The behaviour of parents toward their children was assessed through personal interviews designed, among other things, to rate parental behaviour on four dimensions (rejecting, exploiting, indifferent, positive). Where the father's behaviour was being assessed, economic loss was found to be positively correlated with the first three dimensions and negatively correlated with the third. Economic loss appeared to have less effect on maternal than paternal behaviour.

Lempers, Clark-Lempers and Simons (1989) examined the effects of a rural economic recession in a mid-western rural community in the United States. The subjects in the study were 622 school students enrolled in schools throughout the community. Measures of economic stress were obtained by interviewing students about recent income-related changes in their family's lifestyle. Measures of parental nurturance and consistency in administering discipline were obtained through a questionnaire dealing with changes in parental behaviour during the previous six months, as perceived by the students. Lempers et al. found a strong negative association between the perceived level of financial hardship experienced by the family over the last six months and the perceived level of parental nurturance. This effect obtained for both sons and daughters. They also found a strong relationship between the perceived level of financial hardship and the use of inconsistent discipline by the parents. The children of families subjected to greater economic stress were much more likely to rate the disciplinary practices of the parents over the preceding six months as inconsistent.

Silbereisen, Walper and Albrecht (1990) examined the effect of income loss on parental stress and family integration amongst a sample of 134 families drawn from a longitudinal survey of youth in Berlin. The site of their study is of particular significance because of the rapid economic change which occurred in West Germany in the ten to fifteen years prior to the conduct of the first wave of the survey in 1982–83. At that time the West German unemployment rate was 9 per cent and a large proportion of those unemployed were young people with dependent children. To assess the effects of economic stress the researchers constructed three categories of family, based on the income loss sustained by the family over the year preceding the survey. The 'no-loss' group were those who experienced an income loss equal to or less than 5 per cent. The 'moderate loss' group were those who experienced an income loss of up to 25 per cent. The 'high loss' group were those who lost more than 25 per cent of their income. Parental strain was measured through parental responses to questions pertaining to the perceived level of stress experienced by the parents over the past year. Family integration was measured through a series of self-report questions dealing with the level of friction and conflict in the family. Silbereisen et al. found that parents who suffered high income loss exhibited higher levels of stress and had more poorly integrated families than those who did not suffer such loss. In fact significantly higher levels of parental stress were found even among families which suffered moderate income loss.

McLoyd and Wilson (1990) examined the relationship between economic hardship and single parent family functioning in a sample of 155 low-income single parent families recruited through the local school and Department of Social Services. Measures of economic hardship were obtained both from data on income and from self-reports of financial hardship provided by the mothers. Measures of nurturant versus punitive parenting behaviour were obtained from self-reports by the mothers who were asked to indicate on a five-point scale how often they used nine different methods to punish and reward their children (such as verbal compliment, show of affection, scolding, taking away privileges). The mothers participating in the study also completed questionnaires designed to measure their levels of anxiety and depression. McLoyd and Wilson found that income and perceived economic stress significantly increased the level of anxiety in the mother, which in turn reduced the level of nurturance she exhibited toward her children. The more efforts mothers saw themselves as having to make to balance family needs and family income, the more distressed and the less nurturant they became.

Larzelere and Patterson (1990) examined the effect of socioeconomic status on parental monitoring and discipline through interviews with a sample of 206 fourth grade boys drawn from the Oregon Youth Study. Socioeconomic status was measured using both the parents' educational level and a standard scale of occupational prestige. Although these measures of economic stress are less direct than those employed in the studies reviewed above, it is not unreasonable to assume that average income levels were lower among the lower socioeconomic status families. Measures of parental monitoring were based on interviews with the boys and their parents. The interviews with the boys touched on issues such as the extent to which they told their parents when they would be back from an outing, whether they checked in after school and whether they left a note to say where they were going. The interviews with the parents touched on issues such as the amount of time spent with their son, the amount of time their son was unsupervised, whether the son was allowed out after dark and whether the parents talked to their sons about their plans for the next day. Measures of parental discipline were designed to assess its consistency and appropriateness and were based on parental interviews and on direct observation. Three measures of discipline were constructed. One tapped the extent to which the parents followed up with threatened punishments and/or engaged in different patterns of discipline according to their mood. The second tapped the extent to which parents engaged in ambiguous discipline, such as making vague or ambiguous threats. The third tapped the extent to which parents engaged in discipline which was consistent, firm and reasoned. Larzelere and Patterson found that there was a significant association between socioeconomic status (as measured by occupational status) and both parent and observer ratings of the level of parental supervision. There was also a significant association between socioeconomic status and the three measures of parental discipline. Parents from low socioeconomic status backgrounds were more likely to engage in harsh, erratic and inconsistent discipline.

Conger et al. (1992) examined the influence of economic stress on (among other things) parenting behaviour amongst a sample of 205 middle-class two-parent families, a large proportion of whom had been adversely affected by the rural recession in the United States in the mid-1980s. The families were recruited through a large number of public and private schools. Economic hardship was assessed both through objective measures – such as income, family debt-to-asset ratio, unstable work record – and subjective measures – such as self-reports of financial pressure and ability to purchase desired goods and services. Separate measures of parental nurturance and hostility were obtained both from self-reports and from trained observers who videotaped the families discussing a range of family problems and issues put to them by the observer. The observers also rated the level of conflict between the parents. Measures of parental depression were also obtained, both through standardised questionnaires and observer ratings. Conger et al. found that both objective and subjective measures of economic hardship were directly related to ratings of depressed mood in both parents, while ratings of depressed mood, in turn, were inversely related to the level of nurturance shown by parents toward their children. This effect held up when measures of nurturance were based on self-reports and when they were based on ratings by observers.

Sampson and Laub (1994) assessed the impact of economic stress on discipline style, maternal supervision of children and parent–child attachment by reanalysing data originally collected by the Gluecks for their classic study

Unraveling Juvenile Delinquency (Gluech and Gluech 1950). The Glueck data were obtained from extensive personal interviews with the families of 500 delinquent boys aged 10–17 – and 500 matched controls – born between 1924 and 1935 and raised in the slum environments of central Boston. Sampson and Laub based their measures of economic stress on average weekly income and the family's reliance on outside aid. Three measures of family functioning were constructed. These were style of discipline (inconsistent, erratic or harsh punishment), level of parental supervision (of children) and parent–child attachment. Family economic stress was found to be positively correlated with the use of erratic/harsh discipline and negatively correlated with the levels of parent–child attachment and maternal supervision. This was true even after controls were introduced for residential mobility, family size, family disruption, maternal employment, ethnicity, parental deviance and parental instability. Furthermore, even when controls for child misbehaviour were introduced, the positive relationship between family economic stress and the use of erratic/harsh discipline and level of parent–child bond remained strong.

Harris and Marmer (1996) examined the impact of economic stress on the emotional and behavioural involvement of parents with their adolescent children using data from the National Survey of Children (NSC), a panel study of a nationally representative sample of children interviewed in 1976, 1981 and 1987. Their analysis was based on 748 children who lived continually in a two-parent family at all three waves of the study. Because they monitored the families of the children over all three waves of the study they were able to examine the effect of both chronic and temporary economic stress. Families were classified as chronically poor if their income remained within 150 per cent of the (US) economic stress line at all three waves of the study; they were classified as never poor if their income remained above 150 per cent of the economic stress line over the same period. Families who experienced economic stress at only one of the three survey waves were classed as temporarily poor. Poverty was also measured at each wave of the survey by whether or not the families received welfare. Parent–child emotional involvement was measured through interviews with the child on matters such as how close he/she felt to the father/mother and the level of affection provided by the parents. Parent–child behavioural involvement was measured by the number of activities engaged in by parents and child which were perceived to be mutually satisfying. Harris and Marmer did not find any effects of temporary economic stress but did find a strong positive effect of chronic economic stress (whether measured by household income or welfare receipt) on the level of emotional and behavioural involvement between fathers and their adolescent children. They also found that when families received welfare, mothers were less likely to be behaviourally involved with their children. Both these effects were obtained in the presence of controls for race, gender, age, urbanicity, parental education and maternal education.

The nature of the economic stress: parenting relationship

Taken together, these findings show that the aggregate-level evidence linking economic stress to reported rates of child maltreatment is not just an artefact of higher rates of detection of neglect/abuse in poorer areas, and that economic stress really does disrupt the parenting process in ways which encourage child neglect and abuse. Increased irritability, arbitrary discipline, parent–child conflict, physical punishment and weak parental supervision appear to be common parental responses to poverty and unemployment (Vondra 1990).

The question arises as to why this might be so. There is clearly no mechanical relationship between the objective level of economic privation experienced by a family and the level of child neglect or abuse. Rates of family dissolution and child neglect are not noticeably higher in some Asian and southern European countries although many of their inhabitants enjoy material standards of living far below that which would be classed as extreme poverty in any Western nation. Indeed, if anything, Asian and southern European cultures seem to foster more cohesive family units and more intensive concern for the welfare of children than the cultures of more affluent Western nations. It is interesting to observe, moreover, that even in Western countries the association between economic stress and disrupted parenting disappears under certain conditions.

Silbereisen, Walper and Albrecht (1990), for example, found that the direct effect of income loss on family integration disappeared once controls were introduced for parental perceptions of increased strain and increased maternal influence on family decision making. Conger et al. (1992) found that when controls were introduced for parental depression and parental conflict there was no significant association between most measures of economic stress and parental nurturance. Similar results have been reported by Vondra (1986). She found a strong relationship between parental socioeconomic status and child maltreatment but when controls were introduced for the effects of family assistance, family/leisure time and income satisfaction, socioeconomic status was no longer helpful in predicting maladaptive parenting.

These findings serve as a reminder that the effects of low household income on an individual's parenting practices are regulated by the extent to which it produces negative emotional effects, such as anxiety, depression and frustration. The likelihood of these emotional responses, in turn, is probably shaped by the extent to which material privation blocks the fulfilment of socially inculcated desires and expectations. After all, life on a subsistence income will invariably prove more stressful, depressing and frustrating to someone inured in a consumer oriented culture than someone in a culture or social environment which places less emphasis on material consumption.

We may think of incompetent or inadequate parenting, then, as produced by economic stress for the same reasons which Merton regarded it as productive of crime. In other words, problems such as neglect and child abuse appear in response to economic stress, not because there is some intrinsic relationship between the level of household income and the quality of parenting but because poverty, at least in our culture, creates a disjunction between socially inculcated aspirations and the means available to achieve them. It follows that while we may choose to gauge the level of economic stress by objective indicators such as unemployment rates or the percentage of families living in poverty, these indicators gain their significance from the fact that they are contingently associated with emotional conditions which are disruptive to parenting.

Once this point is accepted it becomes clear that the role of economic stress in shaping parental behaviour will depend upon the other factors which impinge upon the psychological well-being of parents. In the next section we examine some of these factors and the role they play in elevating or alleviating the risk of child maltreatment. The results of this discussion will prove fruitful not only in understanding the effects of economic stress on crime but also in our later discussion (see Chapter 4) of various theories concerned with the spatial distribution of crime.

The role of social stressors in child maltreatment

Two obvious sources of additional strain on poor families with dependent children are the lack of a partner and/or the presence of large numbers of dependent children. In their review of relevant literature Giovannoni and Billingsley (1970) argued that, after socioeconomic status, the most frequently observed correlates of child neglect and/or abuse were sole parent status and the number of children per household. Many early studies of the link between child maltreatment and family structure, however, failed to control for other factors which might influence child maltreatment. Evidence supportive of the importance of sole parent status as a correlate of child neglect and/or abuse has since emerged from a variety of studies employing appropriate controls

(Cotterell 1986; Young and Gately 1988; Creighton and Noyes 1989; Coulton and Pandey 1992; Garbarino and Kostelny 1992; Nelson, Saunders and Landsman 1993; Pett, Vaughan-Cole and Wampold 1994; Coulton et al. 1995; Kotch et al. 1995; Chaffin, Kelleher and Hollenberg 1996; Zuravin and DiBlasio 1996).

It has sometimes been observed that the effects of single parent family status on child maltreatment diminish or appear insignificant in the presence of controls for psychiatric problems or substance abuse (e.g. Kotch et al. 1995; Chaffin, Kelleher and Hollenberg 1996). This finding is not necessarily in conflict with the assumption that single parent family status increases the risk of child neglect and/or abuse. Psychological problems such as drug abuse, depression and anxiety are common reactions to the pressures of poverty and single parent family status. There is every reason to expect these problems to affect adversely the quality of parenting, and in so doing to mediate at least some of the effect of single parent family status on child neglect and/or abuse. We should hardly be surprised, then, to find that regression analyses employing single parent family status as a predictor of child maltreatment find that its effect is attenuated or absent in the presence of variables tapping psychological problems such as depression, anxiety and substance abuse.

Large family size is another well-documented risk factor for child neglect and abuse. In their prospective longitudinal study Kotch et al. (1995) found that the number of children in a household was a predictor of child maltreatment even in the presence of controls for maternal depression, lower maternal education, infant illness, receipt of Medicaid (assistance with medical expenses for people with low incomes), separation of a mother from her own mother, emotional support given to a mother by her own mother and maternal experience of violence. In a separate prospective longitudinal study Chaffin, Kelleher and Hollenberg (1996) confirmed the importance of house-hold size as an independent predictor of both child neglect and abuse even in the presence of controls for (the child's) age, marital status, maternal substance abuse and maternal depression. This latter study is of particular significance because, as noted earlier, it relied on personal interviews rather than official reports to determine whether neglect or abuse was present in the family.

Other studies relying on official records have obtained similar results. Zuravin and DiBlasio (1996) examined the factors which best discriminated between neglecting, abusing and control families all receiving benefits under a US Government program known as Aid to Families with Dependent Children (AFDC). They found that the number of dependent children was the best single discriminator of the difference between neglecting and control families, and of the difference between abusive and control families. Nelson, Saunders and Landsman (1993) conducted a similar discriminant analysis designed to identify the factor which best discriminated parents reported for child neglect but in which the neglect had not been confirmed, parents newly reported for child neglect where the neglect had been confirmed, and parents with chronic histories of confirmed child neglect. The number of children in the family emerged as a strong discriminator of all three groups. The importance of crowded households as a predictor of child maltreatment has also been strongly confirmed at the aggregate level. Zuravin (1986) examined the relationship between per cent residential density (defined as per cent of dwellings with 1.51 or more persons/room) and reported rates of child abuse and neglect across 202 census tracts in Baltimore, Maryland. The results of her analysis indicated that residential density was significantly related to reported rates of child neglect and abuse in the presence of controls for race and socioeconomic class.

Although family structure and family size are among the most frequently cited correlates of child neglect and abuse a range of other factors have also been implicated. Rates of neglect and abuse are generally higher in areas with higher levels of geographical mobility (Spearly and Lauderdale 1983; Coulton and Pandey 1992; Garbarino and Kostelny 1992; Coulton et al. 1995; Krishnan and Morrison 1995). There is also evidence that rates of child neglect and/or abuse are higher amongst disadvantaged minority groups, such as Blacks and Mexican-Americans (Spearly and Lauderdale 1983; Coulton and Pandey 1992; Garbarino and Kostelny 1992; Coulton et al. 1995; Krishnan and Morrison 1995; Chaffin, Kelleher and Hollenberg 1996). Both these effects hold up in the presence of controls for family economic status and family structure.

It seems likely that geographical mobility and ethnicity derive their significance as predictors of child maltreatment at least partly from the fact that they both signal defects in the strength of neighbourhood social supports. Most researchers examining the effect of geographical mobility as a predictor of child maltreatment maintain that families in neighbourhoods with high levels of mobility have fewer material and emotional resources to call on to ameliorate the stresses of parenting and poverty. Similar arguments have been put in relation to ethnic minority groups (see, for example, Spearly and Lauderdale 1983: 95). In the case of ethnic minority groups this disruption to social networks stems from the fact that the family and kinship structure of indigenous groups in the United States, Canada and Australia suffered massive disruption in the wake of European invasion (Weeks 1988; York 1989). The appropriation of land by Europeans for pastoral use typically resulted in whole communities of indigenous people being uprooted from their traditional lands. In Australia the disruption to indigenous life was further exacerbated with the forcible removal of Aboriginal children from their families, ostensibly for their benefit but with generally calamitous results (Human Rights and Equal Opportunity Commission 1997).

Among the black population in the United States, different processes appear to have produced similar results. According to Martin and Martin (1978), the urban environment has had a destructive effect on the supportive functions of the black extended family. This disruption to the social networks of black families appears to have been further exacerbated during the 1980s by the deindustrialisation of central cities and the exodus of middle- and upper-income black families from the inner city (Sampson and Wilson 1995: 42).

Family structure, family size, geographical mobility and ethnicity are the principal exogenous sources of social stress on families with dependent children. But there are also a range of other factors which have been found to exacerbate the risk of child neglect and/or abuse. As we intimated above, these include depression (Gaudin et al. 1993; Hubbs-Tait et al. 1994; Kotch et al. 1995; Chaffin, Kelleher and Hollenberg 1996; Zuravin and DiBlasio 1996) and substance abuse (Davis 1990; Kelley 1992; Dore, Doris and Wright 1995; Jaudes, Ekwo and Van Voorhis 1995; Harrington et al. 1995). In her review of the literature on risk factors associated specifically with child neglect, Salmelainen (1996) also cites factors such as the level of conflict between parents, deficiencies in maternal problem-solving skills and the presence in the family of a child with a handicap or developmental disability. Furthermore Tomison (1996c) cites a body of evidence supporting the hypothesis that parents exposed as children to neglect and/or abuse are at increased risk (regardless of their circumstances) of neglecting or abusing their own children.

The role of social supports in child maltreatment

Since the lack of adequate social support appears to exacerbate the effects of economic stress on child maltreatment, we might expect the provision of support to buffer its effects. Although studies examining this issue often fail to employ adequate statistical controls, their findings generally confirm this expectation. Several studies, for example, have shown that the social networks of neglecting or abusive mothers are smaller than those of non-maltreating mothers matched in terms of at least some of the key factors known independently to affect the risk of child maltreatment. Gaudin et al. (1996) compared the social network size of non-neglecting and neglecting parents who had been matched on household income and a range of other demographic characteristics (but had not been matched in terms of the number of children or the mother's education). Asked to list 'persons important in your life' the primary caregivers from the control group listed significantly more members than did providers from the neglect group. Coohey (1996) obtained similar findings in her comparison of neglecting parents with controls matched on the basis of poverty level, number of dependent children and the mother's race and age (but not matched in respect of mother's education level and family structure). Neglecting and abusing parents generally listed fewer close friends and relatives and also indicated that they experienced fewer contacts on average from each member of their social network than their matched control counterparts. The Western Australian Child Health Survey (Zubrick et al. 1995: 44) found that caregivers who know their neighbours well enough to ask them 'to mind a child for an hour in an emergency, water the garden or feed a pet when away on holiday' were only about half as likely as those who did not know their neighbours this well to report a high level of family discord. Kotch and Thomas (1986) found that the use of regular childcare and the presence of an extended family reduced the likelihood of substantiated child maltreatment amongst families otherwise at risk of such maltreatment.

The social network differences between maltreating and non-maltreating parents are mirrored in their perceptions of the extent of social support enjoyed by each group. Lacharité, Ethier and Couture (1996), for example, found that neglectful mothers in two-parent families generally rated their partners as less supportive and their relationship with their partner less satisfactory than mothers not reported for neglect who had been matched on maternal and paternal age, number of children, family occupational status, family income, marital duration and biological status of the father. Similar findings have been reported by those comparing perceived levels of social support among maltreating and non-maltreating parents from sources other than the marital partner (Cotterell 1986; Caliso and Milner 1994; Coohey 1995, 1996). These differences in social support appear to be linked, at least in part, to variations in neighbourhood social structure. Garbarino and Sherman (1980) examined various forms of neighbourhood interaction in two neighbourhoods which had been matched in terms of socioeconomic and racial profile but which had very different reported rates of child maltreatment. Compared with the low-rate neighbourhood, mothers in the high-risk neighbourhood tended to assume more exclusive and direct responsibility for childcare, used children in the neighbourhood as playmates for their own children less frequently, engaged in fewer neighbourhood exchanges, made less use of neighbourhood resources and rated their neighbourhood more poorly as a place to live.

There is some limited evidence that direct material support may act as a buffer against the effects of economic stress on child maltreatment. In their ecological study of the structural determinants of child maltreatment, Spearly and Lauderdale (1983) found that county rates of child abuse were lower in counties which had higher average monthly AFDC payments than in counties with lower average monthly payments. This effect held up even after controlling for differences between counties in household income, family structure and the number of dependent children aged less than six years. Coohey (1995, 1996), in the studies cited earlier, also found that neglecting mothers received fewer material and instrumental resources from friends and relatives than mothers in non-neglecting or non-abusing control groups. While these studies raise the possibility that direct financial or material support may act as a buffer against the effects of economic stress on child maltreatment, their results should be treated with some caution. In the studies by Coohey material support was just one among a number of factors which discriminated between maltreating and non-maltreating families. The evidence presented by Spearly and Lauderdale in relation to income support, on the other hand, is open to other interpretations. It is possible, for example, that the counties spending smaller amounts per capita on AFDC in their study also provided a smaller range of non-material services to families with dependent children.

Whatever the relative importance of various forms of social support as buffers against the effects of economic stress on parenting, it is plain that the effects of economic stress on child maltreatment cannot be considered in isolation from the effects of social stressors and supports. As Belsky (1993) points out, child maltreatment is determined not just by the level of household income available to a family but by the overall balance of stressors and supports they experience. The available evidence suggests that poverty and unemployment are probably less likely to lead to child maltreatment in families which have strong social supports but more likely to lead to maltreatment among parents or caregivers whose parenting capacity is already weakened by factors such as lack of support from a partner, a weak social network, psychological disorder, substance abuse, prior history of maltreatment, lack of parenting skills or the presence of a maladjusted or disabled child. If we accept this argument we should expect poor communities in general to have higher rates of child neglect and abuse, but the strength of the cross-sectional relationship between economic stress and child maltreatment will depend on the extent to which those communities can call upon resources which attenuate or buffer the effects of poverty.

The interaction between economic and social stress

So far we have treated economic and social stress as if they were processes which exert similar but nevertheless independent effects on the prevalence of criminogenic child-rearing practices. Considered over time, however, economic and social stress are best viewed as two mutually interacting social processes. This is because economic stress appears to increase the risk of parental separation (and the absence of a supportive partner is an important source of social stress for parents with dependent children), while parental separation, in turn, appears to increase the risk of economic stress.

Wilson (1987) cites a variety of studies in the United States attributing the rise in family dissolution among black families after the Second World War to increasing rates of unemployment among young black men. Junankar and Kapuscinski (1992) examined the effect of unemployment on the annual divorce rate in Australia between 1921 and 1989, controlling for the age structure of the population, the urbanisation rate and gender-specific wage rates. They found a significant positive relationship between the unemployment rate and the divorce rate. Divorce, in turn, has been found by others to exert a depressing effect on income. Weston (1986) examined the effect of divorce on income using data collected as part of a large-scale longitudinal study conducted by the Australian Institute of Family Studies on the effects of divorce on families. She observed that, while the real incomes of both males and females declined several years after divorce, the income of men in the lowest income categories actually rose slightly several years after divorce. Furthermore, even where the income of both male and female divorcees decreased, in every category of pre-separation income, women experienced a larger drop in income following divorce than men. Whereas, for example, the median real incomes of men in the top income category had declined by 27 per cent, the median real incomes of women declined by 51 per cent (Weston 1986: 103).

These findings indicate that, over time, the combined effects of economic and social stress on the prevalence of problems such as child neglect and abuse are probably much greater than the separate contributions of these stressors to the same problems at a given point in time. Exposure to economic stressors, such as unemployment, appears to increase the risk of exposure to social stressors, such as family dissolution. Exposure to social stressors such as family dissolution, on the other hand, increases the risk of exposure to economic stressors, such as a significant drop in income. The two types of stress in this way would appear to amplify each other's effects over time, each increment in the percentage of families living in poverty producing a further increase in problems such as family dissolution, which in turn produce a further increase in poverty and so on.

This interaction is strengthened in another important way which turns out to be of some significance when we consider the relationship between parenting and crime. Individuals or families who are chronically poor are likely to find themselves quarantined into neighbourhoods where housing and rental accommodation is cheap. But, as we saw above, individuals and families who are poor include a disproportionate number who are exposed to some form of social stress. This is true not only because economic stress increases the risk of family dissolution. Most other forms of social stress (e.g. large family size, psychiatric problems, drug abuse, inability to communicate in the dominant language group) also restrict the earnings potential and increase the risk of unemployment amongst those exposed to them. The result is that, instead of the various forms of economic and social stress being geographically distributed more or less independently of each other, they tend to be concentrated together in certain neighbourhoods.

The spatial concentration of economic and social stress may exert effects which ramify into successive generations of individuals growing up in poor neighbourhoods. Children growing up in impoverished neighbourhoods are more likely to show poorer educational attainment and cognitive skills, and are more likely to give birth as a teenager, than children with the same characteristics who do not grow up in impoverished neighbourhoods (Jencks and Mayer 1990). Lower educational attainment and teenage parenthood are themselves risk factors for child neglect and abuse (Nelson, Saunders and Landsman 1993; Kotch et al. 1995; Zuravin and DiBlasio 1996). The spatial concentration of economic and social stress is therefore likely to exert deleterious effects on child-rearing practices above and beyond those which would be expected if individuals exposed to these stresses were not concentrated in certain areas.

Summary and conclusion

There is strong evidence to suggest that economic stress exerts a very disruptive effect on the parenting process, increasing the risk that parents will neglect or abuse their children or engage in discipline which is harsh, erratic and/or inconsistent. This evidence comes from aggregate-level studies, which show that the incidence of child neglect and abuse (but particularly the former) is more prevalent in areas with a larger percentage of poor households. It also comes from individual-level studies which have charted the effects of economic stress on families.

The effects of economic stress on parenting, however, cannot be considered in isolation from those of social stress. Social stressors – such as the lack of a supportive partner, a larger than average number of dependent children, social isolation, drug abuse and psychiatric disorder – increase the risk that economic stress will lead to disrupted parenting. Social supports, however – in the form of a close family network or close relationships with friends and neighbours – can buffer the effects of economic stress.

Economic and social stress also interact in two other important ways. Over time, families which experience economic stress are at elevated risk of experiencing social stress because factors such as unemployment increase the risk of family dissolution. Family dissolution, on the other hand, often leads to increased economic stress because the level of household income, particularly for the parent left with principal responsibility for the children, declines sharply in the wake of family dissolution.

Economic and social stress reinforce each other in another way. The nature of the housing market means that those exposed to either form of stress are likely to find themselves quarantined in the same neighbourhoods. The spatial concentration of poverty and social disadvantage can be expected to produce adverse effects on parenting above and beyond those which would be expected if they were distributed across neighbourhoods independently of each other.

CHAPTER THREE

Parenting, peers and delinquency

The control theory position

If economic stress in the absence of social supports increases the risk of parenting behaviour which is neglectful or abusive or is marked by harsh, inconsistent, erratic discipline, then does such behaviour, in turn, increase the risk of juvenile involvement in crime? If it does, are all the effects of economic stress on delinquency mediated through parenting deficiencies? If they are, is the relationship between parenting defects and delinquency direct, or are the effects of inadequate parenting on delinquency mediated through some other process, such as association with delinquent peers? These questions form the central focus of this chapter.

The classical answer to them was given by control theory. The theory rejects the hypothesis that economic stress or association with delinquent peers plays any role in the production of delinquency. However, it is entirely consistent with the proposition that parenting behaviour which is neglectful or abusive or is marked by harsh, inconsistent and erratic discipline increases the risk of juvenile involvement in crime. In the original version of the theory (Hirschi 1969) inhibitions about involvement in crime are acquired partly as a result of attachments which form between juveniles and their parents or other law-abiding authority figures, partly as a result of commitments to conventional society, partly as a result of involvement in conventional activities and partly as a result of beliefs about the importance of adhering to conventional social norms. Defective parenting is treated by the theory as disruptive of these processes.

Despite recent modifications, control theory remains no less committed to the implication of a strong association between defective parenting and juvenile involvement in crime. In the revised theory, delinquency will occur unless someone with whom a child has an emotional bond (1) monitors his/her behaviour; (2) recognises deviant behaviour when it occurs; and (3) punishes such behaviour in a consistent and loving manner (Gottfredson and Hirschi 1990: 97). Since child neglect or maltreatment, or inconsistent, erratic or harsh discipline can be expected to interfere with (1), (2) and (3), such parental behaviours can also be expected to elevate the risk of juvenile involvement in crime.

Parental controls and delinquency

The central thesis of control theory must be regarded as one of the best supported hypotheses in criminology. Research evidence on the importance of parental variables to delinquency began accumulating nearly twenty years before the publication of *Causes of Delinquency* (Hirschi 1969). In their classic study *Unraveling Juvenile Delinquency*, for example, Glueck and Glueck (1950), found that poor parental supervision of children and a weak parent–child bond were among the best predictors of subsequent juvenile involvement in crime. The importance to delinquency of the parent–child bond and the level of parental supervision of children has since been repeatedly confirmed in studies relying on official crime data and in studies relying on self-report crime data.

Loeber and Stouthamer-Loeber (1986) have carried out what remains the most thorough and comprehensive review of the relevant literature. They grouped studies of family factors and delinquency into four basic paradigms: *neglect, conflict, deviant behaviours and attitudes* and *disruption*.[1] The results of studies within each of these paradigms were separately analysed according to whether they involved concurrent (i.e. cross-sectional) or longitudinal designs and comparison or normal samples.[2] In order to assess the relative importance of variables examined within each of these paradigms as predictors of delinquency they constructed a common measure of predictive efficacy called RIOC (relative improvement over chance). This index ranged between zero (no predictive efficacy) and 100 per cent (perfect predictive efficacy) and was able to be calculated from data published in most of the studies they reviewed. Where the data from studies within the above-mentioned paradigms could not be converted to RIOC values (e.g. where measures of group differences were based on *t* or *F* values) Loeber and Stouthamer-Loeber employed a standard effect size estimate, called Cohen's *d*.[3]

The results of Loeber and Stouthamer-Loeber's analysis revealed that variables associated with the neglect paradigm consistently outperformed variables from the other paradigms as predictors of juvenile delinquency. Amongst the highest median RIOC values in concurrent comparison samples were parent–child involvement (61.5 per cent), supervision (66.3 per cent), discipline (73.5 per cent) and parental rejection (62.6 per cent). The meta-analysis revealed that the ranking of variables based on the measure of d for these studies was very similar. It also revealed that the ranking of RIOC values for the longitudinal studies (all of which involved normal samples) was very similar to that for concurrent studies, this ranking being: parents' involvement with children (31 per cent), parental rejection of children (35.8 per cent) and supervision (36.4 per cent). Loeber and Stouthamer-Loeber also found evidence that the strength of these control variables grew rather than dissipated over time. As they put it: 'in the concurrent studies, based on normal samples, the median RIOC for supervision and rejection was 14.6 per cent and 24 per cent, respectively, compared with 36.4 per cent and 35.8 per cent in the longitudinal studies'.

The importance of parental control variables to the onset of delinquency has since been confirmed in numerous other studies. Simons, Robertson and Downs (1989) employing a panel design and a sample of 300 adolescents chosen from drug treatment programs and the general community found that parental rejection predicted delinquency even after controls were introduced for other family process variables, such as family conflict, family religiosity and maternal employment.

Widom (1989), employing a prospective matched control design (with matching on race, sex, age and socioeconomic status), found that children registered as having been neglected or abused by their parents were significantly more likely as adults to have a criminal record. About 29 per cent of the neglected/abused group, compared with approximately 21 per cent of their matched controls, were found to have a criminal record. About 16 per cent of the neglected/abused group, compared with approximately 10 per cent of their matched controls, had a criminal record for a violent offence. These differences between maltreated and control groups might not appear substantial but it is important to remember that families in the control group were not screened for the quality of their parenting. It is possible, therefore, that juveniles from the control groups were subjected to forms of parenting which were defective but not serious enough to warrant official intervention.

McCord (1983) in a forty-year longitudinal study of 232 males found that 10 per cent of abused, 15 per cent of neglected and 29 per cent of rejected children had adult criminal records compared with 7 per cent of children rated by social workers as having been 'loved' by their parents. In a follow-up study (McCord 1991) also found that poor child-rearing in the domains of

mother's competence, father's interaction with the family and family expectations all predicted future juvenile delinquency.

Smith and Thornberry (1995), employing a stratified random sample of
1,000 New York students and – controlling for race/ethnicity, social mobility,
sex, socioeconomic status and family structure – replicated the Widom study
and found that officially recorded child neglect was strongly correlated with
both officially recorded and self-reported crime. They also found evidence
that the likelihood of subsequent involvement in crime increased with the
seriousness of the earlier child maltreatment.

The centrality of parenting factors to delinquency has also been confirmed
in studies which measure parenting directly rather than relying on official
records. Larzelere and Patterson (1990) found that the level of parental
monitoring and the consistency of parental discipline among a sample of 206
male high-school students predicted both official and self-reported delinquency, even in the presence of controls for socioeconomic status. Weintraub
and Gold (1991), employing a representative sample of 1,395 American
adolescents, found that parental monitoring predicted delinquency even after
controls were introduced for age, sex and the strength of the affectional
relationship between parents and children. Thornberry et al. (1991) conducted a panel study of 987 students and found that the strength of a student's
attachment to his or her parents was inversely related to delinquency, even in
the presence of controls for the level of attachment to school.

Essentially similar results have also been obtained in cross-sectional studies
by Barnes and Farrell (1992), Martens (1992), Mak (1994), Rankin and Kern
(1994) and Burton et al. (1995), in a retrospective longitudinal study by
Sampson and Laub (1994), and in a prospective longitudinal study by Johnson
et al. (1995).

Nevertheless it has occasionally been suggested that, while there is an
association between child neglect and/or abuse and juvenile delinquency, the
relationship is not as strong as early studies may have suggested. Zingraff et al.
(1993) argue that many of the earlier studies of the relationship between child
maltreatment and delinquency contained serious methodological weaknesses
(e.g. unrepresentative samples, self-reports of prior maltreatment, retrospective research designs, absence of relevant controls). The best designed
matched-control studies (e.g. McCord 1983; Widom 1989) show that the
majority of maltreated children do not end up with a criminal record, even if
they do appear to be at greater risk of offending than their matched control
counterparts.

To remedy the defects they had identified in past studies Zingraff et al.
classified maltreatment according to whether it involved neglect, physical

abuse or sexual abuse and then examined officially recorded rates of juvenile court referral amongst a sample of juveniles officially recorded as having been maltreated, with the juvenile court referral rates of two comparison samples: one drawn from a school population and one drawn from families receiving social security. Juveniles in the comparison samples who had any record of maltreatment were removed, and differences in court referral rates among the samples were then compared after controls had been introduced for age, race, gender and family structure. Zingraff et al. found that, although the joint effect of all types of maltreatment was independently predictive of involvement in minor status offences, none of the individual types of maltreatment was significantly associated with delinquency in the presence of each other. They also found that the majority of juveniles who had been recorded as maltreated had no juvenile court record. This led them to conclude that the maltreatment–delinquency relationship had been exaggerated.

The wealth of studies attesting to the influence of parental supervision and inconsistent, erratic, harsh discipline on delinquency suggests at once that Zingraff et al.'s findings should be regarded with some caution. Officially reported child neglect and abuse are but extreme manifestations of the kinds of behaviours independently shown in the many studies reviewed by Loeber and Stouthamer-Loeber (1986) to produce delinquency. The absence of any relationship between officially recorded neglect/abuse and officially recorded crime raises questions about either the measurement of these variables or the research design in which their relationship was explored.

As it happens there are at least two features of the Zingraff et al. study which call into question its conclusions. First, the tactic of removing juveniles officially reported as maltreated from the comparison samples may not have been enough to ensure that the comparison samples were actually free of maltreated subjects. In fact the comparison samples had characteristics (e.g. a high percentage of poor, black sole-parent households) which would have rendered them likely to have had a proportion of maltreated juveniles even if such maltreatment had not been detected by child welfare authorities. If this occurred it is impossible to gauge the independent effect of maltreatment on the likelihood of delinquency.

The second point to note is that, as Zingraff et al. themselves point out, their measure of delinquency only tapped juvenile court referrals. The study, in other words, did not measure self-reported involvement in crime, juvenile contacts with police which were not referred to a juvenile court, or adult arrest histories. This may not have hampered the capacity of their study to detect *differences* between maltreatment and comparison groups in the rate at which juveniles were referred to court. But it would have limited its capacity to determine differences in the true proportion of maltreated children who ended up involved in unreported crime or crime as adults.

Control theory and the role of economic stress

If control theorists were right in their emphasis on the role of parenting in delinquency, the evidence increasingly suggests they were wrong in their view that economic stress plays no part in the onset of delinquency. The evidence of Chapter 2 indicates that the conditions which control theory treats as central to the prevention of delinquency (i.e. strong emotional attachment to parents, parental supervision of children, consistent discipline) are precisely those which economic stress in the absence of social supports appears prone to disrupt. In fact a number of the studies we reviewed in Chapter 2 directly exhibit the interrelationship between economic stress, parenting and delinquency.

Lempers, Clark-Lempers and Simons (1989) found that, although families experiencing economic stress were more likely to have children involved in delinquency and drug use, the effect of economic stress was substantially reduced once controls were introduced for the level of nurturance shown by the parents to the children and for the consistency of their discipline.

Harris and Marmer (1996) found that poverty reduced the level of paternal emotional and behavioural involvement with adolescents which, in turn, increased the level of their involvement in delinquency. A close affective relationship with the father or a close emotional bond with the mother, on the other hand, appeared to reduce the effect which poverty had on self-reported delinquency.

Silbereisen, Walper and Albrecht (1990) measured juvenile 'transgression proneness' (as evidenced by self-reports by adolescents on their inclination to act against 'common rules and norms') and found that families which had suffered moderate or high income loss over the past year were more likely to have children who were transgression prone. A path analysis, however, revealed that the effects of income loss on transgression proneness were mediated by the level of family integration (i.e. lack of family conflict) and the level of juvenile self-derogation.

The studies by Harris and Marmer, and Silbereisen, Walper and Albrecht, while suggestive, do not permit one to gauge how much of the influence of economic stress on delinquency is mediated by parental variables. The studies best designed to address this question have been conducted by Larzelere and Patterson (1990) and Sampson and Laub (1994). Both set out to determine whether the effects of family economic status on the likelihood of juvenile involvement in crime persisted after controls were introduced for the parental behaviours which putatively mediate the effects of economic stress.

Larzelere and Patterson (1990) examined the interaction between family socioeconomic status, parental monitoring, parental discipline and delinquency amongst a sample of fourth-grade school students in the Oregon Youth Study. As expected, they found a strong bi-variate relationship between the socioeconomic status of the parents and both self-reported and officially recorded offending. When, however, controls were introduced for a composite parental management variable, formed out of separate measures of parental monitoring and consistency of parental discipline, the effect of parental socioeconomic status on delinquency was reduced to zero. They concluded that the usual effects of socioeconomic status on delinquency are mediated entirely by differences in parental discipline and monitoring.

Sampson and Laub (1994) addressed the same issue. Instead of measuring family socioeconomic status, however, they employed a measure of family poverty based on average weekly earnings and the family's reliance on outside aid. The parental variables measured were very similar to those employed in Larzelere and Patterson. Rather than just confine themselves to the question of whether economic stress exerted its influence on delinquency through parenting practices, however, Sampson and Laub constructed indices of social stress (e.g. family size, family disruption, maternal employment and foreign-born status). This enabled them to see whether the effects of social stress on delinquency were also mediated through parenting practices.

Sampson and Laub found a strong bi-variate relationship between family poverty and delinquency. Once again, the relationship disappeared after controls were introduced for the degree of erratic/harsh discipline and the level of parental supervision. They found, moreover, that most of the effect of the social stressors on delinquency was also mediated through its effects on discipline and parental supervision. They concluded that poverty and structural disadvantage influence delinquency by reducing the capacity of families to achieve effective informal social control.

These studies strongly suggest that the influence of economic stress on juvenile participation in crime is mediated through parental controls. The study by Sampson and Laub, taken together with the evidence of Chapter 2, further suggests that the effects of social stress on delinquency are also mediated through those same controls. We need to know, however, whether defects in parental controls influence delinquency directly or through association with delinquent peers. To address this issue we must examine studies which have examined the relationship between parental controls, delinquent peers, parents or siblings and juvenile participation in crime.

Control theory and the role of delinquent peers

Control theorists have been no less emphatic in their rejection of delinquent peers as a stimulus for involvement in crime than they have been of economic stress. They appear to have been no less mistaken on the same issue. At first blush the rejection by control theorists of delinquent peer influence as a proximate cause of involvement in crime would seem a hard position to justify. As Reiss (1986a) points out, the majority of juvenile offending is carried out with an accomplice. The range of different crime types in which a motivated offender becomes involved, moreover, would appear to be constrained by the knowledge and skills that he or she has about the execution of different types of crime. Yet such knowledge and skills, for the most part, can only be acquired from those who already have them. If this were not enough, it is well established that peer influence is one of the strongest correlates of delinquency (Kornhauser 1978; Elliott, Huizinga and Ageton 1985; Matsueda and Heimer 1987; Agnew 1991b; Brownfield and Thompson 1991; Warr and Stafford 1991). Association with delinquent peers is also known to precede and seems to amplify delinquency (Thornberry et al. 1994; Keenan et al. 1995).

The existence of a strong correlation between delinquency and association with delinquent peers was in fact known long before the advent of control theory (Glueck and Glueck 1950). The problem has always been what to make of this observation. It could be taken to mean that when non-delinquents associate with delinquents they are themselves more likely to become delinquents. This could be called the 'rotten apple' theory (because 'one rotten apple spoils the barrel'). On the other hand it could just be taken to mean that like-minded people (including delinquents) tend to form friendships with one another. This might be called the 'birds of a feather' theory.

The former view, of course, is epitomised in differential association theory, the theory that delinquency is learned by association with delinquent peers. Differential association theory fell from grace for reasons which were both partly theoretical and partly empirical. Its theoretical problems stemmed from the fact that it provided what can only be described as an abstruse account of the learning process. The principle of differential association held that 'a person becomes delinquent because of an excess of definitions favourable to violation of law over definitions unfavourable to violation of law' (Sutherland and Cressey 1978: 80–82). Yet the theory assigned no clear operational meaning to the term 'excess of definitions' and no means of determining a priori when an excess of definitions of one kind or another had been experienced by an individual. This left the theory, in a strict sense, practically untestable.

Hirschi himself mounted a number of empirical arguments against the differential association theory. First, he argued that if delinquent peer influence was a causal influence in delinquency then delinquents should be as, if not more closely, attached to their peers than non-delinquents. Otherwise there was little likelihood of a susceptible juvenile being influenced by delinquent attitudes and values. Second, the stronger the attachment to peers, the weaker should be the attachment to parents (Hirschi 1969: 140). Third, he argued that if delinquent peer influence is the central causative factor in juvenile crime then there should be little or no correlation between the level of attachment felt by a juvenile for his or her parents and school, and his or her self-reported delinquency, once controls are introduced for delinquent peer influence (Hirschi 1969: 98).

The data collected by Hirschi did not seem to support any of these implications. He found that juveniles strongly attached to their peers, were less likely to report committing delinquent acts than juveniles not strongly attached to their peers and that the stronger the attachment between juveniles and their peers, the stronger the attachment they felt to their parents (Hirschi 1969: 142–146). He also found that, regardless of the delinquency of their friends, boys who were more closely attached to their parents were less likely to commit delinquent acts than those who were less closely attached (Hirschi 1969: 100).

Hirschi's arguments, however, suffer from a number of weaknesses. Perhaps the most significant of these is the fact that Hirschi failed to consider the possibility that social control variables may exert a distal effect on participation in crime while peer association exerts a proximate effect. In other words, the level of attachment to parents may determine whether and to what extent delinquent friends later increase the likelihood of involvement in delinquency. Warr (1993a), for example, using data from the National Youth Survey, examined the relative effects of time spent with family members and level of attachment to parents on association with delinquent peers and involvement in delinquency. He found that the quantity of time adolescents spend with their family has moderate to strong effects in counteracting delinquent peer influence. Attachment to parents appeared to exert an indirect effect on delinquency by reducing the likelihood that adolescents associate with delinquent peers. Similar findings have been obtained by Agnew (1991a, 1991b). They suggest that in the absence of a strong family bond, association with delinquent peers does in fact increase the risk of juvenile involvement in crime.

A second problem is that Hirschi's own data (Hirschi 1969: 158) show that self-reported offending rates varied much more strongly with the number of delinquent friends than with what Hirschi called their 'stake in conformity' (a composite measure formed from separate measures of attachment to the father, attachment to school and need for achievement). Those same data suggest that the strength of the association between delinquent peers and self-reported delinquency depends on a juvenile's stake in conformity. This is entirely consistent with the differential association theory argument that weak bonds between children and their parents facilitate association with delinquent peers.

A third problem with control theory is that there is no reason to assume that delinquent peer influence is only possible in the context of a close bond between adolescents. Emotional attachments among members of delinquent peer groups are often marked by estrangement rather than intimacy (Pabon, Rodriguez and Gurin 1992). Such estrangement need not impede delinquent peer influence. It could be transmitted through contact with individuals who model and reward deviant behaviour or who ridicule and stigmatise conforming behaviour. It could be transmitted through information about how to carry out certain criminal acts. Alternatively it could be transmitted because neighbourhoods with large numbers of delinquents create a culture of tolerance toward involvement in crime.

Direct empirical support can be found for at least two of these possibilities and arguments may be adduced in favour of the third. Warr and Stafford (1991) compared delinquent peer attitudes and delinquent peer behaviour as predictors of self-reported delinquency. The results of their analysis showed that delinquent peer behaviour was much more important as a predictor of self-reported offending than delinquent peer attitudes. They also showed that, whereas the effects of delinquent peer attitudes largely disappeared when controls were introduced for a respondent's own attitudes toward offending, delinquent peer behaviour exerted effects on self-reported offending which were not mediated by a respondent's own attitudes. These results indicate that it is the behaviour of delinquent peers which is influential in generating delinquency, not the attitudes and values evinced by delinquents or those with whom they come into regular contact.

Evidence on the importance of criminal knowledge and skill as a source of delinquency has come from studies by Bruinsma (1992) and McCarthy (1996). Using survey methods with a cross-section of 1,096 secondary-school students, Bruinsma examined various mechanisms through which contact with delinquent peers might stimulate delinquency, including identification with the source of deviant contacts, positive definitions of deviant behaviour and the frequency of communication with delinquent friends about techniques for committing delinquent acts. His analysis indicated that the frequency of communication with delinquent friends about criminal techniques was by far the most important of the delinquent peer mechanisms through which association with delinquent friends produced delinquent behaviour, being even more influential than parental control variables.

McCarthy (1996) examined the importance of tutelage in criminal techniques in a sample of 390 homeless adolescents in Toronto, Canada. As well as obtaining measures of various aspects of parental control, he constructed measures of various ways in which association with delinquent peers might influence delinquency. In addition to several crime-specific measures of tutelage (e.g. methods of minimising the risk of detection for drug-selling), these measures included the extent of deviant associations at home and on the street and the strength of deviant attitudes held by respondents. He found that the effect of tutelage on self-reported delinquency far surpassed that of any other variable, including, once again, the parental control variables included in the analysis.

Finally, while there is no direct evidence that neighbourhoods with large numbers of delinquents create a culture of tolerance toward involvement in crime the hypothesis is not an unreasonable one. Reiss (1986a) has cited ethnographic evidence that offences such as theft are both endemic to and highly visible occupations in many lower-class or working-class communities. The same communities also usually have a high proportion of males with criminal convictions. In such circumstances, the social stigma attached to visible or proven involvement is likely to be far less than that in communities where rates of juvenile or adult participation in serious crime are low, and visible involvement in delinquency relatively uncommon. Social stigma is known to exert a powerful inhibitory influence on behaviour (Thorsell and Klemke 1976). We would therefore expect communities with high proportions of active offenders to have, for this reason alone, higher rates of initiation into crime.

The role of delinquent parents and siblings

Association with delinquent peers is not the only means by which individuals may come to get involved in crime. If contact with delinquent peers is criminogenic because it provides an opportunity to acquire skills in crime and attitudes conducive to involvement in it, contact with a delinquent sibling or criminal parent should have the same effect. Unfortunately, compared with the amount of research conducted on the influence of delinquent peers, there has been a paucity of research on the effect of delinquent parents and siblings on the likelihood of involvement in crime.

Most studies in the area, nevertheless, find evidence that delinquent parents and siblings increase the risk of involvement in crime. Early suspicions that this might be the case arose from the observation that a small proportion of families account for a large proportion of convicted persons. Loeber and Stouthamer-Loeber (1986: 101) cite a number of studies illustrating this point. These include a study by Wilson (1975) of disadvantaged inner-city families showing that 16 per cent of families studied produced 62 per cent of the delinquent children, a study by Farrington, Gundry and West (1971) showing that 4.3 per cent of families from the Cambridge Study in Delinquent Development produced 49.6 per cent of the convicted children, and a study by the New York City Youth Board showing that about 75 per cent of the city's delinquents came from about one per cent of the city's families.

Loeber and Stouthamer-Loeber also cite a number of studies providing more direct evidence that parental or sibling criminality increases the risk of juvenile involvement in crime. Of the fourteen longitudinal analyses of the effects of parental criminality or aggression on juvenile conduct problems or delinquency they reviewed, nine produced significant results. Eight of the nine analyses examining the influence of deviant parental attitudes on the deviancy of their offspring also found a significant positive relationship.

Of course, the fact that the children of parents with a criminal record or deviant attitudes are at increased risk themselves of becoming deviant may by interpreted in several ways. It could indicate that the offspring of deviant parents are at increased risk of involvement in crime because of a shared genetic predisposition to criminal behaviour (Brennan, Mednick and Volava 1995). It could indicate that adolescents exposed to deviant behaviour by their parents tend to imitate such behaviour. Or it could indicate that deviant parents create a family environment which independently increases the risk of involvement in crime. Deviant parents, for example, may supervise their children less intensively or engage in criminogenic patterns of discipline. Note, however, that if the shared genetic predisposition hypothesis is true, the association between contact with delinquent siblings or parents and increased risk of delinquency is causally spurious. The correlation between the two must be regarded as arising from the influence of a third factor.

Evidence on the mechanisms underpinning sibling and parental criminality effects on delinquency is somewhat mixed. In their reanalysis of the Gluecks' data, Sampson and Laub (1993) found that parental criminality exerted a strong effect on the likelihood of juvenile involvement in crime and that most of this effect was mediated through the family environment. It appeared that paternal criminality increased the risk of erratic and harsh discipline on the part of both the father and the mother and that this, in turn, produced the increased risk of juvenile involvement in crime. Rowe and Farrington (1997), however, have recently re-examined the issue and come to a somewhat different conclusion. Employing stronger controls for the effect of sibling criminality (including, for example, controls for the number and gender of delinquent siblings) but similar controls for family environment they found evidence that parental criminality exerted a direct effect on the criminality of their offspring. Such an effect is consistent with a 'shared genetic inheritance' hypothesis but also with the hypothesis of direct imitation.

The studies by Sampson and Laub (1993) and Rowe and Farrington (1997) also differed in the conclusions they reached concerning the effect of sibling criminality. Sampson and Laub found that neither sibling criminality nor attachment to delinquent siblings exerted any effect on juvenile involvement in crime in the presence of controls for residential mobility, family size, household crowding, maternal employment, foreign-born status and deviance among delinquent peers. Taking a somewhat different tack, Rowe and Farrington estimated the number of delinquent siblings among families with three male children expected under a random distribution of convicted individuals. Their results show that there were more families with exactly no convicted boys or three convicted boys than would be expected by chance alone. They interpreted these results as indicating that relatively conforming siblings discourage other siblings' criminal behaviour while the presence of antisocial siblings encourages such behaviour.

On balance it would seem reasonable to assume, given current knowledge, that one or other or both of parental or sibling criminality increases the risk of juvenile involvement in crime. Whether the effects are direct – as Rowe and Farrington's study seems to suggest – or indirect – as Sampson and Laub's study seems to suggest remains unclear. Even if the effects are direct, however, at least some of the effect would appear to be environmental rather than inherited. If the interpretation given to the sibling effects by Rowe and Farrington is accepted, sibling criminality must be an outcome of the family environment. If the interpretation of the parental criminality effects given by Sampson and Laub is accepted, parental criminality also exerts its effects by environmental means.

Integrated control theories

The consistency and inherent sense of these findings has led to a reappraisal of the role of delinquent peers in generating delinquency. Instead of regarding control and differential association theories as competing explanations of delinquency, an increasing number of theorists have begun looking for ways in which to integrate them. Scholarly interest in the role of delinquent peers has also been strengthened by reformulations of differential association theory which have enhanced its clarity and plausibility. Burgess and Akers (1968) reformulated the theory drawing heavily on the principles of operant conditioning and modelling. These principles, which are underpinned by a substantial body of empirical evidence, gave the learning principles of differential association theory a more secure foundation.

Most integrated theories of delinquency construe it as the outcome of an interaction between strain, social control and differential association variables (Elliott, Huizinga and Ageton 1985; Simons, Conger and Whitbeck 1988). In Elliott et al.'s theory, for example, high levels of strain (as indexed by a perceived inability to fulfil material aspirations by legitimate means) and low levels of social control combine to increase the likelihood of association with delinquent peers. This, in turn, increases the likelihood of involvement in crime.

The theory implies that little or no relationship should be observed between delinquency and either strain or social control variables, once controls are introduced for association with delinquent peers. Elliott et al. tested this implication using survey data from 1,725 individuals who participated in three waves of the National Youth Survey (a longitudinal survey of delinquency and drug use among American youth). Measures of strain and social control were based, respectively, on self-reported discrepancies between aspirations and actual or expected achievements (strain), and self-reported attachment to or involvement with parents and school (social control).

The three waves of the survey enabled two independent tests of the theory: one from criterion variables at wave 1 to delinquency at wave 2, and a second from criterion variables at wave 2 to delinquency at wave 3. In both tests, the results of a path analysis revealed that neither strain nor social control variables exerted any direct effect on delinquency. The only variables exerting a direct effect were delinquent peers and prior delinquency. Furthermore, when controls for prior delinquency were introduced, Elliott et al. observed that persons who were strongly bonded to delinquent peers were more delinquent than those who were not and, furthermore, that the volume (i.e. frequency) of their delinquency was inversely related to the strength of their bond to family and school (Elliott, Huizinga and Ageton 1985: 133). No evidence was found to support the contention that juveniles experiencing higher levels of strain were also more likely to associate with delinquent peers. Instead strain appeared to weaken the bond between parents and children.

A second form of integrated theory is that put forward by Agnew (1993). He rejected the control theory assumption that social control factors, per se, increase the risk of delinquency. His main argument is that the motivation to offend is variable, being influenced by parenting and perceived blockages of social opportunity. Inadequate parental controls are seen as influencing delinquency but only if disadvantage and/or alienation from parents and school produce anger and frustration. In this circumstance juveniles are likely to associate with delinquent peers and thereby become involved in crime (Agnew 1993: 256).

Using data from a nationally representative survey of 2,213 male adolescents Agnew (1993) found evidence confirming his hypothesis that weak parental attachment was most likely to be associated with delinquency among juveniles who rated highly on a composite scale measuring anger/frustration. He also found evidence that association with delinquent peers mediated the influence of social control factors on delinquency. This effect was most pronounced when the delinquents with which juveniles associated were reported as committing a large number of delinquent acts. Agnew concluded on the basis of this finding that weaknesses in social control only affect delinquency when those affected by such weaknesses associate with delinquent peers.

Sampson and Laub (1993, 1994) put forward an integrated theory of delinquency which followed that of Elliott, Huizinga and Ageton. However, whereas Elliott, Huizinga and Ageton viewed strain variables as influencing delinquency both directly and indirectly, Sampson and Laub argued that strain variables influence delinquency through their effects on social control variables. They tested their theory by carrying out a series of reanalyses of the data collected by Glueck and Glueck (Sampson and Laub 1993, 1994). Sampson and Laub (1994) found that family socioeconomic status exerted no effect on delinquency once controls for inconsistent discipline, supervision and parental attachment were introduced. In a separate set of analyses, designed to assess the relative efficacy of different factors as predictors of delinquency, Sampson and Laub (1993) found that school attachment, mother's supervision and delinquent peer attachment exerted the strongest effects on both official and self-reported delinquency (Sampson and Laub 1993: 120). Delinquent peer influence was the strongest of these factors; having delinquent friends increased the probability of officially recorded delinquency by 90 per cent.

Interestingly, Sampson and Laub (1993: 116) also found that children from large families were more likely to be attached to delinquent peers or siblings than children from smaller families. Since family size was found to be associated with delinquency (even in the presence of controls for residential mobility, parental supervision, problematic child behaviour and delinquent peer attachment) this result suggests that the effects of social stress on delinquency were transmitted through the same mechanisms as those of economic stress. Both appeared to influence the likelihood of juvenile involvement in crime by eroding the capacity or willingness of parents effectively to monitor and supervise the behaviour of their children, thereby leaving them vulnerable to delinquent peer influence.

Further support for the hypothesis that economic and social stress exert their effects through common mechanisms can be found in a study by Steinberg (1987). Noting the common observation of an association between single parent family status and delinquency, Steinberg set out to assess whether the children of single parent families were more susceptible to delinquent peer pressure. Employing a convenience sample of 865 adolescent school students, he presented each student in the sample with a series of hypothetical dilemmas involving antisocial activity (e.g. vandalism, cheating, stealing). The task in respect of each dilemma was to choose between two courses of action: one suggested by the student's 'best friends' and the other suggested by what the student 'really' thought he or she should do. Even after controlling for sex, age, socioeconomic status and maternal employment status, Steinberg found that family structure exerted a strong effect on susceptibility to peer influence. Students from single parent families were significantly more susceptible to peer influence than students from families where both biological parents were present.

A more complex form of integrated control theory, known as coercion theory, has been developed by Patterson and his colleagues at the Oregon Social Learning Centre (Patterson and Dishion 1985; Snyder and Patterson 1987; Patterson, Capaldi and Bank 1991). As with the integrated control theories of Elliott, Huizinga and Ageton, and Sampson and Laub, coercion theory views economic stress as disruptive of the parenting process (Larzelere and Patterson 1990). However, instead of assuming that there is a single path to delinquency, coercion theory postulates two paths to delinquency: one for so-called 'early starters' (defined as those whose antisocial behaviour becomes apparent roughly between the ages of four to nine) and one for so-called 'late starters' (defined as those whose antisocial behaviour does not become apparent until early adolescence). The role of social controls and peer influence in generating delinquency is seen to be somewhat different for early and late starters. Peer influence, in particular, is assigned a stronger influence on delinquency among late starters than among early starters.

According to coercion theory it is not so much the failure of indirect social controls (e.g. the lack of a close emotional bond between parent and child) which is the key to the onset of delinquent behaviour among early starters, or even the failure of direct social controls, in the form of adequate parental supervision. Instead, disruption in socialisation occurs in two stages. In the first pre-adolescent stage inept family socialisation practices (e.g. frequent severe but non-contingent punishments which, in effect, reinforce coercive and threatening behaviour in the child) result in high frequencies of antisocial but largely trivial behaviours by the child, such as non-compliance, fighting, temper tantrums, petty theft and lying. The outcome of this process is a child who is antisocial and lacks interpersonal skills. These characteristics increasingly place the child at risk for rejection by peers and adults and, as a result, for later academic failure.

In the second stage, as a result of being rejected by peers and adults, the child begins to gravitate toward other unskilled coercive children. These children may later amplify each other's delinquency but inadequate parenting practices are held principally responsible both for delinquent peer association and for involvement in delinquency.

For late starters, by contrast, delinquent peers are held to be much more important. Late starters are at least marginally successful in peer relations and academic studies. In early adolescence, however, their parents' marginal family management skills are disrupted by forces such as divorce, unemployment, substance abuse, illness or the 'normal perturbations that accompany their son's drift into adolescence' (Patterson, Capaldi and Bank 1991). As a result the 'late starter' falls under the influence of delinquent peer groups. His or her greater social competence, however, ensures that their period of involvement in crime and association with deviant peers is relatively short-lived by contrast with that of the early starter.

The putative difference between early and late starters in the role of delinquent peers as a cause of involvement in crime is a point of some significance to the present discussion. Early starters are known to have longer criminal careers than late starters and, for this reason, are likely to exert a stronger influence over aggregate rates of offending. But if coercion theory is right in its assumption that association with delinquent peers is more a correlate than a cause of involvement in crime amongst early starters, we are forced to conclude that association with delinquent peers does not play a strong role in precipitating involvement in crime in those whose behaviour exerts the most potent effects on aggregate crime rates. As it happens, the evidence suggests that delinquent peer influence is an important precipitator of involvement in crime even amongst those who begin their criminal career early. Patterson, Capaldi and Bank (1991: 160) found that for many so-called 'early starters' the acquisition of an antisocial personality does in fact serve to promote later association with delinquent peers which in turn increases the risk of involvement in crime. Similar findings have been obtained by Simons et al. (1994).

The salience of contact with offenders as a mediating variable

We will not attempt an assessment of which of the theories discussed in the previous section is best supported by the available evidence. For our purposes their differences are less important than their basic similarity. To the extent that they address the issue, all are consistent with the proposition that the effects of social and economic stress on delinquency are mediated through parenting defects. Each is also consistent with the proposition that the effects of defective parenting on delinquency are mediated, either in whole or in part, through association with delinquent peers. These hypotheses have been confirmed in the studies conducted to test the theories. They have also been confirmed in numerous other studies.

Simons and Robertson (1989) found empirical support for a model of adolescent drug use which argued, in part, that parental rejection lowered adolescent self-esteem which then increased association with delinquent peers and thereby increased involvement in substance abuse. The same model was successfully tested in relation to general delinquency by Simons, Robertson and Downs (1989). Simons et al. (1991) found empirical evidence suggesting that inept parenting practices, weak identification with parents, prosocial values and problems at school all affected delinquency indirectly through their influence on delinquent peers. Matsueda and Heimer (1987) obtained evidence that delinquent peer influence explained the stronger association between family dissolution and delinquency in black American families than in white families. Blackson et al. (1996) found that paternal substance abuse and difficult paternal temperament increased the level of affiliation of their sons with deviant peers. A number of studies have shown that association with delinquent peers remains a predictor of delinquency even in the presence of parental control variables (e.g. Simons and Robertson 1989; Lawrence 1991; Burton et al. 1995; Sorenson and Brownfield 1995). Agnew (1991a, 1991b) has provided longitudinal evidence that delinquent peer influence and delinquency amplify and reinforce each other over time and Warr (1996) has recently highlighted the key role which older, more experienced offenders play in instigating criminal behaviour on the part of novice juvenile offenders.

To the extent that the integrated control theories differ in ways which are important to the present discussion, it is principally over the question of whether all or only some of the influence of social control variables on delinquency is transmitted through delinquent peers or whether control variables exert both direct and indirect effects on delinquency. The evidence on this issue is somewhat inconclusive. All studies converge in showing a greatly attenuated relationship between parental factors and delinquency when controls are introduced for delinquent peer influence. However, some of the studies we have reviewed find that the effects of social control variables disappear in the presence of controls for delinquent peer influence while others find that social control variables continue to exert direct effects on delinquency even in the presence of variables measuring delinquent peer influence.

The central finding by Elliott, Huizinga and Ageton (1985) that delinquent peer influence mediated all the effects of social control variables on delinquency has been confirmed in several other studies. Weintraub and Gold (1991), for example, found that when controls were introduced for association with delinquent peers, the effect of parental monitoring on delinquency declined to insignificance. Similar results have been obtained by Agnew (1993). Evidence that delinquent peers may not mediate all of the influence of social control variables on delinquency was obtained in a study by Patterson and Dishion (1985). They conducted an interview study of 136 male school students employing multiple sources of information about parenting practices, social skills and involvement in delinquency. Poor social skills and inadequate parental monitoring were both found to increase the likelihood of association with delinquent peers which was, in turn, strongly correlated with the level of self-reported and official delinquency. Although association with delinquent peers was the strongest single predictor of both official and self-reported delinquent behaviour, the results of a path analysis indicated that parental monitoring and academic skills influenced delinquency both indirectly, through their effects on association with delinquent peers, and directly.

In the final analysis it may be difficult to resolve the question of whether parenting factors exert an effect on delinquency independently of delinquent peer influence. Evidence of a residual effect of parenting factors on delinquency after controls have been introduced for peer influence may just signal a failure to measure delinquent peer influence adequately. This is an important point because there is no consensus on how best to measure the salience of delinquent peer influence as a proximate cause of involvement in crime. Some studies measure attachment to delinquent peers, others measure the extent of association with delinquent peers. Yet others concentrate on the level of transmission of information about techniques for committing crime. To the extent that any one of these measures is inadequate, its inclusion in a regression equation with parental control variables will give the appearance that the latter exert direct effects rather than effects mediated through delinquent peers. There are unquestionably multiple pathways to delinquency (Huizinga, Esbensen and Weiher 1991; Paternoster and Brame 1997) but on balance it would seem reasonable to assume that peer group influence provides the dominant pathway through which parenting variables (and therefore economic stress) exert their effects on the proclivity of juveniles to become involved in crime.

Parental controls, delinquent peers and neighbourhood effects on crime

The evidence we have just reviewed is consistent with the thesis that the aggregate-level relationship between economic stress and crime is mediated by family and peer group processes. If contact with delinquent peers plays an important proximal role in precipitating juvenile involvement in crime it becomes possible to see how economic and social stress, acting through family and neighbourhood processes, might jointly influence the rate of delinquent population growth in a neighbourhood. The higher the prevalence of parenting problems in an area, the larger the potential pool of juveniles susceptible to delinquent peer influence in the area. The rate at which juveniles susceptible to delinquent peer influence *become* delinquent, however, is limited by the frequency or probability of contact with juveniles already involved in crime. To put the matter another way, the rate at which *potential* delinquents in a neighbourhood are converted into *active* delinquents should depend upon the prevalence of delinquency in the neighbourhood.

In Chapters 4 and 5 we explore this hypothesis and the assumptions underpinning it. We do this, first using individual-level data drawn from a large-scale survey of families in Western Australia, and then using aggregate-level data drawn from official records of child maltreatment and delinquency in New South Wales. The object of the individual-level analysis is to show that (economic and social stress induced) parenting problems have a greater effect on the likelihood of a juvenile becoming involved in crime when they occur in a 'delinquent-prone' neighbourhood. The object of the aggregate-level analysis is to show that the processes mapped out at an individual level are significant enough to exert measurable aggregate-level effects. This is important if only because parenting and peer influence may provide a pathway between socioeconomic stress and crime without carrying all or even most of the traffic.

Summary and conclusion

The evidence presented in this chapter suggests that the children of families exposed to economic and social stress are more likely to become involved in crime. The effect is not direct. Instead, it appears to arise because such stress produces parental behaviour which is lax in supervision, which weakens the bond between parent and child and/or which involves harsh, erratic and inconsistent discipline. Each of these parental behaviours has been consistently shown to increase the risk of involvement in crime.

Just as the effects of family economic stress on delinquency are mediated through defective parenting, the effects of defective parenting on delinquency are mediated in whole or in part by association with delinquent peers, siblings and/or criminal parents. Precisely how such associations increase the risk of delinquency is not fully understood. It would appear that delinquent peer behaviour is more important than delinquent peer attitudes in stimulating delinquent behaviour. It is also known that delinquent peer influence is particularly strong when it involves communication about techniques for carrying out certain kinds of criminal activity (or reducing the risks associated with them). Parental and sibling criminality is also associated with increased risk of involvement in crime. This association may be produced by the existence of a shared genetic susceptibility to involvement in crime. But there is also evidence to suggest that criminal parents and delinquent siblings exert a direct or indirect causal effect on the likelihood that previously non-delinquent siblings will become involved in crime. These findings support the hypothesis that economic and social stress exert most of their effects on aggregate crime rates through parental and peer group processes. If this is true, the rate of entry into crime in a neighbourhood should be a joint function of the prevalence of parenting problems in the neighbourhood and the prevalence of involvement in crime in that neighbourhood. Chapters 4 and 5 explore this hypothesis, first using individual-level data and then using aggregate-level data.

CHAPTER FOUR

Delinquency generation at the individual level

The general approach

While the principal focus of this chapter is upon testing whether poor parenting is more likely to produce delinquency in 'delinquent-prone' neighbourhoods, we also seek to provide confirmation of earlier findings about the role of parenting as a mediator of the effects of economic and social stress on crime. We begin by showing the effect of economic and social stress on participation in crime. We then examine the effect of economic and social stress on parenting, followed by the effect of parenting upon participation in crime. We then examine the relative effects of parenting variables on delinquency in crime-prone versus non crime-prone communities. Finally we test whether all of the effects of social and economic stress on delinquency are channelled through poor parenting.

Data and methods of analysis

The source of individual-level data is a large scale epidemiological survey of child health and well-being conducted in Western Australia in 1993. The survey was not conducted to explore the correlates of offending. The focus of the survey was on estimating the prevalence and distribution of mental health problems and other chronic medical conditions, and on estimating the prevalence and distribution of adverse health behaviours (Zubrick et al. 1995). It targeted children aged 4–16 and was conducted jointly by the Institute for Child Health Research and the Australian Bureau of Statistics.

A number of different survey instruments and data collection methods were used in the survey. The following measures of specific interest to us were either collected directly or were derivable from data collected in the survey:

- family type;
- family income;
- neighbourhood type;
- parenting style;
- parental supervision;
- involvement in crime.

Information on family type and family income came from questions which were asked of primary caregivers in face to face interviews about their family background. Family type was categorised as either single parent or couple, and family income was categorised as either at most $16,000 per annum or more than $16,000 per annum.

Information on neighbourhood type came from questions about neighbourhood problems. The questions were included in a questionnaire on family health and activity which was self-administered by caregivers. A respondent's neighbourhood was classified as 'crime-prone' if the respondent indicated that the family was affected by one or more of the following problems in their neighbourhood: vandalism or graffiti, house burglaries, car stealing, harassment or violence in the streets.

Information on parenting style came from questions about methods and frequency of disciplining and rewarding children. These questions were asked of caregivers in a child health questionnaire which was administered in face to face interviews. We used a categorisation of parenting style which only took account of the frequency of coercive methods of discipline used by parents (low or high frequency) regardless of their use of rewards and reinforcements.[1]

A self-report questionnaire completed by 12–16-year-old youths provided information on parental supervision and involvement in crime. Youths were asked to indicate whether, in the last six months, their parents let them go out any evening *never, sometimes, often* or *very often*. They were also asked about their recent contact with the criminal justice system. We classified them as being involved in crime if, in the last six months, they reported they had (1) been questioned by the police about anything they might have done such as stealing, damaging property or something else; or (2) been to the Children's Panel or had a warning from the police for anything they had done; or (3) been to the Children's Court or some other court for anything they had done.

We use information on family type to measure social stress, information on family income to measure economic stress, information on neighbourhood type to measure neighbourhood differences in participation in crime, and information on parenting style and supervision to measure criminogenic parenting practices.

To test our hypotheses *generalised estimating equations* (see, for example, Liang and Zeger 1993) were used to fit models similar to logistic regression models. In ordinary logistic regression it is assumed that the observations are independent of each other. However, the assumption of independence did not hold for the Western Australian Child Health Survey data because the sampling design used a two-stage selection process: a sample of districts (Census Collection Districts) was selected first, then a sample of dwellings was selected within these districts. All children aged 4–16 resident in the selected dwellings were eligible for inclusion in the survey. There were therefore two main sources of correlation between observations, within districts and within families. This correlation structure was modelled in the generalised estimating equations used to fit regression models to the data.[2] However, in reporting the results, we have used odds ratio estimates and confidence intervals based on robust (empirically based) estimates of error variance. Age and gender were included in all regression models as control variables. Age was split into two categories: 12–14 year-old and 15–16 year-old.

The effect of social and economic stress on participation in crime

Our first step was to confirm, for this set of data, that there is a relationship between involvement in crime and social and economic stress. Hence we fitted a model with involvement in crime as the response variable and family type, family income, age and gender as predictor variables. The results are shown in Table 4.1.

The table shows the odds ratios, and their 95 per cent confidence intervals, for each of the significant terms in the model. It can be seen that, in the presence of family type, there is no significant effect of family income. The odds ratios show that: (1) the odds of juveniles from single parent families being involved in crime are 2.9 times greater than the odds of juveniles from couple families being involved in crime; (2) the odds of 15–16-year-olds being involved in crime are 2.0 times greater than the odds of 12–14-year-olds being involved in crime; and (3) the odds of males being involved in crime are 3.8 times greater than the odds of females being involved in crime. These results confirm a relationship between social stress and crime. The significant effects of age and gender indicate the necessity to control for these effects when testing for the effects of other variables.

A clearer idea of the effect of being in a single parent family is evident from

Table 4.1. *Involvement in crime: Model with family type and family income as predictors*

Terms in the model	Odds ratio	95% confidence interval
Family type (single parent versus couple)	2.9	1.1–7.7
Family income (low versus other)	NS	
Age (15–16 versus 12–14)	2.0	1.1–3.7
Gender (male versus female)	3.8	1.7–8.4

Note: 'NS' indicates the odds ratio is not statistically significant from 1.0.

Table 4.2. *Estimated percentage of juveniles involved in crime: Family type, family income*

	Percentage	95% confidence interval for percentage
Family type		
Single parent	22.4	13.6–31.3
Couple	6.8	4.4–9.2
Family income		
Income ≤ $16,000	22.3	13.6–31.1
Income > $16,000	7.7	5.0–10.5

Table 4.2 which shows the estimated percentages of 12–16-year-olds involved in crime for both single parent and couple families (the percentages are population estimates averaged over all other variables). The table shows that 22.4 per cent of juveniles from single parent families are involved in crime (i.e. recent contact with police, a Children's Panel or a court) compared with 6.8 per cent from couple families.

Table 4.2 also shows the estimated percentages of 12–16-year-olds involved in crime for low- and higher-income families. It indicates that, when averaged over other variables, there is an effect of income on involvement in crime. There are 22.3 per cent of juveniles from low-income families involved in crime compared with 7.7 per cent from families with higher incomes (and the non-overlapping confidence intervals indicate these two percentages are significantly different from each other). The fact that low income was not significant in the fitted regression model, once the effect of single parent families was taken into account, indicates that it is probably predominantly the single parent families who have low incomes.

To test whether there was an interaction effect between family type and family income, a model similar to that shown in Table 4.1 was fitted, the only difference being that family income was replaced as an explanatory variable by an interaction effect between family type and family income. As was the case with family income, the interaction effect was not significant in the presence of family type.

The effect of social and economic stress on parenting

Our next step was to examine the effects of family type and family income on parenting as measured by parental supervision. For the purpose of fitting a regression model with supervision as a dichotomous response variable, parental supervision was classified into two groups: (1) juveniles who were allowed out any evening *very often*, and (2) juveniles who were allowed out any evening *never, sometimes* or *often*. (The reason for this particular split will become clear later.)

Table 4.3 shows the results of fitting a regression model using family type, family income, age and gender as predictors of supervision. Neither age nor gender significantly affected supervision. However, both family type and family income had significant effects. The odds of juveniles from single parent families being poorly supervised (*very often* allowed out any evening) are 2.6 times greater than the odds of juveniles from couple families being poorly supervised. The odds of juveniles from low-income families being poorly supervised are 3.2 times greater than the odds of juveniles from families with higher incomes being poorly supervised.

These effects on supervision are more clearly seen in Table 4.4 which shows the estimated percentages of juveniles *very often* allowed out any evening, together with their associated 95 per cent confidence intervals. The table is in two parts. The first part shows that 11.9 per cent of juveniles from single parent families are allowed out *very often* any evening, compared with 3.4 per cent of juveniles from couple families; and similarly, that 14.0 per cent of

Table 4.3. *Supervision: Model with family type and family income as predictors*

Terms in the model	Odds ratio	95% confidence interval
Family type (single parent versus couple)	2.6	1.0–6.3
Family income (low versus other)	3.2	1.2–8.1
Age (15–16 versus 12–14)	NS	
Gender (male versus female)	NS	

Note: 'NS' indicates the odds ratio is not statistically significant from 1.0.

Table 4.4. *Estimated percentage of juveniles poorly supervised: Family type, family income, family type by family income*

	Percentage	95% confidence interval for percentage
Family type		
Single parent	11.9	7.2–16.6
Couple	3.4	1.5–5.2
Family income		
Income ≤ $16,000	14.0	7.3–20.8
Income > $16,000	3.3	1.4–5.3
Single parent families		
Income ≤ $16,000	19.8	9.9–29.8
Income > $16,000	3.7	−0.5–7.9
Couple families		
Income ≤ $16,000	2.2	−5.9–10.3
Income > $16,000	3.3	1.4–5.2

juveniles from low-income families are allowed out *very often* any evening, compared with 3.3 per cent of juveniles from higher income families. These percentages are averaged over all other variables.

The second part of the table shows the percentages for the two-way cross-tabulation of family type by family income. It is clear from this part of the table that the critical combination is a single parent family with a low income. Nearly one in five juveniles from such families is allowed out *very often* any evening. By comparison there are small, and very similar, percentages of poorly supervised juveniles for all other combinations of family type and income.

We also tested whether social and economic stress affected parenting using parenting style as the measure of parenting. However, neither family type nor family income was found to be a significant predictor of parenting style.

The effect of parenting on delinquency

The next step was to test the effects of supervision on involvement in crime. Before discussing the fitted regression model we present the population estimates of the percentages of juveniles involved in crime, tabulated by supervision. The percentages in Table 4.5 are proportions of juveniles

Table 4.5. *Estimated percentage of juveniles involved in crime: Supervision*

Allowed out any evening:	Percentage	95% confidence interval for percentage
Never	6.2	2.3–10.1
Sometimes	9.3	5.5–13.0
Often	8.8	−0.8–18.3
Very often	43.7	23.5–64.0

involved in crime according to their level of self-reported supervision by parents (or caregivers), averaged over all other variables. It is clear from the table that there is little difference between the proportions involved in crime for those allowed out any evening *never, sometimes* or *often*. However, four out of ten (43.7 per cent) juveniles allowed out any evening *very often* are involved in crime. This proportion is significantly different from the other three percentages in the table (as indicated by their non-overlapping confidence intervals). It is because of the relationship evident in Table 4.5 that the supervision variable used in the regression models was categorised as either (1) *very often* or (2) *never, sometimes* or *often*.

Table 4.5 indicates a strong effect of supervision on involvement in crime. Fitting a regression model allows us to explore this effect while controlling for other factors. The results of fitting a model with supervision, age and gender as predictors of involvement in crime are shown in Table 4.6. The table shows that the odds of being involved in crime for juveniles who are allowed out *very often* any evening are 8.9 times greater than the odds of being involved in crime for juveniles allowed out less frequently. We also fitted a similar model with parenting style as a predictor of involvement in crime but parenting style was found to be non-significant.

The relationship between parenting, neighbourhoods and delinquency

We now come to one of the main objectives of this chapter, that is, to test whether delinquency is more likely to result from poor parenting in crime-prone neighbourhoods than in neighbourhoods which are not crime-prone. Table 4.7 shows the results of fitting a model similar to that in Table 4.6 except that the model includes an additional predictor variable, neighbourhood type. Table 4.7 shows there is a significant neighbourhood effect on involvement in crime even after taking account of the effects of supervision.

Table 4.6. *Involvement in crime: Model with supervision as predictor*

Terms in the model	Odds ratio	95% confidence interval
Parental supervision (poor supervision versus other)	8.9	3.3–23.9
Age (15–16 versus 12–14)	NS	
Gender (male versus female)	3.5	1.6–7.6

Note: 'NS' indicates the odds ratio is not statistically significant from 1.0.

Table 4.7. *Involvement in crime: Model with supervision and neighbourhood type as predictors*

Terms in the model	Odds ratio	95% confidence interval
Parental supervision (poor supervision versus other)	8.3	3.2–21.4
Neighbourhood type (crime-prone versus other)	2.0	1.0–4.1
Age (15–16 versus 12–14)	NS	
Gender (male versus female)	3.6	1.6–7.9

Note: 'NS' indicates the odds ratio is not statistically significant from 1.0.

The odds of juveniles from crime-prone neighbourhoods being involved in crime are twice as great as they are for juveniles from neighbourhoods without crime problems.

Table 4.8 shows the estimated percentages of juveniles involved in crime by both supervision and neighbourhood type. For poorly supervised juveniles the estimated percentages involved in crime are 51.0 per cent for those living in crime-prone neighbourhoods compared with 33.8 per cent living in neighbourhoods which are not crime-prone.[3]

The interrelationship between social and economic stress, parenting and delinquency

Using data from the Western Australian Child Health Survey, we have now confirmed that, compared with juveniles from other types of families, juveniles from poor single parent families are more likely to be poorly supervised and more likely to be involved in crime. Further, we have seen that juveniles who

Table 4.8. *Estimated percentage of juveniles involved in crime: Supervision by neighbourhood type*

Allowed out any evening:	Not crime-prone neighbourhood		Crime-prone neighbourhood	
	Percentage	95% confidence interval	Percentage	95% confidence interval
Never	5.0	0.4–9.6	8.8	2.0–15.7
Sometimes	6.9	2.6–11.2	14.1	6.2–22.1
Often	9.1	−1.5–19.8	5.0	−2.6–12.6
Very often	33.8	0.2–67.3	51.0	24.5–77.6

are poorly supervised are much more likely to be involved in crime than those who are not poorly supervised. We now turn to assessing the extent to which social and economic stress exert their effects on delinquency through their effects on parenting.

If social and economic stress influence delinquency by causing incompetent parenting, which then causes delinquency, we would expect social and economic stress to have no effect on delinquency in the presence of a measure of incompetent parenting (because all of the social and economic stress effects would be channelled through incompetent parenting). Table 4.9 shows the results of fitting a regression model using supervision, family type, age and gender as predictors of involvement in crime. Family income was not included in this model because it had no significant effect on involvement in crime in the presence of family type (see Table 4.1). Table 4.9 shows that there are significant effects of both supervision and family type. Nevertheless the odds ratio for supervision is greater than that for family type.

The effects of supervision and family type on involvement in crime can be seen in Table 4.10. An estimated 82.0 per cent of juveniles from single parent families who are poorly supervised are involved in crime. Even though the confidence interval for this percentage is quite large its lower bound is 57.6 per cent. This means that well over half the juveniles from single parent families who are allowed out very often any evening are involved in crime (to the extent of having recent contact with the criminal justice system). While the table also shows that the percentages of juveniles involved in crime are generally greater for single parent families than for couple families and that, for couple families, the percentage of poorly supervised juveniles involved in crime is greater than for those not poorly supervised, the confidence intervals are so large that none of these pairwise comparisons is significantly different.

Table 4.9. *Involvement in crime: Model with supervision and family type as predictors*

Terms in the model	Odds ratio	95% confidence interval
Parental supervision (poor supervision versus other)	6.7	2.8–16.3
Family type (single parent versus couple)	3.4	1.6–7.2
Age (15–16 versus 12–14)	NS	
Gender (male versus female)	3.8	1.7–8.3

Note: 'NS' indicates the odds ratio is not statistically significant from 1.0.

Table 4.10. *Estimated percentage of juveniles involved in crime: Supervision by family type*

	Percentage	95% confidence interval for percentage
Never allowed out any evening		
Single parent	12.1	0.3–23.9
Couple	5.3	1.9–8.7
Sometimes allowed out any evening		
Single parent	18.5	5.8–31.2
Couple	7.1	4.2–10.1
Often allowed out any evening		
Single parent	8.4	−25.8–42.6
Couple	8.9	0.7–17.2
Very often allowed out any evening		
Single parent	82.0	57.6–106.4
Couple	11.6	1.5–21.8

Summary and conclusion

Using data on individual juveniles and their families from a representative household survey we have seen that our hypothesis about the way in which economic and social stress generate delinquency is, to a large extent, confirmed.

Social stress and economic stress affect parental supervision. An estimated 19.8 per cent of 12–16-year-olds from single parent low-income families are allowed out very often any evening, compared with less than 4 per cent from any other combination of family type and income.

Supervision has an effect on involvement in crime. More than 40 per cent of juveniles allowed out very often any evening have recent contact with the criminal justice system for something they have done. By comparison, less than 10 per cent of better supervised juveniles are involved in crime.

Neighbourhood type also has a significant effect on involvement in crime even after taking account of the effect of supervision. The odds of being involved in crime are twice as great for those who live in crime-prone neighbourhoods than the odds for those who don't. This finding does not provide direct evidence that interaction between juveniles whose parenting has been inadequate and those who are already involved in crime is the principal mechanism by which new delinquents are generated. It does, however, provide powerful indirect evidence that this is likely to be the case. It also runs directly counter to theories which assign no role to social context in the supply of motivated offenders.

Not all of the effects of social stress are channelled through supervision. Family type and supervision are both found to have significant effects on involvement in crime when included together as predictors in a regression model. Nevertheless supervision has a higher odds ratio than does family type indicating that a greater increase in involvement in crime would result from an increase in poorly supervised juveniles than from an increase in juveniles from single parent families (assuming the latter could be increased without affecting parental supervision). It is also possible that the finding that family type is significant, even after taking account of the effect of supervision, may just reflect that supervision is not a strong measure of all the aspects of incompetent parenting which result from social and economic stress.

When self-reported parenting style was used as a measure of incompetent parenting there were no significant effects. This result deserves some comment. It should be remembered that it is parenting of young children which is the most critical. It would have been preferable to have a measure of how parents disciplined their children when they were young rather than at their present age of 12–16. Silburn et al. (1996) quote results from the Western Australian Child Health Survey showing that coercive parenting methods are used far less frequently for adolescents than for younger children. About 30 per cent of parents of 4–11-year-olds smack their children often or sometimes, compared with 6 per cent of parents of 12–16-year-olds. It seems reasonable to assume that parenting styles change as children grow older. The self-reported methods of disciplining a 12–16-year-old are therefore probably not a good measure of incompetent parenting.

CHAPTER FIVE

Delinquency generation at the aggregate level

Individual-level research studies make a convincing case that incompetent parenting is one of the major causal pathways through which economic and social stress influence individual offending behaviour. Yet, by themselves, they are incapable of resolving the question of whether the aggregate-level association between economic stress and crime is mediated mainly by such parenting. There may be other more important ways in which economic stress influences juvenile participation in crime. To show that the economic stress and aggregate crime rate relationship can be explained in terms of the effect of economic stress on parenting we need to examine the interrelationship between economic stress, parenting and juvenile participation in crime at both individual and aggregate levels.

The first aim of this chapter, then, is to assess whether economic and social stress increase rates of juvenile involvement in crime largely because they increase the prevalence of criminogenic parenting practices. The second aim is to see whether there are any measurable neighbourhood effects at the aggregate level. We examine these effects for both property and violent crime. We also examine the relationship between economic stress and parental behaviour for both adult and juvenile participation in crime. Finally, to assess how important rates of participation in crime are as determinants of the level of crime, we examine the relationship between criminal participation rates and aggregate crime rates.

In order to address these issues we must construct aggregate-level measures of economic and social stress, juvenile participation in crime and the prevalence of criminogenic parenting practices in a neighbourhood. This last task is far from easy. Although the individual-level research literature is quite specific about the kinds of parental behaviour and family environments which are criminogenic (e.g. weak parental supervision; weak parent–child bond; erratic, harsh and inconsistent discipline), no aggregate-level measures of these variables exist. To obtain aggregate-level measures of poor parenting we were obliged to work with official classifications of parental behaviour devised for the purpose of protecting children from criminal maltreatment rather than for the purpose of monitoring trends in the antecedents of juvenile or adult participation in crime. In New South Wales the Department of Community Services identifies two general forms of child maltreatment. These are child neglect (comprising physical and/or emotional neglect) and child abuse (comprising physical or sexual abuse). Separate measures were calculated for neglect and for abuse as a means of tapping the prevalence of criminogenic parenting practices.

As a measure of juvenile involvement in crime we used Children's Court appearances for property or violent offences. Court appearances for other offences (e.g. drug offences) were excluded because they can vary with police practice, whereas property and violent offences usually come to police attention when reported by victims. As measures of social and economic stress we used data from the 1991 census. Indicators of poverty and unemployment were used as measures of economic stress and indicators of single parent families, residential stability and crowded dwellings (as a proxy for large families) were used as measures of social stress.

All measures were calculated for each postcode area of New South Wales and were calculated as rates based on the relevant population in each postcode. Specifically, the variables included in our analysis were defined as follows:

- *neglect*: the number of children with at least one notification during the five-year period 1 July 1986 to 30 June 1991 for either neglect or emotional abuse (but not for physical or sexual abuse), divided by the number of 0–15-year-olds resident in the postcode at the 1991 census;
- *abuse*: the number of children with at least one notification during the five-year period 1 July 1986 to 30 June 1991 for either physical or sexual abuse (but not for neglect or emotional abuse), divided by the number of 0–15-year-olds resident in the postcode at the 1991 census;
- *juvenile participation in crime*: the number of juveniles with at least one court appearance during the five-year period 1 July 1990 to 30 June 1995 where the most serious offence was a property or violent offence, divided by the number of 10–17-year-olds resident in the postcode at the 1991 census;
- *juvenile participation in property crime*: the number of juveniles with at least one court appearance during the five-year period 1 July 1990 to 30 June 1995

where the most serious offence was a property offence, divided by the number of 10–17-year-olds resident in the postcode at the 1991 census;

- *juvenile participation in violent crime*: the number of juveniles with at least one court appearance during the five-year period 1 July 1990 to 30 June 1995 where the most serious offence was a violent offence, divided by the number of 10–17-year-olds resident in the postcode at the 1991 census;

- *poverty*: households with an annual income of less than $16,000, as a proportion of all households at the 1991 census;

- *unemployment*: unemployed persons, as a proportion of the labour force at the 1991 census;

- *single parent families*: single parent families with dependent offspring, as a proportion of all families at the 1991 census;

- *stability*: families who had a different address five years earlier, as a proportion of all families at the 1991 census;

- *crowded dwellings*: dwellings with more than 1.5 persons per bedroom, as a proportion of all dwellings at the 1991 census.

It will be noted that the measures of neglect, abuse and participation in crime were each based on a five-year period. Given the nature of the hypothesis being tested (i.e. that delinquency is caused by child neglect and/or abuse) the data for child neglect and abuse were deliberately drawn from an earlier time period than the data for juvenile participation in crime.

The postcode areas were split into two groups, one for urban areas and one for rural areas. The urban group included postcodes in Sydney, Newcastle and Wollongong, the three major cities in New South Wales. We present here only the analysis for this group of 262 urban postcodes. Our report of this study (Weatherburn and Lind 1997) includes the results of the rural postcode analysis. It also provides detailed descriptions of the data and of the method of analysis, which we cover only briefly here.

To test the hypotheses we used multiple linear regression and path analysis. In the regression models parameters were estimated using weighted least squares because the response variables were proportions (and the variance of a proportion is dependent on the sample size on which it is based). The measures of neglect, abuse and juvenile participation in crime, which all had skewed distributions with long upper tails, were normalised by applying a logistic transformation, in which y is replaced by its logit function $\ln[y/(1-y)]$. The variables were transformed only when they served as response variables in regression models. Predictor variables were left untransformed in all regression models.

Because we were analysing spatial data, to account for possible spatial autocorrelation, we included in each regression a measure of the relevant response variable for the surrounding neighbourhood.[1] For the analysis of juvenile participation in crime, this neighbourhood measure also allowed us to test for neighbourhood effects.

For each linear regression model fitted, the adequacy of the fitted model was assessed in a number of ways. Variance inflation factors were calculated to check for multicollinearity. The normality of the residuals from each fitted model was checked by examining probability plots of the residuals. Finally, studentised residuals were examined to check for outliers. Generally, there were at most one or two outliers for any fitted regression model. No outliers were removed because the focus was on hypothesis testing rather than prediction and, for this purpose, the influence of one or two outliers was deemed to be negligible.

No transformations were applied to data for the path analysis. Path coefficients were estimated using the best linear predictor method, applied to standardised variables, as described by Kang and Seneta (1980). Using this method, no assumptions need be made about the variables in a path analysis other than that they are random (i.e. not controlled as in an experiment) and that the sample size is relatively large (so that large sample theory can be applied to use the sample correlation matrix as an estimate of the population correlation matrix).

There was one postcode with zero rates of neglect and abuse. This postcode was always included in each analysis. However, the zero rates for this one postcode were replaced with a very small non-zero number (0.00000001) when either abuse or neglect was the response variable in a regression (because the logistic transformation cannot be applied to zero values). There were five postcodes with zero rates of juvenile participation in violent crime. These postcodes were excluded from the models used to predict juvenile participation in violent crime.[2]

Correlations

We begin with a brief description of the data and examine their pairwise correlations before moving on to the tests of hypotheses.

The rates of children reported for *neglect* in the 262 postcodes ranged from zero to 185.0 per thousand children, with an average of 30.7 and 90th percentile of 57.5. The rates of children reported for *abuse* ranged from zero to 62.7 per thousand children, with an average of 14.4 and 90th percentile of 27.2.

The rates of Children's Court appearances for a property or violent offence in the 262 urban postcodes ranged from 6.1 to 231.9 per thousand juveniles, with an average of 45.3. Ninety per cent of postcodes had juvenile crime participation rates of less than 80.4.

Table 5.1 shows the matrix of pairwise correlations between all the variables of interest, that is, the measures of neglect, abuse, juvenile participation in crime and of social and economic stress. All of these correlations are of the variables measured in their original scales (i.e. before any transformations made for the regression analyses).

From this table of correlations it can be seen that juvenile participation in crime is significantly positively correlated with each of the measures of social and economic stress. This result is consistent with the common finding of an association between crime and social disadvantage.

Neglect and abuse are also significantly positively correlated with each of the measures of social and economic stress. These correlations indicate that rates of child neglect and child abuse tend to be higher in areas with higher rates of social and economic stress.

More importantly, it is clear that juvenile participation in crime is highly correlated with both neglect and abuse, indicating that rates of juvenile participation in crime are generally higher in areas with higher rates of neglect and abuse.

Because they are based on reports to authorities, rates of recorded neglect, abuse and juvenile participation in crime may vary from one area to another merely because there are different rates of reporting in different areas. In Chapter 2 we drew attention to the surveillance hypothesis, that is, the thesis that such rates may be higher in poorer areas merely because neglect, abuse and juvenile participation in crime are more easily discovered in poor areas. If this were the case, one would not expect to find significant correlations if the analysis were restricted only to poor areas. To test the surveillance hypothesis, the correlations were recalculated for the 10 per cent of urban postcodes which had the highest proportions of low-income households (i.e. the top 26 urban postcodes ranked on *poverty*). These revised correlations are presented in Table 5.2. Neglect, abuse and juvenile participation in crime remain significantly correlated with *poverty* even for this restricted set of postcodes.

The effect of social and economic stress on participation in crime

Regression models were fitted to determine which combination of the measures of social and economic stress was best in explaining juvenile participation in crime. Table 5.3 shows the results of fitting two multiple linear

Table 5.1. *Pearson correlation coefficients for New South Wales urban postcodes*

	Neglect	Abuse	Juvenile participation in crime	Juvenile participation in property crime	Juvenile participation in violent crime	Poverty	Unemployment	Single parent families	Stability	Crowded dwellings
Neglect	1.00									
Abuse	0.90	1.00								
Juvenile participation in crime	0.80	0.74	1.00							
Juvenile participation in property crime	0.78	0.71	0.99	1.00						
Juvenile participation in violent crime	0.73	0.69	0.93	0.90	1.00					
Poverty	0.60	0.50	0.64	0.63	0.58	1.00				
Unemployment	0.59	0.53	0.62	0.61	0.55	0.65	1.00			
Single parent families	0.57	0.53	0.58	0.58	0.55	0.57	0.64	1.00		
Stability	0.17	0.19	0.24	0.25	0.16	NS	NS	0.30	1.00	
Crowded dwellings	0.29	0.31	0.37	0.35	0.34	0.33	.64	0.21	NS	1.00

Note: 'NS' indicates that the correlation is not significantly different from zero ($p > 0.05$).

Table 5.2. *Pearson correlation coefficients for 10 per cent of New South Wales urban postcodes with highest proportions of low-income households*

	Neglect	Abuse	Juvenile participation in crime	Juvenile participation in property crime	Juvenile participation in violent crime	Poverty	Unemployment	Single parent families	Stability	Crowded dwellings
Neglect	1.00									
Abuse	0.92	1.00								
Juvenile participation in crime	0.72	0.62	1.00							
Juvenile participation in property crime	0.68	0.58	0.99	1.00						
Juvenile participation in violent crime	0.60	0.51	0.93	0.93	1.00					
Poverty	0.55	0.59	0.74	0.73	0.76	1.00				
Unemployment	NS	NS	NS	NS	NS	0.44	1.00			
Single parent families	NS	NS	NS	NS	NS	0.52	0.76	1.00		
Stability	NS	NS	NS	NS	NS	NS	NS	NS	1.00	
Crowded dwellings	NS	NS	NS	NS	NS	NS	0.72	0.56	NS	1.00

Note: 'NS' indicates that the correlation is not significantly different from zero ($p > 0.05$).

Table 5.3. *Juvenile participation in crime (262 urban postcodes): Models with socio-economic measures as predictors*

Terms in the model	Model 1		Model 2	
	Parameter estimate	p	Parameter estimate	p
Intercept	−4.74	0.0001	−4.68	0.0001
Poverty	1.94	0.0001	2.00	0.0001
Unemployment	0.75	0.3201	−	−
Single parent families	6.13	0.0001	6.82	0.0001
Stability	0.40	0.2929	−	−
Crowded dwellings	2.02	0.0006	2.48	0.0001
Neighbourhood delinquency	7.98	0.0001	8.30	0.0001
R^2 for fitted model	0.61		0.60	

regression models: the first (Model 1) includes all the socioeconomic measures as predictors of juvenile participation in crime; the second (Model 2) includes only *poverty, single parent families* and *crowded dwellings* as predictors. Both models also include the measure of neighbourhood juvenile participation in crime (which we call *neighbourhood delinquency*). As noted earlier, the response variable in the regression models was transformed using the logistic transformation and the parameters were estimated using weighted least squares.

Table 5.3 shows that in Model 1 the regression coefficients for *unemployment* and *stability* are not significantly different from zero. Model 2 excludes both these variables. As there is very little difference in the R^2 values between the two models, it is clear that Model 2 explains virtually the same amount of variation in juvenile participation in crime as does Model 1. We can therefore conclude that, in the presence of the other socioeconomic variables, neither *unemployment* nor *stability* is a necessary explanatory variable for juvenile participation in crime. It is clear, however, that juvenile participation in crime is strongly associated with the remaining three measures of social and economic stress, as well as with the rate of juvenile participation in crime in the surrounding neighbourhood.

The effect of social and economic stress on parenting

If, as we hypothesise, social and economic stress influence juvenile participation in crime because they are causal factors for child neglect and abuse, then we would expect *poverty, single parent families* and *crowded dwellings* to be

Table 5.4. *Neglect and abuse (262 urban postcodes): Models with socioeconomic measures as predictors*

Terms in the model	Neglect		Abuse	
	Parameter estimate	p	Parameter estimate	p
Intercept	−5.13	0.0001	−5.55	0.0001
Poverty	1.51	0.0002	1.09	0.0031
Single parent families	11.40	0.0001	8.84	0.0001
Crowded dwellings	1.83	0.0001	1.43	0.0003
Neighbourhood neglect	11.40	0.0001	–	–
Neighbourhood abuse	–	–	23.89	0.0001
R^2 for fitted model	0.64		0.58	

good predictors of child neglect and abuse. Table 5.4 presents the results of fitting linear regression models using these variables as predictors of neglect and abuse. The models also include relevant neighbourhood measures to account for possible spatial autocorrelation. It is clear from Table 5.4 that each of the three measures of social and economic stress is a significant predictor of both neglect and abuse.

The effect of parenting on delinquency

If parental neglect is a causal factor in child delinquency then neglect should be a predictor of juvenile participation in crime. A linear regression model was fitted with neglect and neighbourhood delinquency as the only predictors of juvenile participation in crime. This model had an R^2 value of 0.65, indicating that neglect alone explains more variation in juvenile participation in crime than do the measures of social and economic stress. (The details of the two models are presented in Table 5.5.)

Figure 5.1 shows the observed rates of juvenile participation in crime plotted against the neglect rates. There is a strong linear relationship between juvenile participation in crime and neglect as can be seen more clearly in Figure 5.2, in which the data have been averaged over groups of postcodes.[3] (The straight line in Figure 5.2 is a software-generated line of best fit.)

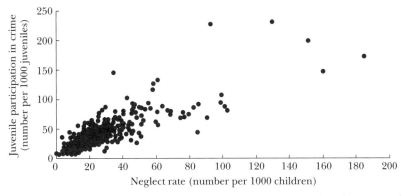

Figure 5.1 Rates of juvenile participation in crime and neglect in urban postcodes of New South Wales

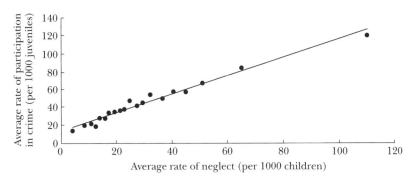

Figure 5.2 Average rates of juvenile participation in crime in groups of urban postcodes of New South Wales

The interrelationship between social and economic stress, parenting, neighbourhood delinquency and delinquency

We now turn to determining whether social and economic stress have any effect on juvenile participation in crime once the effects of neglect have been taken into account. Table 5.5 shows the results of fitting three models to explain the variation in juvenile participation in crime. All the models include neighbourhood delinquency as an explanatory variable but use different combinations of the other explanatory variables: social and economic stress only (measured by *poverty*, *single parent families* and *crowded dwellings*); neglect only; and neglect together with social and economic stress. (The first of these models has already been presented in Table 5.3 but is shown again for ease of comparison.)

Table 5.5. *Juvenile participation in crime (262 urban postcodes): Models with neglect and socioeconomic measures as predictors*

Terms in the model	Model with social and economic stress		Model with neglect		Model with neglect and social and economic stress	
	Parameter estimate	p	Parameter estimate	p	Parameter estimate	p
Intercept	−4.68	0.0001	−4.02	0.0001	−4.48	0.0001
Neglect	–	–	14.08	0.0001	11.56	0.0001
Poverty	2.00	0.0001	–	–	1.38	0.0001
Single parent families	6.82	0.0001	–	–	0.72	0.3869
Crowded dwellings	2.48	0.0001	–	–	2.08	0.0001
Neighbourhood delinquency	8.30	0.0001	11.02	0.0001	8.05	0.0001
R^2 for fitted model	0.60		0.65		0.73	

Comparing the first two models in Table 5.5 it can be seen that the variation explained by neglect and neighbourhood delinquency is greater than the variation explained by the measures of social and economic stress and neighbourhood delinquency. The table also shows that the full model, including all the predictors, explains 73 per cent of the variation in juvenile participation in crime, only an additional 8 percentage points more than the percentage of variation explained by the model containing neglect and neighbourhood delinquency alone. In the absence of neglect, however, the measures of social and economic stress, together with neighbourhood delinquency, explain 60 per cent of the variation. It is clear then that a substantial amount of the variation explained by social and economic stress is accounted for by neglect.

Nevertheless the association between juvenile participation in crime and social and economic stress is not fully explained by neglect. The increase in R^2, from the neglect and neighbourhood delinquency model to the model with all variables included, is statistically significant ($F_{3,\ 256} = 24.2$). The additional explanatory power is due only to *poverty* and *crowded dwellings*. In the presence of neglect, the regression coefficient for *single parent families* is not significantly different from zero.

It is also clear from Table 5.5 that the neighbourhood measure of juvenile participation in crime is significant in the presence of both neglect and

Table 5.6. *Juvenile participation in crime (262 urban postcodes): Models with abuse and socioeconomic measures as predictors*

Terms in the model	Model with social and economic stress		Model with abuse		Model with abuse and social and economic stress	
	Parameter estimate	p	Parameter estimate	p	Parameter estimate	p
Intercept	−4.68	0.0001	−4.11	0.0001	−4.59	0.0001
Abuse	–	–	35.08	0.0001	27.48	0.0001
Poverty	2.00	0.0001	–	–	1.68	0.0001
Single parent families	6.82	0.0001	–	–	1.09	0.1903
Crowded dwellings	2.48	0.0001	–	–	2.01	0.0001
Neighbourhood delinquency	8.30	0.0001	11.32	0.0001	7.93	0.0001
R^2 for fitted model	0.60		0.63		0.72	

the measures of social and economic stress, indicating that the level of delinquency in the surrounding neighbourhood has an effect on juvenile participation in crime which is independent of the effects of neglect and social and economic stress.

Table 5.6 presents information similar to that presented in Table 5.5 except that abuse replaces neglect as a predictor of juvenile participation in crime. Together with neighbourhood delinquency, the three models in Table 5.6 use the following combinations of variables to explain the variation in juvenile participation in crime: social and economic stress only (measured by *poverty*, *single parent families* and *crowded dwellings*); abuse only; and abuse together with social and economic stress.

Given that neglect and abuse are highly correlated with each other ($r =$ 0.90; see Table 5.1), it is not surprising that the results in Table 5.6 are very similar to those we obtained for neglect. The model with all predictors included explains 72 per cent of the variation in juvenile participation in crime. When we compare the last two models in the table, we find that adding social and economic stress as predictors to a model which already contains abuse increases the R^2 from 0.63 to 0.72. While abuse accounts for most of the total explained variation, the increase in R^2 is significant ($F_{3, 256} = 26.7$) indicating that the measures of social and economic stress are still significantly associated with juvenile participation in crime after taking account of abuse.

Table 5.7. *Juvenile participation in property crime (262 urban postcodes): Models with neglect and socioeconomic measures as predictors*

Terms in the model	Model with social and economic stress		Model with neglect		Model with neglect and social and economic stress	
	Parameter estimate	p	Parameter estimate	p	Parameter estimate	p
Intercept	−4.86	0.0001	−4.20	0.0001	−4.67	0.0001
Neglect	–	–	14.14	0.0001	11.54	0.0001
Poverty	1.92	0.0001	–	–	1.31	0.0001
Single parent families	7.06	0.0001	–	–	0.82	0.3310
Crowded dwellings	2.49	0.0001	–	–	2.06	0.0001
Neighbourhood property delinquency	9.63	0.0001	12.92	0.0001	9.65	0.0001
R^2 for fitted model	0.62		0.66		0.74	

Once again the level of juvenile participation in crime in the surrounding neighbourhood has a significant effect on juvenile participation in crime, independently of the effects of abuse and of social and economic stress.

The effects of parenting and social and economic stress on participation in property and violent crime

We also wish to know whether the effects of social and economic stress are mediated through parenting effects for both property crime and violent crime. Tables 5.7 and 5.8 show the results of fitting regression models for juvenile participation in *property* crime. The models are the same as those fitted for juvenile participation in (property and/or violent) crime. Results for the models where neglect is a predictor are shown in Table 5.7 and those where abuse is a predictor are shown in Table 5.8. In the tables, *neighbourhood property delinquency* refers to the neighbourhood measure of juvenile participation in property crime.

The results are similar to those shown in Tables 5.5 and 5.6. The model with neglect and neighbourhood delinquency (in property crime) as the only predictors explains about two-thirds of the variation in juvenile participation in property crime (Table 5.7); there is a similar result for abuse (Table 5.8). Comparing the last two models in Table 5.7 (i.e. the model with neglect and

Table 5.8. *Juvenile participation in property crime (262 urban postcodes): Models with abuse and socioeconomic measures as predictors*

Terms in the model	Model with social and economic stress		Model with abuse		Model with abuse and social and economic stress	
	Parameter estimate	p	Parameter estimate	p	Parameter estimate	p
Intercept	−4.86	0.0001	−4.30	0.0001	−4.78	0.0001
Abuse	–	–	34.95	0.0001	26.62	0.0001
Poverty	1.92	0.0001	–	–	1.63	0.0001
Single parent families	7.06	0.0001	–	–	1.37	0.1087
Crowded dwellings	2.49	0.0001	–	–	2.00	0.0001
Neighbourhood property delinquency	9.63	0.0001	13.45	0.0001	9.54	0.0001
R^2 for fitted model	0.62		0.63		0.72	

the neighbourhood measure as the only predictors and the model with all predictor variables included), the increase in R^2 is significant ($F_{3, 256} = 23.6$). The same is true for the models in Table 5.8 where neglect is replaced by abuse ($F_{3, 256} = 26.1$). In the presence of neglect or abuse, *single parent families* ceases to be a significant predictor. The neighbourhood measure of juvenile participation in property crime is significant in all models.

Tables 5.9 and 5.10 show the results of fitting similar regression models for juvenile participation in *violent* crime. Results for the models where neglect is a predictor are shown in Table 5.9 and those where abuse is a predictor are shown in Table 5.10. In the tables *neighbourhood violent delinquency* refers to the neighbourhood measure of juvenile participation in violent crime.

It is apparent that the percentage of variation explained in juvenile participation in *violent* crime is less than the percentage of variation explained in juvenile participation in *property* crime. Nevertheless there is a familiar pattern in the results. When measures of social and economic stress are added to a model, which already includes neglect and neighbourhood (violent) delinquency as predictors, the percentage of variation explained increases by only 6 percentage points, from 55 per cent to 61 per cent. In contrast, in the absence of neglect, the neighbourhood and social and economic stress measures explain 50 per cent of the variation in juvenile participation in violent crime, indicating that most of the effect of social and economic stress is

Table 5.9. *Juvenile participation in violent crime (257 urban postcodes): Models with neglect and socioeconomic measures as predictors*

Terms in the model	Model with social and economic stress		Model with neglect		Model with neglect and social and economic stress	
	Parameter estimate	p	Parameter estimate	p	Parameter estimate	p
Intercept	−5.81	0.0001	−5.16	0.0001	−5.63	0.0001
Neglect	–	–	13.82	0.0001	11.73	0.0001
Poverty	1.93	0.0001	–	–	1.36	0.0011
Single parent families	6.80	0.0001	–	–	0.51	0.6434
Crowded dwellings	2.38	0.0001	–	–	2.02	0.0001
Neighbourhood violent delinquency	24.97	0.0001	33.27	0.0001	23.66	0.0001
R^2 for fitted model	0.50		0.55		0.61	

Table 5.10. *Juvenile participation in violent crime (257 urban postcodes): Models with abuse and socioeconomic measures as predictors*

Terms in the model	Model with social and economic stress		Model with abuse		Model with abuse and social and economic stress	
	Parameter estimate	p	Parameter estimate	p	Parameter estimate	p
Intercept	−5.81	0.0001	−5.27	0.0001	−5.75	0.0001
Abuse	–	–	34.86	0.0001	28.60	0.0001
Poverty	1.93	0.0001	–	–	1.68	0.0001
Single parent families	6.80	0.0001	–	–	0.72	0.5138
Crowded dwellings	2.38	0.0001	–	–	1.91	0.0001
Neighbourhood violent delinquency	24.97	0.0001	34.66	0.0001	24.08	0.0001
R^2 for fitted model	0.50		0.54		0.61	

mediated through neglect. Nevertheless the results for the model including both neglect and measures of social and economic stress show that, after taking account of neglect, *poverty* and *crowded dwellings* still have a significant effect on juvenile participation in violent crime. The increase in R^2 is statistically significant ($F_{3,\ 251}$ = 12.3). The final point to note is that once again, after controlling for the effects of both neglect and social and economic stress, there is still a significant neighbourhood effect.

As can be seen in Table 5.10, the results for models containing abuse instead of neglect as a predictor are almost identical to those in Table 5.9. There is a significant increase in R^2 ($F_{3,\ 251}$ = 13.9) from the abuse and neighbourhood (violent) delinquency model, to the model with abuse and neighbourhood delinquency plus social and economic stress. The neighbourhood measure is again significant in all models.

The relative importance of neglect and abuse

Up to this point we have not included neglect and abuse together as predictors in the same regression model for any of our measures of juvenile participation in crime. Because they are highly correlated with each other, we would expect there to be multicollinearity if they were both included as predictor variables in a regression model.

This indeed proved to be the case when we attempted to fit such models. For each of our measures of juvenile participation in crime (property and/or violent crime; property crime only; violent crime only) we fitted a regression model with neglect *and* abuse as predictors together with the three measures of social and economic stress and the appropriate neighbourhood measure of delinquency. In each case there were variance inflation factors of about 10 or 11 for neglect and abuse, indicating high multicollinearity. For this reason we do not present the results from fitting these models other than to note that, in every case, in the presence of neglect the regression coefficient for abuse was not significantly different from zero.

Path analysis

We now consider a path analysis for our main measure of juvenile participation in crime (either property or violent crime). The path analysis allows us to assess the relative importance of neglect as a cause of juvenile participation in crime.

Figure 5.3 shows the path diagram for juvenile participation in crime. It includes as posited causes of juvenile participation in crime the following variables: poverty, single parent families, crowded dwellings, neglect, abuse and neighbourhood delinquency. The largest path coefficient is that from neglect to juvenile participation in crime (0.51), indicating that of all the posited causes of juvenile participation in crime, neglect has the greatest

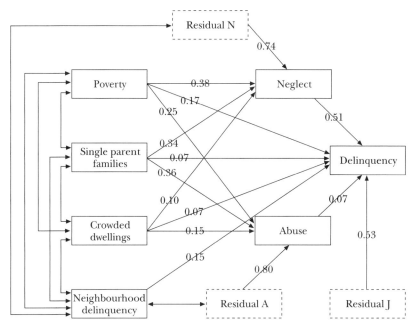

Figure 5.3 Path diagram for juvenile participation in crime

causal influence. We note in particular that the path coefficient from abuse to juvenile participation in crime is relatively small (0.07). The path analysis also shows that poverty and single parent families have a greater causal influence on neglect than does crowded dwellings.

Figures 5.4 and 5.5 show similar path diagrams for juvenile participation in *property* crime and juvenile participation in *violent* crime. The results are similar in that, of the specified causal variables, neglect has the greatest causal influence on both juvenile participation in property crime and juvenile participation in violent crime. It is, however, of interest to compare the relative size of the path coefficients from neglect and abuse in Figures 5.4 and 5.5. For juvenile participation in property crime the path coefficient from neglect is quite large (0.55) whereas the path coefficient from abuse is negligible. By contrast, for juvenile participation in violent crime, the path coefficient from neglect is smaller (0.44) and the path coefficient from abuse is larger (0.07). The other interesting feature is that, of the posited causes for juvenile participation in violent crime, the second largest path coefficient is for neighbourhood juvenile participation in violent crime (0.21).

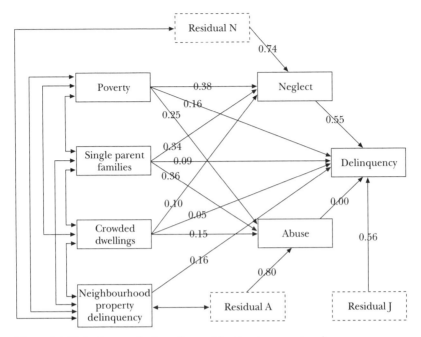

Figure 5.4 Path diagram for juvenile participation in property crime

Adult participation in crime and aggregate crime rates

In testing the implications of our hypothesis that economic and social stress exert their effects on crime through parenting variables we have been concerned solely with explaining variation across areas in juvenile participation in crime. For reasons given in earlier chapters we have concentrated on *offender* rates (i.e. participation rates), rather than *offending* rates (i.e. aggregate crime rates), and, because of the link with parenting, we have concentrated on *juvenile* offenders.

The extent to which our hypothesis can explain variation in adult offender rates and in overall crime rates depends on how closely related these measures are to juvenile offender rates. In this section we address the question of whether adult offender rates are predictable from juvenile offender rates and whether our models also explain adult participation in crime. Further we examine to what extent offender rates explain the variation in aggregate crime rates.

Using Local Court appearance data for New South Wales from the years 1990 to 1993 we calculated a measure of adult participation in crime similar

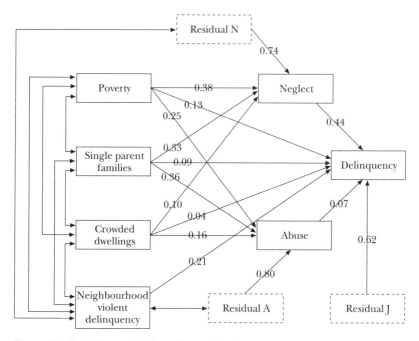

Figure 5.5 Path diagram for juvenile participation in violent crime

to our measure of juvenile participation in crime. That is, for each postcode, we calculated the number of persons with at least one Local Court appearance for a property or violent offence over a four-year period (January 1990 to December 1993) divided by the resident population of the postcode aged 18 and over (1991 census data).[4]

This measure of adult participation in crime has a correlation of 0.83 with our measure of juvenile participation in crime.[5] The high correlation provides evidence that juvenile participation in crime is a good indicator of adult participation in crime: areas with high rates of juvenile participation in crime also tend to have high rates of adult participation in crime and therefore high rates of offenders overall.

We fitted the same models as those in Table 5.5 to this measure of adult participation in crime, again using a logit transformation (to normalise adult participation in crime for the regression model). The results are shown in Table 5.11. In the table, *neighbourhood offender rate* refers to the neighbourhood measure of adult participation in crime. Not surprisingly, given the high correlation between adult and juvenile offender rates, the results are very similar to those in Table 5.5. There is, however, one interesting difference. Whereas for juvenile offenders there was no significant effect of single parent

Table 5.11. *Adult participation in crime (261 urban postcodes): Models with neglect and socioeconomic measures as predictors*

Terms in the model	Model with social and economic stress		Model with neglect		Model with neglect and social and economic stress	
	Parameter estimate	p	Parameter estimate	p	Parameter estimate	p
Intercept	−5.96	0.0001	−5.27	0.0001	−5.66	0.0001
Neglect	–	–	12.70	0.0001	10.02	0.0001
Poverty	0.71	0.0504	–	–	0.19	0.5492
Single parent families	8.12	0.0001	–	–	2.24	0.0210
Crowded dwellings	2.37	0.0001	–	–	1.95	0.0001
Neighbourhood adult offender rate	42.74	0.0001	41.68	0.0001	36.43	0.0001
R^2 for fitted model	0.62		0.66		0.71	

Note: Adult participation data were missing for one postcode.

families once the effect of neglect was taken into account, this was not the case for adult offenders. Instead, there is no significant effect of poverty on adult participation in crime once the effect of neglect is taken into account.

Finally we consider the relationship between crime rates and participation rates. The amount of crime in an area is not determined solely by the number of offenders resident in the area. Other factors affecting crime, as we have noted previously, are the extent to which offenders commit offences in the areas where they reside and the frequency with which they offend. As a measure of crime we used criminal incidents, involving property or violent offences, reported to New South Wales police in 1995. To calculate a rate for each postcode we used the number of such incidents occurring in the postcode divided by its resident population at the 1991 census.

The postcode for the inner city area of Sydney was excluded for the purpose of assessing the relationship between aggregate crime rates and participation rates because crime rates on a *resident* population basis are very high in the inner city which includes most of the city's night-time entertainment areas.

Our measure of aggregate crime rates has a correlation of 0.52 with juvenile participation in crime. Figure 5.6 shows a scatter plot of the relationship. The reasonably strong linear relationship is to some extent masked in this scatter

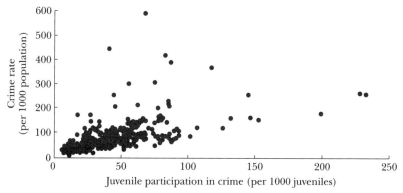

Figure 5.6 Aggregate crime rates and rates of juvenile participation in crime in urban postcodes of New South Wales

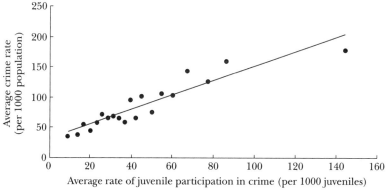

Figure 5.7 Average rates of juvenile participation in crime in groups of urban postcodes

plot by a small number of postcodes with high crime rates. Figure 5.7 shows a scatter plot of average crime rates and average rates of juvenile participation in crime for 20 groups, each of 13 postcodes (which were first ordered according to their rates of juvenile participation in crime). (The straight line in Figure 5.7 is a software-generated line of best fit.) The linear relationship is more evident in this figure, indicating that in general, areas with high rates of juvenile participation in crime also have high crime rates.

Table 5.12 shows the results of fitting a regression model using juvenile and adult participation in crime to predict aggregate crime rates. (Because our purpose here is only to assess how much of the variation in crime rates is explained by participation rates, the response variable was not transformed and no neighbourhood measure was included in the model.) Thirty-one per cent of the variance in aggregate crime rates is explained by participation

Table 5.12. *Aggregate crime rates (259 urban postcodes): Model with juvenile and adult participation in crime as predictors*

Terms in the model	Parameter estimate		p
Intercept	0.03		0.0001
Adult participation in crime	1.08		0.1230
Juvenile participation in crime	0.91		0.0001
R^2 for fitted model		0.31	

Note: Only 259 postcodes are included in this analysis because adult participation data were missing for one postcode and crime data were missing for a second postcode.

rates. In the presence of juvenile participation in crime, adult participation in crime has no significant effect on aggregate crime rates.

Summary and conclusion

Table 5.5 provides strong support for the hypothesis that economic and social stress increase the level of juvenile participation in crime by increasing the prevalence of child neglect. Comparison of the models in Table 5.5 shows, first, that rates of reported neglect account for more of the variation in juvenile participation in crime than do *poverty, single parent families* and *crowded dwellings* combined. Second, comparison of the models shows that most of the variation explained by the measures of social and economic stress is accounted for by neglect. We can therefore conclude that the effects of social and economic stress on juvenile participation in crime are mostly mediated through the effects of these measures on neglect.

For some observers these results will be interpreted in terms of the surveillance hypothesis, that is, the thesis that the association between economic stress, child maltreatment and juvenile involvement in crime arises simply from the fact that poor households are subjected to greater official surveillance than non-poor households. It is worth observing, therefore, that the strong positive pairwise correlations between *poverty* and child neglect, child abuse and juvenile participation in crime (see Table 5.1) were just as strong, if not stronger, when they were computed across the bottom 10 per cent of postcodes in terms of *poverty*. This last observation is difficult to explain in terms of the so-called surveillance hypothesis.

Table 5.5 also provides evidence of strong neighbourhood effects. The measure of delinquency in the surrounding neighbourhood remains significant in the presence of both neglect and social and economic stress.

Table 5.6 shows findings for abuse which are similar to those for neglect. Tables 5.7 to 5.10 show that the effects revealed in Tables 5.5 and 5.6 hold up if we separately examine the pathways linking economic and social stress to participation in property crime and to participation in violent crime. It is true that the relationships are not quite as strong for violent crime as they are for property crime. A substantial amount of the effect of economic stress on rates of both property and violent crime, however, is clearly mediated by neglect (or abuse).

The finding from the path analyses that neglect is more influential than abuse as a pathway between social and economic stress and juvenile participation in crime is an interesting result. It appears to indicate that the significant results obtained from fitting regression models with abuse as a predictor may be due to the high correlation between abuse and neglect (i.e. that abuse was a proxy measure of neglect in these regressions). When neglect and abuse are both present, as in the path analysis, it is neglect which is the important factor. This result mirrors the common finding among individual-level studies that, while neglect and abuse are often found together, measures tapping the level of parental supervision or the strength of the parent–child bond are better predictors of juvenile involvement in crime than variables tapping the level of family conflict or the harshness of parental discipline (Loeber and Stouthamer-Loeber 1986).

The symmetry between the results of individual-level studies on the correlates of delinquency and the present aggregate-level study is also exhibited to some extent in another feature of the path analysis. As we noted earlier, although neglect is more important than abuse as a pathway to juvenile involvement in crime, in the shift from the predictors of participation in property crime to the predictors of participation in violent crime, the relative importance of neglect declines while the relative importance of abuse increases (although the path coefficient for neglect is still more than six times as large as that for abuse). In her prospective longitudinal study of neglected and abused children McCord (1979, 1980) also found that aggressive offenders were more likely to have had parents whose behaviour was abusive than non-aggressive offenders.

Our model of juvenile participation in crime clearly works equally well as a model of adult participation in crime. Though not surprising given the high correlation between juvenile and adult participation in crime, this finding lends support to the assumption that juvenile and adult participation in crime stem from similar developmental processes. Of course this does not mean there are no worthwhile distinctions to be made between the factors underpinning juvenile and adult offending rates. We have been concerned with the supply of motivated offenders. We have not been concerned with factors which influence offending frequency amongst individuals once they have become disposed to involvement in crime. Thus, it is entirely possible that juvenile and adult offenders are alike in their antecedents but quite different in relation to what governs the frequency with which they offend.

This said, unless there is a significant positive correlation between criminal participation rates and aggregate crime rates the hypothesis we have been testing clearly offers no useful explanation for the spatial distribution of crime. Table 5.12 therefore provides valuable confirmation that a substantial proportion of the variation in aggregate crime rates can in fact be accounted for by a model which limits itself to explaining how economic and social stress influence the spatial distribution of motivated offenders. Given the crudeness of our measure of participation in crime the fact that participation rates explain 31 per cent of the variation in aggregate crime rates is an entirely satisfactory result. Presumably some percentage of the variation in aggregate crime rates would have remained impossible to account for no matter how complex the model being applied. Some of the unexplained variation must also be regarded as reflecting the influence of criminal opportunity and incentive on offending frequency.

In summary, then, the data presented in Chapter 5, reinforce the conclusion reached in Chapter 4 that a substantial part of the effect of economic and social stress on aggregate crime rates is mediated by the effect of such stress on parenting and its effect, in turn, on susceptibility to delinquent peer influence. Perhaps the most discordant empirical note for this hypothesis lies in the path analysis which shows that some of the effect of economic and social stress on juvenile participation in crime appears to be transmitted directly rather than through parenting factors. It is possible, however, that this observation simply reflects our inability to obtain adequate measures of the relevant parenting factors at the aggregate level.

CHAPTER SIX

An epidemic model of offender population growth

An outline of the model

The broad picture of the relationship between economic stress and crime which has emerged so far is this. Other things being equal, parents with dependent children who experience higher levels of economic stress are more likely to neglect or abuse their children or engage in disciplinary practices which are harsh, erratic and inconsistent. This pattern of parenting behaviour increases the likelihood that children affected by it will gravitate toward or affiliate more strongly with their peers. To the extent that these peers are involved in crime, this association increases the likelihood that susceptible juveniles will become involved in crime. These effects are attenuated when parents facing economic stress are enmeshed in a strong social support network but they are exacerbated in the absence of such a network or when parents face added parenting burdens, such as the absence of a partner (or the presence of an unsupportive partner), marital conflict, a larger number of children, children with behavioural or developmental problems of some kind, or when parents face particular personal problems such as drug addiction or depression. The process is depicted schematically in Figure 6.1.

The important point to note about Figure 6.1 is that it depicts an epidemic process. Since susceptibility to involvement in crime is converted to active involvement in part through the medium of peer influence, the rate at which juveniles become involved in crime in an area may be seen to depend upon both the number of juveniles susceptible to delinquent peer influence (hereafter *susceptibles*) and the number of contacts between *susceptibles* and juveniles already involved in crime (hereafter *delinquents*). Since, however, the number of possible contacts between *susceptibles* and *delinquents* in an area will depend, in

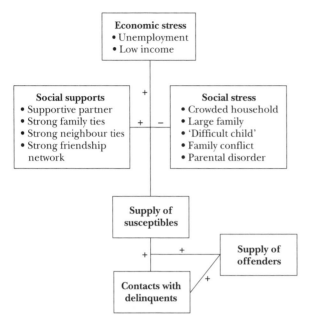

Figure 6.1 An epidemic model of offender population growth

part, on the number of *delinquents*, the effect of an increase in economic stress on rates of juvenile involvement in crime in a neighbourhood is going to depend, in part, on the size of its resident population of active offenders.

In this chapter we develop a formal model of this process and explore its implications. It should be emphasised, at the outset, that our purpose in building a formal model is not primarily to permit the derivation of detailed quantitative predictions concerning temporal or spatial variation in aggregate offending rates. For reasons that we explain below, the lack of data pertaining to the processes depicted in Figure 6.1 makes the task of obtaining precise estimates of the model parameters difficult, if not impossible. The primary reason for developing a formal model of those processes is that it will enable us to draw out certain general implications of the relationship between economic stress and crime not readily apparent from the purely schematic account of the delinquency generation process depicted in Figure 6.1. These general implications will prove of central importance in dealing with the anomalies we discussed in Chapter 1.

The model we present is an adaptation of the 'mass-action' model of disease transmission (Fine 1993) but couched in the criminal career framework developed by Blumstein et al. (1986). Before presenting the mass-action or epidemic model, therefore, we digress briefly to discuss the relevance of criminal career and epidemiological theory to the process of delinquency generation.

The relevance of criminal career theory

Blumstein et al. (1986) and others working within the criminal career paradigm have argued that the aggregate rate of any offence can usefully be decomposed into two components: one reflecting the size of the population of active offenders and the other reflecting the frequency with which those active offenders commit offences. They have also argued that the population of active offenders at any given point in time can usefully be thought of as a product of two other components: one reflecting the rate at which individuals initiate a period of involvement in crime and the other reflecting criminal career duration (i.e. the period of involvement in crime). The notion of a criminal career is an extremely useful concept in making sense of aggregate crime rate variation for two reasons. First, research has consistently shown that those who become involved in crime as adolescents or teenagers tend to persist for a period of several years, engaging in a wide variety of different offences (West and Farrington 1977; Chaiken and Chaiken 1982; Sampson and Laub 1990). Second, those who persist in crime account for a large proportion of all recorded crime (Wolfgang, Figlio and Sellin 1972; Coumarelos 1994).

The distinction between offending frequency, criminal career initiation and criminal career duration is also useful for other reasons. Blumstein et al. suggested, for example, that variation in unemployment might have little effect on the rate of initiation, since most offenders begin their period of involvement in crime during their teenage years, before most people have begun working (Blumstein et al. 1986: 13). On the other hand, unemployment may have a significant effect on criminal career duration since one might reasonably expect the opportunity for full-time work to exert an influence on the duration of a teenager's criminal activity.

This framework for analysing aggregate crime rate variation has been forcefully rejected by Gottfredson and Hirschi (1986). They argue that individuals simply differ in their underlying propensity to commit criminal acts and the factors which affect this propensity can be expected to affect all three components of offending in much the same way. The debate over whether crime can be explained solely by reference to an underlying criminal propensity or whether separate reference to different components of offending has spawned a number of studies designed to see whether the correlates of initiation into crime, criminal career duration and/or offending frequency are the same or different (e.g. Paternoster and Triplett 1988; Nagin and Smith 1990; Loeber et al. 1991; Smith, Visher and Jarjoura 1991; Smith and Brame 1994; Salmelainen 1995).

The results of these studies are somewhat inconclusive. Nagin and Smith (1990) examined the correlates of participation in crime and frequency of offending amongst juveniles interviewed as part of the National Youth Survey. They found little difference in the two sets of correlates and concluded that there was no strong reason for distinguishing between participation in crime and frequency of offending. Other studies, however, have reached rather different conclusions. Paternoster and Triplett (1988) found that the perceived certainty of police apprehension for a property offence exerted much stronger effects on the prevalence of juvenile involvement in crime than on the incidence of offending of those who were involved. Smith and Brame (1994) found that negative labelling exerted no effect on criminal initiation but did affect persistence in crime. Salmelainen (1995) found that drug use and risk of apprehension exerted strong effects on the frequency of vehicle theft and break and enter. However, she also found that many of the factors which predict participation in crime exerted no effect on offending frequency.

The inconclusiveness of these study findings might seem to call into question the wisdom of putting forward a model of offender population growth couched within the framework of criminal career theory. However, we have two reasons for drawing on this framework, neither of which hinges on the assumption that criminal participation rates and offending frequency are determined by the same variables. First, although we do not propose to make use of the notion of offending frequency in offering an account of the way in which economic stress affects aggregate crime rates, we do propose to argue that an individual is capable of stimulating new entrants into criminal activity only for as long as he or she remains an active offender. It follows from this conception of criminal participation that rates of initiation into crime will actually be a function (in part) of the average period of involvement in crime. The period of involvement in crime is therefore central to our account of the rate of initiation into crime. Second, we seek to give an account of the time course of change in aggregate crime rates in response to changes in levels of economic stress. The period spent by offenders in crime turns out to be of central importance in this task.

To see why this is so imagine we have a population of offenders in a neighbourhood, each of whom spends (say) five years involved in crime before quitting. Let us assume that each year this population receives five new entrants. The size of the offender population therefore will be $(5 \times 5 =)$ 25. Now suppose economic stress increases the number of new entrants to the population of offenders in a neighbourhood from 5 to 10 per annum. The size of the offending population will eventually rise to $(10 \times 5 =)$ 50 but this change will not occur immediately. In the first year after the rise in economic stress, 10 people will commence their involvement in crime and 5 will desist. This will increase the offender population from 25 to 30. The same will occur again in the second year, increasing the offender population to 35. This process will continue until the fifth year following the rise in economic stress when, instead of 5 offenders desisting, 10 will desist. Thus, it will take five years before the offending population rises to its new stable level of 50 offenders as a result of our growth in economic stress. Now if, as seems reasonable, we assume that the aggregate rate of offending is determined (in part) by the number of offenders, it will also take five years for the full effect of a rise in economic stress on aggregate crime rates to be felt. Clearly, then, in order to predict when aggregate crime rates will respond to changes in criminal initiation rates we need a clear understanding of the characteristic period of involvement in crime. This is true regardless of whether criminal initiation rates and criminal career duration are affected by the same or different factors.

The epidemiology of offender population growth

Having considered criminal career theory we now consider the relevance of epidemic models to the explanation of delinquency. There have been very few systematic attempts to apply epidemic concepts to the explanation of delinquency. The most significant contribution in recent years has been that put forward by Jonathan Crane (1991). Crane suggested that social problems were contagious and were spread through peer influence. Drawing on the work of Granovetter (1978) and Granovetter and Soong (1983) he proposed a model of the contagion process which assumed that each individual's likelihood of involvement in some form of socially deviant activity depended on whether or not a threshold number of other individuals had engaged (or were engaging) in similar behaviour. According to the model, two basic conditions determine a community's susceptibility to social epidemics: (1) the residents' risk of developing social problems and (2) their susceptibility to peer influence.

One of the central implications of Crane's model is that the relationship between neighbourhood quality and the incidence of particular social problems should be non-linear. Crane attempted to test this implication using rates of high-school dropout and teenage pregnancy as measures of the incidence of social problems and the percentage of high socioeconomic status residents as a measure of neighbourhood quality. The empirical relationship observed between this measure of neighbourhood quality and his measures of social problems were strongly in accord with theoretical expectations. While the rate of high-school dropouts and the rate of teenage pregnancy rose steadily as the percentage of high status residents in a neighbourhood fell, the slope of the relationship increased very sharply once neighbourhoods were reached in which the percentage of high socioeconomic status residents fell below 5 per cent. Crane took this observation as confirming the general thrust of his model.

Unfortunately there is no independent empirical warrant for the assumption that susceptible individuals will only become delinquent if a threshold number of other individuals in the surrounding neighbourhood are or have become delinquent. More importantly, the empirical observations Crane took as providing confirmation of his model are susceptible to other interpretations. In order to determine the effect of neighbourhood quality on high-school dropout rates and teenage pregnancy he fitted a piece-wise linear logit model to the two sets of data. Having fitted each model he obtained an estimate – for each segment of the neighbourhood quality scale – of the probability of a dropout (or teenage pregnancy) in that segment. The graph joining these estimates showed the non-linearity which, according to Crane, provided confirmation of his model. The problem with this approach is that the non-linearity may reflect nothing more than the fact that the raw dropout and teenage pregnancy data were subjected to a log transformation. A plot of the predicted relationship between any pair of variables X and Y will always appear exponential in form if the predicted values were obtained by fitting a model where log Y is a linear function of X.

We propose to take a somewhat different tack than Crane in applying epidemic concepts to the explanation of crime problems. In particular we seek to give a more explicit account of the factors which control the supply of *susceptibles* and the process by which peer influence converts them into *delinquents*. Furthermore, instead of *assuming*, as he did, that the likelihood of a susceptible individual becoming a delinquent is some function of the number of delinquents in the neighbourhood we propose to develop a model in which threshold effects are *derived* from empirically defensible assumptions. Since the model we propose to develop is based on the mass-action model of disease transmission, it will serve our purpose to examine the mass-action model before showing how it might be adapted to model the dynamics of offender populations.

In the most basic form of the standard mass-action model of disease transmission (Fine 1993), the number of new cases of a disease at epoch $t + 1$, C_{t+1}, is given by:

$$C_{t+1} = C_t \, S_t \, r \tag{1}$$

where C_t is the number of cases of the disease at epoch t, S_t is the number of individuals susceptible to infection at epoch t, and r is the transmission parameter, that is, the proportion of all possible contacts between susceptible and infectious individuals which lead to new infections. In order to simulate growth in the size of a diseased population over time, the number of new individuals susceptible to disease is recalculated for each new time period as:

$$S_{t+1} = S_t - C_{t+1} + B_t \tag{2}$$

where S_{t+1} is the population of *susceptibles* in the next time period and B_t is the number of new *susceptibles* added to the population in time period t.

The relationship shown in equation (1) – that the number of new cases in the future is a function of the current number of cases times the current number susceptible – is known as the epidemiologic 'law of mass-action' by analogy with the principle of physical chemistry that the rate or velocity of a chemical reaction is a function of the product of the initial concentrations of the reagents.

There is an obvious and striking analogy between the basic processes postulated by this model and what we know about juvenile involvement in crime. As we have already seen, there is clear evidence that economic stress stimulates certain kinds of parental behaviour which render juveniles susceptible to delinquent peer influence. Contact between *susceptibles* and delinquent peers appears to be the stimulus which transforms this susceptibility into active involvement in crime. Even the notion that individuals remain 'infectious' over the period of their involvement in crime is not without a modicum of empirical support. Warr (1993b) has shown that rates of involvement in crime rise and fall with the level of contact with delinquent peers. Notwithstanding these points of correspondence, however, three of the assumptions underpinning equation (1) are unsatisfactory from the standpoint of offender population growth.

First, it assumes that individuals remain infected for a period which is very short relative to that over which an epidemic (i.e. growth in the number of infected persons) occurs. This is evident in the fact that the value of C_{t+1} is determined solely by the number of 'new' cases of infection which occur at time t. This is a fair assumption in relation to many diseases but it is not a fair assumption in relation to criminal career duration. Blumstein et al. (1986) cite several studies giving estimates of criminal career duration ranging from five to twelve years. These estimates were all based on offenders who had more than one conviction, arrest or court appearance. In his analysis of the conviction patterns of a cohort of persons born in four weeks in 1953 and followed up until the age of 31 by the Research and Statistics Department of the Home Office, Tarling (1993) found that, when those for whom only one conviction was recorded (and who therefore had a criminal career duration of zero) were included in the estimate of average career duration the average career duration for males was 3.3 years for males and 3.1 years for females. When attention was restricted to those with more than one court appearance, however, the corresponding figures were 7.4 years and 4.9 years. Estimates of criminal career duration clearly vary very widely. Nevertheless if we assume that offenders remain capable of stimulating new entrants to crime while active, even the smallest estimates of criminal career duration suggest that criminal peers probably remain 'infectious' over a period which is substantial relative to that over which offender population growth occurs.

A second problematic assumption embedded in the mass-action model is the idea that individuals who become susceptible to disease remain so. If the period of susceptibility to involvement in crime can be judged from the period over which individuals commit their first offence there appears to be no similar point of correspondence in relation to crime. Indeed, the available evidence suggests that the age of onset of involvement in crime rises rapidly from about the age of 12 years, reaches a peak between the ages of 14 and 17 years and declines almost as rapidly from about the age of 20 years (Visher and Roth 1986). Thus, it seems reasonable to suppose that susceptibility to involvement in crime is largely a transient and youthful condition. Any application of the mass-action model to offender population growth would therefore need to make explicit allowance for this fact.

Third, it assumes what epidemiologists refer to as 'homogeneous mixing', or, in other words, that there is random mixing between susceptible and infected persons. This assumption is problematic, even in the context of disease transmission, because individuals do not mix randomly, even in small communities. Contacts between individuals are circumscribed by considerations of gender, race, ethnicity, geography and institutional membership.

We can deal with these problems by making some simple changes to the standard mass-action model. We begin by assuming that the population of individuals involved in crime at time $t + 1$ consists of a portion of those already active at time t plus any new initiates to crime which occur as a result of contact between *susceptibles* and *delinquents*. Of course the influence of the existing population of offenders in a neighbourhood on rates of new entrants into that population may not always be transmitted by direct personal contact between delinquents and non-delinquents. It would be consistent with the model we are putting forward to argue, for instance, that the number of persons known to a susceptible juvenile to have engaged in criminal behaviour in a neighbourhood shapes the likelihood that the susceptible juvenile will also engage in criminal behaviour. Alternatively it could be argued, following De Fleur and Quinney (1966), that the probability of transition from susceptibility to delinquency is some function of the ratio of exposure to law-abiding versus law-breaking criminal norms. Rather than introduce unnecessary complexity into the model at this stage, however, we prefer to start with the simplest assumption possible concerning the mechanism by which susceptible juveniles make the transition to involvement in crime.

Although contact between *susceptibles* and *delinquents* is a necessary condition of involvement in crime, we will assume that the rate of criminal initiation is constrained by two factors. The first is that, during any given time period, only a proportion ($p < 1$) of the possible contacts between *susceptibles* and *delinquents* actually occurs. The second is that, during any given time period, only a proportion ($r < 1$) of the contacts between *susceptibles* and *delinquents* results in a *susceptible* becoming *delinquent*. Finally, we will assume that both susceptibility to involvement and active involvement in crime are transient conditions and that *delinquents* exert no influence on the likelihood of *susceptibles* becoming involved in crime once they cease their involvement in crime.

In this modification of the basic mass-action model individuals are assumed to be in one of three states. They may be immune to involvement in crime, either because family factors have rendered them thus or because they have already terminated their involvement in crime. They may be susceptible to involvement in crime but not yet involved. Finally, they may be actively involved in crime. Figure 6.2 illustrates the possible transitions between these states in any two adjacent time periods.

Between time period t and time period $t + 1$, an individual may either remain susceptible, pass from being susceptible to being a delinquent or pass from being susceptible to being immune. An individual involved in crime at time t may continue his or her involvement at $t + 1$ or pass from being involved to being immune. Individuals who are delinquent at time t cannot return to being susceptible at time $t + 1$. Individuals who are immune at time t must remain immune at time $t + 1$. In other words, we assume that once individuals decide to terminate their involvement in crime they do not recommence their criminal careers and are not susceptible to doing so.

Now let:

S_t = the number of susceptible individuals at time t;
D_t = the number of delinquents at time t;
I_t = the number of delinquents at time t who are either immune to

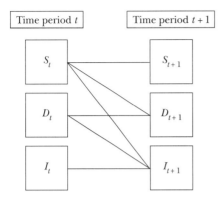

Figure 6.2 State transitions in the epidemic model

involvement in crime or past their period of susceptibility to such involvement;

B_t = the number of new individuals reaching their crime-prone years who are susceptible to involvement in crime;

q = the probability of a delinquent quitting crime and becoming immune;

p = the probability that a susceptible individual comes in contact with a delinquent;

r = the probability of a susceptible becoming delinquent on contact with a delinquent; and

m = the probability of a susceptible individual becoming 'immune' to involvement in crime.

Now for practical purposes p and r are not separately measurable. Accordingly, we define $k = pr$ and the model depicted schematically in Figure 6.1 may be summarised in the following three equations:

$$D_{t+1} = D_t + kS_tD_t - qD_t \tag{3}$$

$$S_{t+1} = S_t - kS_tD_t + B_t - mS_t \tag{4}$$

$$I_{t+1} = I_t + qD_t + mS_t \tag{5}$$

The relevant equations in modelling offender population growth are equations (3) and (4). Equation (5) simply describes the time course of growth in the number of individuals who were either 'born' immune or who became immune after passing their 'window' of susceptibility to involvement in crime (without becoming involved) or ceasing their involvement in crime. Equation (3) states that the population of offenders at time $t + 1$ is determined by its size at t, plus any new cases of involvement in crime which occur at t, minus any departures from crime which occur at t. New cases of involvement in crime are generated at a rate kS_tD_t because there are pS_tD_t contacts between *susceptibles* and *delinquents*, a proportion r of which results in a *susceptible* becoming a *delinquent*. Equation (4) regulates the offender population growth process because it states that the number of individuals susceptible to involvement in crime at $t + 1$ is given by the number who were susceptible at t, minus those *susceptibles* who become *delinquents* at t, plus any new *susceptibles* who enter the population of *susceptibles* at t, minus those *susceptibles* who ceased being *susceptibles* at t. The parameter B_t – which reflects the rate at which new *susceptibles* are added to the existing population of *susceptibles* – mediates the influence of economic stress. It can be seen that economic stress influences the offender population because it controls the size of the pool of potential delinquents.

One feature of this model is that the numbers in the total population (*susceptibles* plus *delinquents* plus *immunes*) is not constant but increasing. It would be possible to change the model to assume a constant population. This could be done by introducing three new parameters: a birth rate, a death rate, and the probability of a new birth being susceptible. A constant population would be achieved by setting the birth rates and death rates equal to each other. A growing population could be modelled by making the birth rate greater than the death rate. The numbers of *immunes* in each time period, as well as increasing by the numbers who become immune from susceptibility and from delinquency, would increase by the numbers of new immunes born and decrease by the number who die. A number of *delinquents* and *susceptibles* would also die in each time period. This variation of the model does not behave substantially differently from the simpler version, except for the numbers of immunes, in which we have little interest. We have chosen, therefore to use the simpler version of the model for demonstrating its properties.

Stable condition values in the epidemic model of delinquency

To derive detailed quantitative predictions from the model we would need to be able to obtain estimates of its parameters. Given the current state of research and the unavailability of relevant data this is simply not possible. Although the assumptions we have made in constructing the model are all supported by research, there are no data on which one could reliably estimate, for example, the probability of a susceptible juvenile becoming delinquent on contact with a delinquent. As a first step toward assessing the model, however, it is worth seeing whether its basic implications accord with both common-sense and existing empirical research.

Ideally one would like to solve equation (3) and obtain explicit confirmation of these implications for both offender populations which are undergoing change and for those which have attained stability. Unfortunately this is impossible for the circumstance where offender populations are unstable. We can, however, examine how the value of D_t is affected by changes in the model parameters in circumstances where the value of D_t is assumed to have stabilised. We do this in the following way:

Under stable conditions, $D_{t+1} = D_t$ and $S_{t+1} = S_t$.

$$D_{t+1} = D_t \text{ if } kS_tD_t - qD_t = 0$$

$$\text{i.e. if} \qquad S_t = q/k \qquad\qquad\qquad (6)$$

$$S_{t+1} = S_t \text{ if} \qquad\qquad B_t = kS_tD_t + mS_t$$

$$\text{i.e. if} \qquad D_t = B_t/q - m/k \qquad\qquad\qquad (7)$$

It is clear from equation (7) that, where the offender population stabilises, its value will be:

(1) positively related to the flow of new *susceptibles*, and therefore, other things being equal, the level of economic stress in a community;

(2) positively related to the rate at which susceptible individuals become delinquent on contact with another delinquent;

(3) negatively related to the rate at which individuals quit crime, i.e. positively related to criminal career duration; and

(4) negatively related to the rate at which juveniles quit susceptibility to involvement in crime, i.e. positively related to the duration of susceptibility to delinquent peer influence.

It is interesting to note at this point that if we take the notifications for neglect as an index of the supply of new susceptibles in a neighbourhood, the result shown in Figure 5.2 is precisely what one would expect from the epidemic model among neighbourhoods where the population of offenders is stable. The other implications of the model are also in accord with what we would expect on the basis of empirical evidence. At the same time, the model also contains some surprising implications about the effect of economic stress on offender population growth.

'Tipping points' and the offender population growth threshold

Criminologists and others who study crime have occasionally remarked on the existence of what have become known as 'tipping points' (see Gladwell 1996). These are points in a neighbourhood or city where crime rates abruptly begin to increase or decrease without any previous indication that this was likely to occur. The phenomenon has been taken as indicative of the existence of epidemic effects in crime. One of the most notable features of the epidemic model is the implication of a population growth threshold. Inspection of equation (3) indicates that $D_{t+1} > D_t$ only when $kS_tD_t > qD_t$, that is, when $S_t > q/k$. In short, q/k defines an offender population growth threshold. We can illustrate the significance of the offender population growth threshold, however, by simulating the effects on offender population levels of changes in B_t. Given the impossibility of fitting equation (3) to any extant body of data the question of how to choose values for q, k and m is an issue which deserves some preliminary comment.

First, it should be noted that, like many deterministic mathematical models of contagious processes, the epidemic model only produces sensible growth patterns under certain combinations of parameter values. These combinations of parameter values act as constraints on the model's validity and, in principle, provide a basis on which it could be tested. Unfortunately, we have not been able to determine the general relationships which must exist between parameters to produce stable patterns of growth in the delinquent population. As we shall show, however, there is no doubt that stable growth patterns can be obtained under realistic combinations of parameter values. Although it is impossible to estimate them directly, the choice of parameter values for q and m is not entirely arbitrary. In the first set of simulations which follow we have assumed that 20 per cent of offenders cease their involvement in crime each year (i.e. set $q = 0.2$) on the grounds, as we discussed earlier, that the average period of time in crime appears to be around five years. On the other hand, because the window of greatest susceptibility to involvement in crime extends between the ages of 10 and 20 years (i.e. ten years) we have also assumed that 10 per cent of susceptible individuals cease being susceptible to involvement in crime each year (i.e. $m = 0.1$). That leaves us with the task of choosing a value for k and starting values for the population of offenders (D_1) and the population of individuals susceptible to involvement in crime (S_1).

The choice of starting point is somewhat arbitrary but, since we are interested in simulating the growth of an offender population in a small

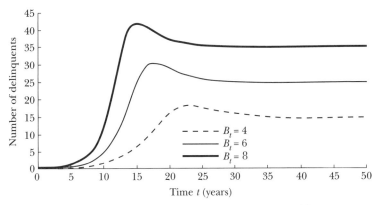

Figure 6.3 Offender population growth for different values of B_t
($q = 0.2$, $m = 0.1$, $k = 0.02$, $S_I = 0$, $D_I = 1$)

community, such as a suburb, in the first set of simulations we will consider, we have assumed that $D_1 = 1$ and $S_1 = 0$. That is, we start with no *susceptibles* and only one *delinquent*. It is impossible to find any empirical basis for separately estimating k. Accordingly we make the arbitrary assumption that $k = 0.02$, that is, we assume that the probability of a contact between a *susceptible* and a *delinquent* which results in the *susceptible* becoming *delinquent* is 0.02. This assumption, though admittedly arbitrary, does not seem implausible.

Figure 6.3 shows the consequences for offender population growth in our hypothetical suburb of changing B_t, that is, the number of new *susceptibles* added to the suburb in each new time period. Each curve is generated on the assumption that B_t is constant over time. However, separate curves show the effect on offender population growth of different values of B_t, ranging from 4 to 8.

The first thing to note about Figure 6.3 is that, regardless of whether the flow of *susceptibles* is 4, 6 or 8, the offender population does not grow at all until the supply of *susceptibles* rises above the epidemic threshold. The second thing to note is that increasing the flow of *susceptibles* into our community both hastens the onset of offender population growth and changes the ultimate level to which the offender population grows. With four additional *susceptibles* added per time period the population of offenders barely grows at all for the first ten years, then rises to a maximum of about 18 offenders over the next thirteen years before settling back to a more or less stable population of about 15 offenders. With six *susceptibles* added per time period, the population of offenders shows little change for about eight years, then rises over the next ten years to about 30 offenders before settling back to a stable level of about 25

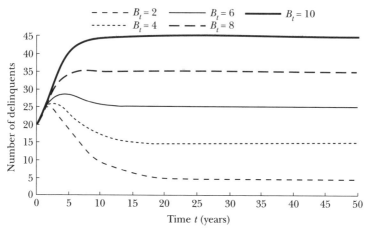

Figure 6.4 Offender population growth for different values of B_t
($q = 0.2$, $m = 0.1$, $k = 0.02$, $S_I = 20$, $D_I = 20$)

offenders. Finally, with eight *susceptibles* added per time period, the population
of offenders begins to rise steeply after about five years, reaches a maximum of
about 42 offenders over the next ten or so years before settling back to a stable
level of about 35 offenders.

Another interesting consequence of the model is its implication that
offender populations will not always grow in response to an increase in B_t.
This is actually implicit in Figure 6.3 but may more clearly be drawn out by
considering the impact of increasing the flow of *susceptibles* into a community
or suburb which already has a small population of offenders. In Figure 6.4 we
have assumed that $D_1 = 20$ and $S_1 = 20$. The remaining parameters have
been set at the values used to construct Figure 6.3. The salient feature of
Figure 6.4 is the sensitivity of offender population growth to the flow of
susceptibles. With two *susceptibles* added per time period, the population of
offenders falls toward five. With four added per time period, the population
declines to a little below 15 before stabilising. Six additional *susceptibles* added
per time period produces a slight growth in the offender population before
stabilising at 25. Values of B_t above six produce significant offender population
growth, with $B_t = 10$ essentially doubling the size of the offender population
over five years.

It should be emphasised that we are not arguing that offender populations
behave in the precise manner described in Figures 6.3 and 6.4. The precise
behaviour of an offender population in response to changes in the number of
susceptibles is quite dependent on the choice of model parameter value. The
parameter values we have chosen to illustrate the model's implications,

although plausible, are somewhat speculative. The processes described by those figures may be slower or faster than we have depicted them. We turn next to the question of what light the model can shed on the anomalies we discussed in Chapter 1. Before doing so, however, we need to discuss two important preliminary issues. The first concerns the link between criminal participation rates and aggregate crime rates. The second concerns the short-run effect of economic conditions on aggregate crime rates.

Criminal participation rates and aggregate crime rates

From the viewpoint of criminal career theory the epidemic model is a theory of criminal participation. If we wish to apply the theory to problems involving aggregate crime or victimisation rates we must therefore make some assumption about the extent to which variation in aggregate crime or victimisation rates is influenced by variation in rates of criminal participation. This creates something of a problem because, according to criminal career theory, variation in aggregate crime rates could arise from variation in criminal participation rates or from variation in offending frequency or both. While there are methods for separately measuring both components of offending when dealing with individual offenders, there is no obvious way of determining the relative contribution made by each component to any given pattern of aggregate variation in crime.

The most appropriate approach to this problem would seem to be to make the most parsimonious assumption until confronted with evidence inconsistent with it. Our general approach to the link between criminal participation rates and aggregate offending rates will therefore be the obvious one; that is, we assume that areas or time periods which have higher criminal participation rates will also have higher crime rates. This assumption is supported both by the data presented in Table 5.12 and by a range of other considerations.

First, the distances travelled by offenders from homes to crime sites appear to be short, with the number of offences declining rapidly as one moves further from the offender's home (Capone and Nichols 1976; Phillips 1980; Rhodes and Conley 1981). Second, several studies of spatial variation in crime have found that residential proximity of crime victims to motivated offenders accounts for a significant proportion of the spatial variation in criminal victimisation rates (Cohen, Kluegel and Land 1981; Miethe, Stafford and Long 1987). Third, offenders are themselves known to be at higher risk of crime victimisation than non-offenders (Sampson and Lauritsen 1990). On this account alone we should expect higher rates of criminal victimisation in areas with large rates of participation in crime. Fourth, there is direct evidence that, when the city centre and other 'offence-attracting' areas are excluded, there is a strong correlation between the spatial distribution of offenders and the spatial distribution of offences. Bottoms and Wiles (1986), for example, found support for this in a comparison of offence and offender rates in Sheffield. Similar results have been obtained by Herbert and Hyde (1984) in Swansea who, after considering various possible explanations for the pattern of victimisation in that city, concluded that variations in offender residence come the closest to a general explanation of offence rates. Outside of the city centre and other 'offence-attracting areas', then, it would seem reasonable to assume that the spatial distribution of offending generally follows the spatial distribution of offenders.

Short- and long-run effects of economic stress on aggregate crime rates

This brings us to the second preliminary issue we need to discuss. If the parameter values chosen to construct Figures 6.3 and 6.4 are any guide, the epidemic model itself implies that the time course of change in the level of participation in crime in response to economic deterioration is fairly pro-tracted, taking place over a period of years rather than months. There is evidence to support this implication. Schuerman and Kobrin (1986) examined the twenty-year histories of Los Angeles County's highest crime rate neigh-bourhoods in 1970. They classified the census tracts in their study into three groups, according to the trend in crime over the period 1950–70. The three groups were *emerging* (i.e. areas of low crime in 1950 which became moderately crime-prone by 1970), *transitional* (i.e. areas with moderate crime rates in 1950 which had high crime rates by 1970) and *enduring* (i.e. areas with high crime rates from 1950 to 1970). It is only the first of these three groups which is of interest to us. *Emerging* high-crime areas were distinguished by a steady decline in their share of professional and skilled occupational groups and of popu-lation with advanced education, an increase in the share of unskilled labourers and unemployed persons, combined with a rising share of the country's overcrowded and deteriorated housing. They were also marked by a rise in residential mobility and broken families. Using cross-lagged panel analysis Schuerman and Kobrin were able to show that changes of this sort in one decade explained much of the variance in subsequent decades of accelerated transformation into high-crime areas. These observations are clearly in accord with the predictions of the epidemic model.

Time series studies of the relationship between economic factors and crime, however, also often find significant short-run effects (see Allen 1996). In fact, in his review, Chiricos (1987: 201) concluded that contemporaneous studies of the relationship between unemployment and aggregate offending rates were more likely to find evidence of a significant positive association than studies examining the lagged effect of unemployment. The observation that variables such as unemployment and income exert short-run effects on aggregate crime rates cannot be explained by the epidemic model. Given the inconsistent results obtained in time series studies of the relationship between unemployment and crime, it is tempting to treat these short-term effects with a degree of scepticism, especially as the effects in question are sometimes quite small (e.g. see Land, Cantor and Russell 1995). However, we do not believe that the short-run effects of economic factors on crime should be dismissed as inconsequential. In our view the explanation for the short-run effect of unemployment on crime probably lies in the evidence provided by Farrington et al. (1986), noted in Chapter 1, that unemployment does not appear to induce otherwise law-abiding individuals to commit crime but it does seem to increase the frequency of offending amongst those already disposed to commit crime. This finding is consistent with the view that short-term changes in the level of economic stress probably exert little effect on rates of participation in crime but do exert some effect on the average offending frequency of the existing population of offenders. Such a conclusion would be consistent with studies showing short-run effects on crime of other economic variables (e.g. Field 1990). It would also be consistent with other evidence suggesting that offending frequency is shaped largely by the supply of opportunities and incentives for involvement in crime (Salmelainen 1995).

Dealing with the anomalies

We turn, then, to the question of whether the epidemic model can shed any new light on the anomalies surrounding the ESIOM paradigm. For convenience of exposition we once again list the anomalies we described at the conclusion of Chapter 1. They were:

1. The *individual-level evidence anomaly*: the fact that there is limited and somewhat ambiguous evidence available to support the claim that economic adversity increases individual offending rates.
2. The *non-utilitarian crime anomaly*: the fact that aggregate rates of non-utilitarian violent crime are strongly affected by economic stress.
3. The *early onset anomaly*: the fact that many of the processes which shape involvement in crime substantially precede entry into the labour market and, in some cases, precede entry into school.

4. The *inconsistency problem*: the fact that studies examining the relationship between economic stress and crime have frequently produced non-significant and occasionally negative results.
5. The *neighbourhood effect anomaly*: the fact that the effect of economic stress on rates of juvenile offending appears to be influenced by the level of economic stress in the surrounding neighbourhood.
6. The *income inequality anomaly*: the fact that income inequality appears to be a better predictor of area crime rates than absolute levels of income.

It is obvious, to begin with, why the first three problems cease to exist. They arise because ESIOM theories assume that economic stress exerted its effects on crime by motivating individuals to offend. We have abandoned this hypothesis in favour of the (empirically better supported) claim that economic stress exerts its effects on delinquency by eroding the quality of parental supervision, weakening the bond between parent and child and/or increasing the frequency of inconsistent, harsh and erratic parental discipline. Since incompetent or inadequate parenting is known to increase the risk of all forms of delinquent behaviour it is also clear why economic stress is correlated with both property and (non-utilitarian) violent crime. Moreover, since the processes by which economic stress leads to juvenile involvement in crime occur during the early years of a child's life, it is equally clear why juvenile involvement in crime can be predicted long before his or her entry into the labour market.

The epidemic model also sheds some light on why higher levels of economic stress (whether measured by unemployment or income) may not always be accompanied by higher levels of crime. Recall that the supply of juveniles susceptible to involvement in crime in a neighbourhood is not determined solely by the level of economic stress but also by the extent to which the effects of economic (or social) stress are buffered by strong social supports (or compounded by social stress). We should accordingly expect an attenuated relationship between economic stress and crime in communities which are highly cohesive and in which, as a result, those experiencing poverty are able to call upon neighbours, friends and family members for material or emotional support.

More importantly, it is clear from our discussion of the implications of the epidemic model that the effects of economic stress on the supply of *susceptibles* may be quite rapid but growth in an offender population will not even begin until the supply of *susceptibles* in a community crosses the epidemic threshold. Depending upon the infection rate and the period of involvement in crime, this may not occur until several years after the economic contraction actually ends. The model suggests, moreover, that the long-term effect of a deterioration of economic conditions will not necessarily be felt equally in all communities. In areas where the impact of economic stress is insufficient to drive the supply of juveniles susceptible to involvement in crime above the epidemic threshold, there will be no observable growth in the offender population, although there may be a slowing down in the rate at which the existing population of offenders declines. In areas where the offender population is already growing, the effect of an increase in economic stress will be to accelerate that growth. In areas where changes in the level of economic or social stress have been sufficient to drive the supply of juveniles susceptible to involvement in crime above or below the epidemic threshold, formerly stable offender populations will experience a 'tipping point' and give way to rising or falling ones.

Though it is almost certainly not the complete answer, this non-monotonic relationship between economic stress and offender population growth may provide a partial explanation for the fact that time series studies of the relationship between measures of economic stress and aggregate offending rates produce much less consistent results than cross-sectional studies. Conventional wisdom suggests that if economic factors influence aggregate offending rates, there should be an orderly relationship over time between changes in those conditions and changes in aggregate offending rates. The present model suggests, however, that a deterioration in economic conditions will not necessarily lead to a uniform increase in aggregate offending rates.

It should be equally clear why rates of neighbourhood economic status will exert effects on offending which are independent of family economic status. In the epidemic model the likelihood of an individual becoming involved in crime is ultimately shaped both by his (or her) own family's economic circumstances and that which prevails among other families in his or her own neighbourhood. The influence of family economic status stems from the fact that it helps to determine whether or not a juvenile will grow up susceptible to delinquent peer influence. The influence of neighbourhood economic status stems from the fact that poor neighbourhoods in general have larger populations of offenders and therefore offer higher rates of contact between delinquent and susceptible individuals. This, in turn, increases the likelihood that the children of any particular family facing economic stress will become involved in crime.

Evidence supporting this explanation can be found in a study by Paternoster and Mazerolle (1994). They measured self-reported delinquency rates among a sample of 1,725 youths from the National Youth Survey, a longitudinal survey of the correlates of delinquency and drug use in the

United States. A notable feature of the study is that it was able to examine the effect of living in a crime-prone neighbourhood on self-reported offending at two points in time one year apart. The study found that the perceived level of neighbourhood crime problems at time one was significantly associated with self-reported delinquency at time two, even after controlling for the strength of the bond between parent and adolescent as seen by the adolescent.

Ordinarily then, the epidemic model would lead one to expect that higher levels of involvement in crime will be found among low economic status juveniles resident in low economic status areas. But there are two important caveats to enter here. First, according to the epidemic model the effects of economic status on juvenile participation in crime are mediated by parental supervision and association with delinquent peers. Once these individual-level factors are controlled for we would expect the contextual effect of economic stress to disappear. Second, higher criminal participation rates in an area do not guarantee higher self-reported rates of offending. The frequency with which an individual offends will be influenced by the supply of opportunities and incentives for involvement in crime. Thus, while the prevalence of involvement in crime (i.e. the participation rate) should be highest in low economic status families resident in low economic status neighbourhoods, offenders resident in wealthier neighbourhoods may actually offend more frequently if, as a result of living in such neighbourhoods, they are exposed to a greater range of opportunities and incentives for involvement in crime. This may explain why studies employing self-report measures of offending fre- quency (e.g. Johnstone 1978; Jarjoura and Triplett 1997) tend to find higher rates of offending amongst juveniles from low economic status families in middle-level economic status neighbourhoods than among juveniles from the same types of families resident in low status neighbourhoods.

Finally, the epidemic model also bears some interesting and important implications concerning the relationship between inequality and crime. The conventional approach to this relationship, as we have seen, is to argue that inequality generates crime because poverty motivates offenders while wealth provides abundant opportunities for crime. Without questioning the relevance of this explanation in certain circumstances, it is possible to offer an alternative account of the impact of inequality on crime. High and/or growing levels of inequality are often associated with high and/or growing levels of residential segregation, with low-income households increasingly concentrated in certain areas of extreme social disadvantage. Between 1975 and 1991, in Australia, for example, the ratio of the mean household income in the lowest 5 per cent of Australian census collection districts (CDs), ranked in terms of socioeconomic status, to the mean household income of the highest 5 per cent of CDs widened by 38 per cent. In constant dollars, the average household income of the lowest 5 per cent of households fell by about $7,500 while the average household income in the highest 5 per cent of households rose in real terms by about $12,500 (Gregory and Hunter 1995).

Gregory and Hunter (1995) argue that much of this change has come about because the unemployed have become increasingly concentrated in certain areas. In 1976, for example, the male employment to population ratio was essentially the same across CDs ranked in terms of socioeconomic status. By 1991, however, the employment to population ratio had fallen by twice as much in the lowest 5 per cent of CDs, ranked in terms of socioeconomic status, than it had in the top 5 per cent of CDs. The relevance of these findings for our purposes stems from the fact that neighbourhoods with a concentration of low-income households (i.e. 'ghettos') can be expected to have a larger supply of individuals susceptible to involvement in crime. Over time they will also suffer higher rates of contact between *susceptibles* and *delinquents*. Thus, communities where those on low household incomes are concentrated in certain areas will generally tend to experience higher rates of mixing between *susceptibles* and *delinquents* and therefore potentially suffer worse crime problems than those with the same average overall level of household income but a more uniform level of income across and within neighbourhoods. It is no surprise to observe, therefore, that over the period during which Australia apparently witnessed a progressive geographical concentration of its poor it also experienced substantial increases in crime. Between 1973–74 and 1988–89 recorded rates of serious assault, robbery, break and enter and motor vehicle theft in Australia more than doubled (Mukherjee and Dagger 1990).[1]

Testing the epidemic model

While the epidemic model can be defended on the grounds that it rests on plausible assumptions and resolves many of the anomalies surrounding the economic stress-crime relationship, it must be acknowledged that proper testing of the model would require detailed longitudinal analysis. Unfortunately the data required for such an analysis are not easy to obtain. Long-term aggregate crime data are not really suitable for the purpose for three reasons. First, they may be affected by factors other than the supply of motivated offenders (e.g. changes in offending frequency). Second, they are usually collected at a level of spatial aggregation which would obscure the neighbourhood-level processes hypothesised by the model. Third, aggregate crime data describe the distribution of criminal offences rather than offenders. It is the latter not the former with which the model is principally concerned.

To test the model ideally one would like to track the impact over time on criminal participation rates of changes in economic and social stress at the neighbourhood level. It would be of particular interest to see how newly forming neighbourhoods, or those where the level of economic and/or social stress has historically been low, respond to a growth in economic and/or social stress. If the epidemic model is correct, the growth in criminal participation rates which occurs in response to such stress should be lagged but preceded by a growth in rates of child maltreatment. The response of criminal participation rates to such maltreatment should be non-linear. That is, initially the population of active offenders should first pass through little or no growth in response to increasing economic and social stress. It should then accelerate rapidly once the epidemic threshold has been reached. Whether these predictions are borne out by evidence will only be known with time. In Chapter 7 we content ourselves with showing how the epidemic model compares with other theories of the spatial distribution of crime.

Summary and conclusion

We have presented a simple model of the offender population growth based on assumptions which, for the most part, are strongly supported by empirical evidence. The model assumes that economic and/or social stress, especially in the absence of social supports, increases the supply of juveniles susceptible to involvement in crime. According to the model, the rate at which susceptible juveniles in an area become involved in crime, that is, initiate criminal careers, depends upon the level of interaction between them and those in the area already involved in crime. The population of active offenders in an area is a function of the rate at which juveniles initiate criminal careers and the rate at which they quit those careers. Differences between areas in the size of their respective offender populations are assumed to be reflected in differences between them in their aggregate crime rates.

The model has been shown to resolve each of the major anomalies confronting ESIOM theories of crime. Because it avoids the ESIOM paradigm assumption that the effects of economic stress on crime are mediated through offender motivation, it does not imply that those directly affected by economic stress will themselves exhibit a greater propensity to become involved in crime. On the other hand, because it proposes that the effect of economic stress is a general increase in juvenile susceptibility to involvement in crime, it is able to explain why economic stress influences both property and violent crime rates and, moreover, why juvenile involvement in crime is predictable from factors which predate entry into the labour market. Furthermore, because the model implies that economic stress will not produce a growth in the size of an offender population in an area unless it produces a threshold number of juveniles susceptible to involvement in crime, the model also offers one possible explanation for why studies examining the effect of economic stress on crime do not always find a significant association between economic disadvantage and crime.

Finally, the model is also able to explain why economically disadvantaged juveniles resident in disadvantaged areas are more likely to be involved in crime and why income inequality is a better predictor of aggregate crime rates than the absolute levels of income. Disadvantaged juveniles resident in disadvantaged areas are more likely to experience contact with those already involved in crime and are, therefore, more likely themselves to become involved in crime. If higher levels of inequality are also associated with a greater geographical concentration of economically and socially disadvantaged people, higher rates of crime would be expected in areas of marked economic inequality than in areas where economically disadvantaged individuals are more uniformly distributed within and across neighbourhoods.

The fact that the epidemic model explains these anomalies lends credence to its validity, as does the fact that it rests on plausible assumptions. To test the model properly, however, it would be necessary to track neighbourhood-level changes in rates of criminal participation over time to see whether they respond to economic and social stress as predicted by the model.

CHAPTER SEVEN

Theories of crime and place

Alternative conceptions of crime and place

The model put forward in Chapter 6 construes neighbourhoods as having both distal and proximate influences on area crime rates. The distal influence of a neighbourhood arises from the fact that it shapes the extent to which the effects of economic stress on parenting practices are buffered by social supports. The proximate influence of neighbourhoods on delinquency generation arises from the fact that the number of active delinquents in a neighbourhood shapes the rate of interaction between juveniles susceptible to involvement in crime and those already involved and, therewith, the rate of entry into crime.

This conception of the factors which shape crime-prone areas differs in some significant ways from a number of other branches of criminological theory concerned with the spatial distribution of crime. Some theorists have argued that the spatial distribution of crime in large measure reflects the way in which geographical mobility, population heterogeneity and family dissolution affect the social equilibrium of neighbourhoods. Later theorists working within the same general paradigm have highlighted the way in which public disorder, fear of crime and public housing policy can influence the 'trajectory' of crime in a neighbourhood. Criminal opportunity theorists have argued that the spatial distribution of crime reflects the spatial distribution of criminal opportunities and incentives rather than the spatial distribution of motivated offenders.

In this chapter we will discuss these three main theoretical perspectives on crime and place, namely, (1) social disorganisation theory, (2) theories which deal with the roles of public disorder, fear of crime and public housing policy as causes of future crime in a neighbourhood, and (3) criminal opportunity theory. We begin with social disorganisation theory, starting with its conception as an explanation for the persistence of crime-prone places, then moving on to criticisms of the theory and more recent research which appears to confirm that informal social controls are a causal mechanism for crime. We then consider those theories which posit that public disorder, fear of crime or an area's 'reputation' have a causal influence on the area's crime rates at some point of time in the future. We include here a discussion on the role of public housing policy. Finally we consider criminal opportunity theory ending with a brief discussion on attempts to integrate theories which deal with the supply of motivated offenders with theories which deal with the supply of criminal opportunities.

There are several reasons for discussing the relationship between these branches of theory and the epidemic model. To begin with we wish to see whether the evidence on which they are based is consistent with the epidemic model of delinquency. Second, we want to identify the points at which our explanation for the spatial distribution of crime does in fact contradict those put forward by other theorists. Lastly, we wish to identify some important limits in the extent to which the epidemic model can account for the spatial distribution of crime.

Social disorganisation theory and the persistence of crime-prone places

One of the most intriguing features of crime-prone places is their persistence over time. This point can be demonstrated by a comparison of crime rates in 1990 with those in 1995 for 44 Local Government Areas in Sydney. The correlations of the 1990 rates with the 1995 rates are 0.83 for break and enter, 0.94 for motor vehicle theft, 0.78 for assault, 0.83 for robbery and 0.53 for sexual offences. (Two Local Government Areas which include inner-city night-time entertainment areas were excluded from these calculations, if included in the calculations all correlations are greater than 0.97 because the rates for the two excluded areas are so much greater than in the other predominantly residential areas.)

One thing which makes these correlations particularly impressive is the fact that the population turnover in these subdivisions is quite substantial. The average period at one address in metropolitan Sydney at the time of the 1991 census was less than five years. Thus, the spatial distribution of crime in metropolitan Sydney has remained stable despite substantial turnover in its resident population.

The stability of area crime rates over time was an observation which greatly impressed the developers of social disorganisation theory (Shaw and McKay 1969). In studying the spatial distribution of delinquents in Chicago, Shaw and McKay also observed that the spatial distribution of crime remained stable despite a complete turnover in its population. Shaw and McKay noted that areas with higher densities of offenders were, regardless of their ethnic mix, generally characterised by three structural factors: low economic status, ethnic heterogeneity and geographical mobility. All three factors, according to Shaw and McKay, lead to higher rates of crime in an area because they disrupt or inhibit the development of the informal social controls which normally limit the scope for juveniles to get involved in crime. By 'informal social controls' Shaw and McKay meant the processes by which neighbours, residents and members of local institutions watch out for each other, supervise the behaviour of adolescents, question strangers about their intentions and generally challenge unacceptable forms of social behaviour.

A distinctive feature of social disorganisation theory is its contention that the process of delinquency generation does not stop with the creation of communities with weakened forms of informal social control. According to Shaw and McKay, the persistence of delinquency in a community for any length of time fosters the emergence of delinquent subcultures (Shaw and McKay 1969: 317). These subcultures offer an alternative system of moral values which, although it never comes to dominate an entire community, is pervasive enough to sustain the flow of juveniles into delinquent activity from one generation of residents to the next. Thus, while economic disadvantage, geographical mobility and ethnic heterogeneity might underpin the emergence of high crime rate areas, their persistence is partially attributable to the fact that the process of delinquency generation can become self-sustaining. It is for this reason, according to Shaw and McKay, that places remain crime-prone long after their original inhabitants have left.

The relationship between the epidemic model and social disorganisation theory

There is clearly much in social disorganisation theory which is consistent with the epidemic model. Although we have chosen to eschew the notion of 'delinquent subculture' in favour of the more transparent (if, some might say, rather more simplistic) concept of 'contact between *susceptibles* and *delinquents*' the thesis that delinquent subcultures serve to sustain the flow of juveniles into delinquent activity is entirely consistent with our point of view. Figure 6.3 shows that under certain conditions it is possible for offender populations to become self-sustaining once they reach a certain size. As long as the supply of juveniles susceptible to involvement in crime exceeds the epidemic threshold, the existing stock of offenders – through their interaction with *susceptibles* – will generate an initiation rate sufficient to offset any departures from crime by those whose criminal careers have come to an end. However, it is possible to reach a point where the rate of departure from crime precisely offsets the rate of initiation into it. In these circumstances the population of offenders and therefore the aggregate rate of offending will remain stable despite a complete turnover in the membership of the population of offenders. In effect, although the mechanisms by which criminal behaviour is acquired remain essentially social-psychological in nature, the dynamics of crime rate change in an area are determined by the rate (and character) of change in its social and economic structure.

There are, however, two crucial differences between social disorganisation theory and the epidemic model. The first concerns the role assigned to economic stress. The second concerns the mechanism through which geographical mobility and ethnic heterogeneity are presumed to exert their effects.

We have argued that economic stress exerts its effects on crime by increasing the prevalence of certain parenting behaviours which are inherently criminogenic. Depending on the interpretation given to it, social disorganisation theory treats economic stress as exerting either no influence on offending rates, or a direct effect along lines similar to those posited by strain theory. The direct effect hypothesis is suggested by the fact that in discussing the effects of economic stress on delinquency rates Shaw and McKay observe that, whereas all individuals are exposed to common ideas about the value of material goods and personal status, low-income families enjoy more limited access to the means by which to acquire such goods and status (Shaw and McKay 1969: 318). This suggests they regard economic stress as playing a role similar to that posited by strain theory. Bursik and Grasmick (1993), however, dispute this interpretation of social disorganisation theory. They argue that economic stress acquires its significance in the theory simply because the poor areas of Chicago studied by Shaw and McKay had higher rates of population turnover and ethnic heterogeneity. If this is true, economic stress has no causal significance within the theory. Fortunately we do not need to resolve which of these interpretations of the role of economic stress in social disorganisation theory is correct. Both are inconsistent with the epidemic model. Both are also poorly supported by empirical evidence. We discussed the difficulties confronting the strain theory account of economic stress in Chapter 1. The evidence reviewed in Chapter 2 runs counter to the proposition that economic stress exerts no independent causal effect on delinquency.

The difference between the epidemic model and social disorganisation theory in terms of the putative mechanism by which these variables are assumed to influence area crime rates is subtle but important. Whereas social disorganisation theory maintains that geographical mobility exerts its effects on crime by decreasing the level of informal social control in a neighbourhood, we would argue that their principal effect is to reduce the level of social support or increase the level of social stress faced by parents with dependent children. We have already provided indirect evidence to support this contention in relation to geographical mobility in Chapter 2, where it was pointed out that rates of child abuse and neglect are also higher in areas marked by high levels of geographical mobility. If our hypothesis concerning the way in which geographical mobility influences aggregate crime rates is correct, the effect of geographical mobility on aggregate crime rates should be most pronounced in areas where it is also associated with higher than average economic stress. Support for this hypothesis can be found in the discovery by Smith and Jarjoura (1988) that geographical mobility is positively associated with violent crime rates in poorer neighbourhoods but not in more affluent areas.

The apparent impact of ethnic heterogeneity on area rates of offending presents a slightly more complex problem of interpretation. As Sampson and Lauritsen (1994) point out, Shaw and McKay's measure of ethnic heterogeneity is in fact better understood as a measure of ethnicity or population composition (see Sampson and Lauritsen 1994: 53). The neighbourhoods they observed with the highest delinquency rates were in fact those with the highest percentage of black/foreign-born residents. This fact can be reconciled with the epidemic model since, as we noted in Chapter 2, neighbourhoods with a high percentage of disadvantaged minority groups, such as Blacks or Mexican-Americans also tend to have higher rates of child neglect and abuse. Interestingly enough, ethnic heterogeneity (as opposed to ethnicity) has also been found to be associated with higher crime rates, independently of poverty and geographical mobility (Smith and Jarjoura 1988). This fact can also be easily reconciled with the epidemic model. We need only suppose that social support networks are more likely to form amongst people who see themselves as sharing the same norms, attitudes and values than amongst people who view their neighbours as not sharing such things. This would lead us to expect weaker social ties and therefore higher rates of social stress within ethnically heterogeneous neighbourhoods than among ethnically homogeneous ones. It turns out, in fact, in the study by Smith and Jarjoura (1988), that the effects of ethnic heterogeneity were rendered insignificant once family structure (per cent single parent families) was controlled. This observation provides further support for the view that both ethnicity and ethnic heterogeneity gain their significance as determinants of area crime rates from the fact that they both signal heightened levels of social stress.

One important implication of the difference between the epidemic model and social disorganisation theory in their respective explanatory mechanisms concerns the time course of change in crime in response to change in conditions, such as the level of geographical mobility. According to the epidemic model, increases in the prevalence of criminogenic parenting behaviour, whether brought on by a growth in economic stress or a breakdown in social support networks, encourage crime by (over time) boosting the supply of motivated offenders. As we have noted, this process is quite protracted. According to social disorganisation theory, on the other hand, a breakdown in social support networks encourages crime because it removes some of the disincentives to particular criminal acts normally faced by motivated offenders (for an elaboration of this point, see Bursik 1988: 521). These two assumptions generate quite different implications concerning the time course of change in crime rates in response to changes in factors such as geographical mobility. If social support networks play the role we have assigned to them we would expect a substantial lag between their breakdown and an increase in crime. If such networks play the role assigned to them by social disorganisation theory, the effect of their dissolution on crime should be relatively short.

Early criticisms of social disorganisation theory

Social disorganisation encountered a great deal of criticism in the years immediately after its formulation. Indeed, as Bursik (1986) points out, fifteen years after being trumpeted as one of the most influential theories of crime, social disorganisation theory was regarded as 'little more than an interesting footnote in the history of community-related research'. Early criticisms of social disorganisation theory focused on Shaw and McKay's reliance on official data to measure the distribution of delinquents, pointing out that self-report data show a fairly even geographical distribution of delinquency (Robinson 1936, cited in Vold and Bernard 1986: 172). Criticism was also made of Shaw and McKay's frequent use of ecological or plant analogies to describe the process by which social conditions spawn delinquent populations (Alihan 1938, cited in Vold and Bernard 1986: 174). Other criticisms have included the complaint that delinquency rates are not always high in deteriorated neighbourhoods, the complaint that Shaw and McKay had committed the ecological fallacy (Vold and Bernard 1986: 177), the complaint that delinquent neighbourhoods often show clear evidence of strong social organisation both among law-abiding and law-breaking citizens (Whyte 1943, cited in Reiss 1986b: 5) and the complaint that Shaw and McKay did not always clearly differentiate the presumed outcome of social disorganisation (i.e. increased rates of crime) from disorganisation itself (Lander 1954, cited in Bursik 1986: 41).

As Bursik (1988) points out, many of these criticisms are poorly founded. We have already had occasion to question the assertion that the results of self-report studies undermine empirical generalisations about delinquency based on official data. Criticism that Shaw and McKay chose the wrong analogies to explicate their theory of social disorganisation must also be regarded as of little account. The basic theoretical claims of social disorganisation theory can be advanced without any reliance on ecological concepts. The complaint that Shaw and McKay committed the ecological fallacy is also misguided. There is no fallacy involved in putting forward conjectures about individual criminal behaviour based on observations about the way in which social and economic factors appear to influence rates of crime in a neighbourhood. It is true that the conjectures Shaw and McKay put forward about individual criminal behaviour cannot be regarded as adequately tested by data on crime-prone areas. But to acknowledge this is not to acknowledge a weakness in the theory so much as in the testing process which follows it. As Kapsis (1978) notes, social disorganisation theory is a plausible *ex post facto* interpretation of the data on crime-prone areas. Its assumptions about individual behaviour can only be judged by seeing whether empirical evidence supports the central tenets of the theory.

Later research on informal social controls

In recent years a resurgence of interest in social disorganisation theory has taken place, spurred on by confirmation of some of Shaw and McKay's findings using more sophisticated analytical methods than they had available. Sampson (1985), for example, found that family structure and geographical mobility exerted strong effects on personal victimisation rates in a neighbourhood even in the presence of controls for economic inequality. Byrne and Sampson (1986) found similar effects when comparing the efficacy of family structure, geographical mobility and unemployment, Smith and Jarjoura (1989) observed that racial heterogeneity was positively related to area victimisation rates even in the presence of controls for income and geographical mobility, Kapsis (1978) found that crime rates were higher in neighbourhoods which have a changing ethnic profile than in neighbourhoods with a stable ethnic profile while controlling for socioeconomic status, family environment and educational attainment. Gottfredson, McNeil and Gottfredson (1991) found that children living in areas characterised by weakened family units and high proportions of poor families on welfare, were less strongly bonded to local institutions, more affected by negative peer influence and more likely to engage in delinquency. Patterson (1991) found that residential instability (i.e. geographical mobility) was significantly corre-lated with burglary rates even in the presence of controls for factors such as family structure, poverty and ethnic heterogeneity.

In the absence of a credible alternative explanation, it has been natural to interpret these findings in terms of social disorganisation theory. Most of the above-mentioned researchers have accordingly sought to explain their findings by arguing that factors such as family dissolution, geographical mobility and ethnic heterogeneity weaken the informal social controls which prevent crime in a neighbourhood. Although some researchers appear to include incompe-tent parenting within their definition of what constitutes a breakdown in informal social controls, for the most part the term appears to have been used to denote an erosion in the extent to which neighbours monitor, supervise and attempt to control the behaviour of juveniles disposed to involvement in delinquent activity. The arguments of those who view informal social controls in this light have to a large extent passed without critical attention. Indeed, some researchers even appear to have taken the view that a disruption to informal social controls can simply be inferred from the factors which ostensibly cause it (for an example, see Gottfredson, McNeil and Gottfredson 1991: 210). And yet there are at least five grounds for questioning the claim that factors such as ethnic heterogeneity, geographical mobility and family dissolution exert their effects on crime by disrupting informal social controls.

First, as Sampson and Groves (1989: 775), point out, studies which simply confirm the importance of geographical mobility, racial heterogeneity and family dissolution as predictors of crime do not go much beyond the steps taken by Shaw and McKay. Specifically, they do not establish the claim that informal social controls mediate the relationship between geographical mobility, racial heterogeneity and family dissolution, on the one hand, and crime on the other. Second, while plausible examples of informal social control are frequently offered (e.g. supervising youth leisure activities, intervention in street corner congregation and challenging youths who seem to be 'up to no good') there is little direct evidence that these kinds of behaviour actually occur with any frequency or that they influence the rate of offending. Third, while one might imagine that informal social controls such as surveillance of public places by neighbours are of value in preventing low-level delinquent acts (e.g. malicious damage to property) committed on or near residential property, it seems less reasonable to suppose that they are of value in preventing predatory crimes, such as commercial robbery or assaults on licensed premises, or crimes where neighbourhood surveillance is of no particular value, such as domestic assault. Fourth, attempts to establish the importance of informal social controls as a source of crime control have not always met with success. In their comparison of high and low crime rate areas, for example, Greenberg, Rohe and Williams (1993) could find no differences in the extent of neighbouring, the scale of local friendship networks, the perceived similarity with neighbours and the exchange of information among residents. Finally, and most importantly, studies which purport to provide evidence of the importance of informal social control in a neighbourhood are equally consistent with the view that factors such as geographical mobility, ethnic heterogeneity and family dissolution influence both minor and serious delinquency by disrupting the parenting process thereby increasing the supply of motivated offenders.

Simcha-Fagan and Schwartz (1986), for example, explored the effects of neighbourhood variables on both self-reported and officially recorded delinquency among a sample of 553 adolescent males drawn from 12 New York City neighbourhoods. The males were selected by taking a stratified random sample of male students from schools in the relevant neighbourhoods. Both they and their parents were then interviewed. By factor-analysing the survey data drawn from these interviews the researchers constructed two composite neighbourhood-level factors, one designed to measure a neighbourhood's capacity to exert informal control over the behaviour of its youth, the other designed to measure the strength of the neighbourhood subculture of deviance. These were labelled, respectively, *community organisational participation* and *community disorder-criminal subculture*. The surveys were also used to construct two composite individual-level factors measuring, respectively, school attachment/commitment and association with delinquent peers. The effect of both neighbourhood and individual-level factors on self-reported and officially recorded delinquency was then examined.

The level of *community disorder-criminal subculture* was found to exert strong direct effects on severe self-reported and officially recorded delinquency, even in the presence of controls for factors such as family income and school attachment. This observation is entirely in accord with the epidemic model. However, the level of *community organisational participation* was also found to be inversely related to the level of self-reported delinquency, even in the presence of controls for adolescent age, family income and association with delinquent peers. Path analysis suggested that this effect was mediated in the main by the level of attachment between a juvenile and his or her school.

Simcha-Fagan and Schwartz argued that this finding provided strong support for social disorganisation theory. But in the areas they surveyed the level of *community organisational participation* was inversely related to the percentage of single parent families (i.e. family dissolution). No controls were introduced for this variable in examining the effect of *community organisational participation* on self-reported or officially recorded offending. It is entirely possible, therefore, that the association between *community organisational participation* and crime arose simply because the former variable was tapping the extent of family dissolution in a neighbourhood. The fact that *community organisational participation* appeared to exert its effects on crime through the level of attachment between a juvenile and his or her school does nothing to disturb this interpretation. High-school dropout rates are known to be higher in areas with high rates of family dissolution (Crane 1991). Simcha-Fagan and Schwartz's study, therefore, cannot be regarded as providing compelling evidence, either that factors such as neighbourhood disadvantage disrupt the informal social controls in a neighbourhood or that such controls are an important influence in preventing crime.

A more direct test of social disorganisation theory is that conducted by Sampson and Groves (1989). They were specifically interested in constructing measures of informal social controls and seeing whether these measures mediated the relationship between 'exogenous sources of social disorganisation' and delinquency. The data source for their study was the first British Crime Survey which, in addition to containing data on crime victimisation rates and possible exogenous sources of social disorganisation, also contained a number of questions useful in measuring the extent of informal control. These included a question pertaining to local friendship networks, one pertaining to attendance at committees and clubs and one pertaining to the prevalence in the neighbourhood of 'teenagers who hang out and make a nuisance of themselves'. Amongst the measures of 'exogenous sources of social disorganisation' included in Sampson and Grove's study were socioeconomic status, social mobility, ethnic heterogeneity, family disruption (i.e. one-parent households) and urbanisation. Separate measures of property and violent crime victimisation were constructed using the British Crime Survey data for each of 238 'ecological areas' in Great Britain. The interrelationship between the hypothesised sources of social disorganisation, the measures of informal social controls (i.e. *sparse local friendship networks, unsupervised teenage peer groups* and *low organisational participation*) and crime victimisation and self-reported offending rates were then examined.

The results revealed that family disruption, urbanisation, *sparse local friendship networks, unsupervised teenage peer groups* and *low organisational participation* all exerted significant and independent effects on the total crime victimisation rate, even in the presence of controls for socioeconomic status, ethnic heterogeneity and residential stability. Very similar results were found for self-reported offending. Among these factors, the variable *unsupervised peer groups* proved by far the most influential mediator of the relationship between economic stress and juvenile offending. This result is entirely consistent with the epidemic model. According to the model socioeconomic stress increases the supply of juveniles susceptible to involvement in crime, but the rate at which those juveniles become involved should depend on the availability of delinquent peer groups with which they can associate. The socioeconomic status of a neighbourhood and the number of unsupervised teenage peer groups might therefore be expected to make separate although inter-dependent contributions to neighbourhood offending rates.

The more important issue from our point of view is the question of why factors such as *sparse friendship networks* and *low organisational participation* should exert any effect on crime and why they should appear to mediate the effect of structural variables, such as geographical mobility and neighbourhood socio-economic status on crime. Sampson and Groves argued that communities characterised by *sparse friendship networks* and *low organisational participation* were less well equipped to maintain the 'informal social controls' required to prevent crime. There are other ways, however, of viewing the same results. As we saw in Chapter 2, it is entirely possible that sparse friendship networks and low levels of organisational participation are associated with higher crime rates in a neighbourhood simply because they are precisely the conditions in which the effects of economic stress on parenting are least likely to be buffered by social supports and/or exacerbated by social stress.

A more elaborate study which purported to have provided direct evidence of the importance of informal social controls in preventing crime is that by Elliott et al. (1996). The data for the study were drawn from census records associated with 33 'block groups' in Denver and 58 census tracts in Chicago, and from interviews conducted with a stratified random sample of residents (adolescents and their parents) of these block groups and census tracts in both cities. Elliott et al. tested whether the effects of social disadvantage on adolescent criminal behaviour were mediated through neighbourhood organisation effects. Their measure of social disadvantage for each neighbourhood was an additive combination of standardised census measures of poverty, mobility, family structure and ethnic diversity. They used three measures of neighbourhood organisation, each of which was a composite measure developed from aggregated parents' responses to questions about their neighbourhood. The three measures were labelled *informal control, social integration* and *informal networks*. The *informal control* measure was a combination of parents' general respect for authority and satisfaction with the neighbourhood, and of their perceptions of whether police cared about neighbourhood problems and whether neighbours would respond if they saw someone in trouble or breaking the law. The *social integration* measure was an indicator of the availability of social organisations and activities, and of the level of neighbourhood support. The third measure, *informal networks*, measured the extent to which relatives and friends lived in the neighbourhood. The dimensionality of these three composite measures of neighbourhood organisation was confirmed using factor analysis.

Adolescent delinquency was measured with yet another composite measure, based on self-reported delinquent behaviour, drug use and numbers of arrests. This measure was calculated for each individual as well as being aggregated to provide a neighbourhood-level measure.

In order to control for other individual-level factors which might be expected to influence crime, measures were taken of age, gender, social class, family structure and length of residence (in the neighbourhood). Two sets of analyses were conducted, one designed to explore the effect of neighbourhood variables on neighbourhood crime rates, the other designed to assess the effect of the same variables on individual offending rates. At the neighbourhood level social disadvantage was found to be independently associated with *informal control* for both cities. *Informal control* was found to be the only mediating variable to exert an independent effect on neighbourhood rates of crime and this was only true of Chicago. *Informal control* and *informal networks* both exerted independent effects on individual offending rates but the former affected individual offending rates only in Chicago whereas the latter affected individual offending rates only in Denver.

Once again, these results are susceptible to at least two interpretations. They might be regarded as providing support for the social disorganisation perspective. But the composite measure of disadvantage includes factors which we would expect to affect crime (at both the aggregate and individual levels) simply by eroding the quality of parenting. The same is true of the factors which underpin *informal networks*, and *social integration*.

The same cannot be said for the variable *informal control* which, it will be recalled, taps respondents' perceptions of the willingness of police or neighbours to assist in dealing with social problems or breaches of the law and residents' level of satisfaction with their neighbourhood. But the fact that residents of neighbourhoods with high crime rates experience low levels of satisfaction with their area and take a dim view of the willingness of police or neighbours to assist in dealing with social problems and breaches of the law can hardly be regarded as unequivocal evidence in support of social disorganisation theory. Residents of areas with high crime rates might be expected to exhibit lower levels of satisfaction with their neighbourhoods and to believe that police and neighbours are unwilling to assist in 'dealing' with crime. Whether such beliefs are well founded and whether public reluctance to assist in 'dealing' with crime is largely responsible for generating neighbourhood crime problems are two entirely different issues. Even if we assume that citizens in high crime areas are more reluctant to confront threats to law and order we cannot safely conclude that informal social controls are vital to the prevention of crime. For one thing a lot of predatory crime is committed at night when the prospect of any informal social control is practically negligible. For another, it is just as reasonable to suppose that crime exerts a destructive effect on neighbourhood social relations as it is to suppose that the reverse causal relationship exists (Skogan 1990).

These same problems afflict perhaps the most ambitious attempt, to date, to demonstrate the importance of informal social controls. Sampson, Raudenbush and Earls conducted a survey of 8,782 Chicago residents drawn from 343 neighbourhood 'clusters' in Chicago. As with earlier studies, their aim was to establish whether informal social controls mediated the effect of structural variables (e.g. disadvantage, social composition) on crime. Measures of informal social control in each cluster were obtained from survey questions tapping such things as residents' perspectives on whether neighbours could be called upon to intervene if children were skipping school or 'hanging out' or showing disrespect to an adult. Measures of social cohesion were also obtained, using questions such as 'whether people around here are willing to help their neighbours' and 'whether this is a close-knit neighbourhood'. The measures of informal social control and social cohesion were then combined into a single variable Sampson et al. labelled 'collective efficacy'. Sampson et al. then set out to determine whether this composite variable known as 'collective efficacy' mediated the effects of the structural variables both on neighbourhood crime perception and on actual rates of interpersonal violence.

Sure enough, although the structural variables were strongly associated – both with neighbourhood perceptions of violence and with actual victimisation rates – the measured importance of these variables declined considerably once controls were introduced for 'collective efficacy'. The results were taken as confirming the hypothesis that 'collective efficacy' mediated the effects of disadvantage and social composition on crime. It is immediately obvious from what we have already said, however, that 'collective efficacy' may be measuring the extent to which social support is available to buffer the effects of economic stress on crime rather than the capacity of a community to ward off nascent threats to law and order. The results of this study therefore do not allow us to discriminate between social disorganisation theory and theories such as that embodied in the epidemic model, which assign a different role to social cohesion and social support in preventing crime.

On the whole, then, unless we take the term 'informal social control' to refer primarily to the effects of parenting on the likelihood of juveniles to participate in crime (which seems inconsistent with the spirit of social disorganisation theory), there is little compelling reason to believe that factors such as family dissolution, geographical mobility and ethnic heterogeneity exert their effects on crime by reducing the level of informal social control in a neighbourhood. Attempts to confirm this hypothesis have proved inconclusive. The available evidence supports the existence of other pathways through which the variables in question may exert their effects. It remains unclear how the informal social controls posited by social disorganisation theorists succeed in preventing the incidence of serious crime. We turn, therefore, to the next branch of criminological theory concerned with the spatial distribution of crime.

'Broken windows', fear of crime and crime-prone places

The epidemic model assumes that crime rates are a reflection of economic and social processes but do not influence those processes. It is possible to advance a contradictory view. Three theoretical contributions to this effect stand out. Wilson and Kelling (1982) and Kelling and Coles (1996) have argued that crime-prone neighbourhoods are those which have failed to confront low-level manifestations of disorder. Skogan (1986) has argued that fear of crime in a neighbourhood can trigger an out-migration of residents whose presence is vital to the control of crime in a neighbourhood. Bottoms and his colleagues (Bottoms and Wiles 1986; Bottoms, Mawby and Xanthos 1989; Bottoms, Claytor and Wiles 1992; Bottoms 1994) have argued that the reputation an area has for being crime-prone can, through its effect on the housing market, serve to reinforce its crime problems. The first two of these ideas are similar enough to be dealt with together. In the next section we deal with the relationship between public housing and crime.

Both Kelling and Coles' and Skogan's views on crime-prone communities draw heavily on social disorganisation theory in that both rely heavily on the notion of informal social controls. They depart from social disorganisation theory mainly in their contention that crime itself can produce a breakdown in such controls. In Wilson and Kelling's hands social disorganisation theory is transformed into a theory about the consequences for neighbourhoods of failing to confront manifestations of public disorder at an early stage. In Skogan's hands, social disorganisation theory is transformed into a theory about the way in which fear of crime erodes the system of informal social controls within a neighbourhood.

The essence of Kelling and Coles' position is captured by the parable that a broken window, left unrepaired, leads on to other broken windows. But failure to confront low-level manifestations of disorder (such as broken windows) does not, according to Wilson and Kelling, just lead on to other low-level manifestations of disorder. Minor crime leads on to serious crime. Once motivated offenders realise a neighbourhood is tolerant of disorder, they are ostensibly drawn toward it and strengthened in the belief that they can commit further more serious offences with impunity. A concentration of supposedly 'victimless' crimes, as Skogan aptly puts Wilson and Kelling's argument, 'can soon flood an area with serious victimising crime' (Skogan 1990: 11). Thus, whereas social disorganisation theory argued that informal social controls mediate the relationship between crime and structural factors, such as geographic mobility and ethnic heterogeneity, Wilson and Kelling argue that informal social controls modulate the relationship between minor and serious forms of crime.

Skogan's own point of departure from social disorganisation theory is somewhat more subtle. While acknowledging the importance of geographic stability to neighbourhood social stability, he maintains that social instability is generated by a much broader range of factors than those traditionally contemplated by social disorganisation theorists. These factors include disinvestment (for example, in building repair and maintenance), certain patterns of building demolition and construction, real estate demagoguery (e.g. exaggerating the size of the crime problem in a neighbourhood in order to make windfall profits when the residents of that neighbourhood sell their houses for less then they are worth) and deindustrialisation. These (and various other) conditions are said to lead to a rise in social disorder which, in turn, increases the level of public anxiety about crime. However, instead of treating public fear of crime as just a by-product of neighbourhood instability (as social disorganisation theorists had) Skogan sees it as playing a central role in generating crime. His argument is that individuals resident in crime-prone neighbourhoods do not respond to the fear of crime by becoming more protective of each other but, instead, increasingly tend to 'go their own way' and engage in fewer informal crime prevention arrangements (Skogan 1990:

70). In the extreme, fear of crime provokes an out-migration of the very residents whose presence, he maintains, is essential to the informal social controls which prevent crime escalating in a neighbourhood. The effect of all these processes is to create a reciprocal causal relationship between fear of crime and actual crime rates.[1]

Perhaps the most salient point to note about Kelling and Coles' and Skogan's theories is that, whatever their merits as hypotheses about the way in which crime at one point in time in an area can influence crime at a later point in time, as general theories of spatial variation in crime they both leave an important question unanswered. Neither theory has much to say about the origin of a nascent threat to crime or disorder in a neighbourhood. They concern themselves predominantly with the consequences which flow if these threats are left unchecked. Kelling and Coles pick up the story of crime in a community only at the point where it fails to confront a threat to law and order. Skogan picks up the same story at the point where fear of crime (or crime itself) precipitates an out-migration of law-abiding residents or a breakdown of informal social controls. Of course it could be argued that spatial variation in fear of crime (or willingness to confront a nascent threat to public order) is precisely what differentiates high-crime from low-crime neighbourhoods. But then we are left with the problem of explaining why fear of crime (or willingness to confront threats to law and order) varies across neighbourhoods in a way which renders poorer neighbourhoods more crime-prone than wealthier neighbourhoods.

Another problem afflicting both theories is the fact that both lean on the assumption that informal social controls play a central role in limiting the growth in crime in an area. We have already questioned most of the evidence adduced in support of this assumption. However, Skogan offers other evidence to support the claims of Kelling and Coles about the existence of a causal interrelationship between public disorder and serious crime. Through a detailed analysis of crime survey data he shows that crime and public perceptions of disorder are closely correlated and, moreover, that the usual social and economic correlates of crime (e.g. poverty) are unrelated to crime victimisation rates when public perceptions of social disorder in a neighbourhood have been taken into account. He also shows that fear of crime can exert an effect on the willingness of individuals to 'watch out for each other' (Lavrakas, Herz and Salem 1981, cited in Skogan 1986: 211). These observations might appear to pose a threat to our arguments but they do not. It is one thing to show that residents of high crime neighbourhoods are less inclined to watch out for each other. It is quite another to show that this failure of neighbourhood surveillance exerts a significant general effect on crime. The correlation between crime and disorder does not secure this claim. According to the epidemic model, economic and social stress disrupt the socialisation process as a whole. It follows that individuals prone to involvement in serious crime would be just as prone to involvement in other forms of deviant activity commonly identified as manifestations of public disorder. It is hardly surprising, therefore, to discover a correlation between crime and disorder. Nor is it surprising to discover that, when public perceptions of disorder are partialled out, there is no apparent relationship between poverty and crime. In partialling out public perceptions of disorder, much of the effect of poverty on crime is automatically removed.

The other leg of Skogan's argument, that an increase in public fear of crime can exacerbate crime by forcing an out-migration of residents, also at best enjoys only indirect empirical support. There is no doubt that fear of crime exerts an effect on the quality of neighbourhood life (e.g. Skogan and Maxwell 1981, cited in Skogan 1986: 210; Burnell 1988). Skogan also shows that rates of geographic mobility are higher in areas marked by public perceptions of disorder (Skogan 1990: 75). But neither of these observations can be regarded as providing compelling evidence that outward migrations from neighbourhoods in response to fear of crime are a significant factor in shaping the evolution of crime in a neighbourhood. At least one study has found evidence suggesting that neighbourhood crime rates are not strongly correlated with the rate of out-migration from a neighbourhood (Katzman 1980). Furthermore, the evidence concerning geographical mobility is just as consistent with the thesis that neighbourhoods with high levels of geographical mobility are those where there is less social support for parents, resulting in parental controls being weaker and crime and disorder therefore more prevalent, as it is with the thesis that high levels of crime generate an out-migration of residents.[2]

Setting these problems to one side, the 'broken windows' theory seems to us to suffer the most from both a want of intrinsic plausibility and supporting empirical evidence. While it is easy to see why tolerance of some forms of crime might encourage other forms of crime, it is hard to see how this sort of relationship could provide a general explanation for the emergence of serious crime in a neighbourhood. For example, it is plausible to suppose that a tolerance of public drug-dealing might lead on to robbery because public drug-dealing could attract an influx of drug-users who rely on robbery to fund their drug purchases. But it strains credulity to suppose that serious forms of criminal conduct emerge mainly in response to tolerance of minor forms of crime and disorder. Certainly there is no direct empirical evidence to support such a claim. In support of their thesis Kelling and Coles draw almost entirely on Skogan's research. As we have already found, this research falls short of establishing the claim that tolerance of public disorder provides the lynch-pin of spatial variation in aggregate offending rates for serious crime.

The idea, then, that crime and disorder are two separate but reciprocally interacting social processes and that variations in neighbourhood tolerance or fear of crime and disorder lie at the heart of spatial variation in crime is not well supported by empirical evidence. We do not discount the possibility that, at the margin, community tolerance of disorder or rampant fear of crime does exacerbate the crime problems of a neighbourhood. It would seem likely, however, that crime and disorder are, for the most part, simply two sides of the one coin minted by the effect of social and economic stress on parental behaviour. On this account many of the signs of a breakdown in informal social controls found in crime-prone neighbourhoods might be described as epi-phenomena. In other words, ubiquitous displays of disrespect for public order may portend the emergence of serious neighbourhood crime problems but they should not be mistaken as playing a significant causal role in the genesis of those problems.

The role of public housing

Whereas Skogan was concerned to highlight the role which out-migration of residents from an area can play in producing such a feedback loop, others have highlighted the role which inward migration to an area can have in maintaining it. Most of this work on inward migration has focused on the role played by public housing policy. Public housing estates, as is well known, often seem to experience more than their fair share of crime problems. Indeed, in some cases public housing estates have achieved widespread notoriety for the crime problems they regularly suffer (e.g. *The Sydney Morning Herald*, 21 Nov. 1995: 11; *The Sydney Morning Herald*, 16 Dec. 1995, Spectrum, p. 2; *The Sun-Herald*, 4 Feb. 1996: 29). From the vantage-point of the epidemic model this is hardly surprising. Public housing is normally allocated only to those who cannot afford to purchase or rent privately-owned housing. Preference is often given to unemployed persons or to low-income single parents with dependent children. Since these individuals (and their children) are particularly likely to become involved in or fall victim to crime, we should expect some association between public housing and crime.

It has been suggested by some, however, that the association between public housing and crime reflects more than just the result of preferential allocation of public housing to crime-prone individuals. This line of argument was initiated by Gill (1977), but has mostly been developed by Bottoms and his colleagues (Bottoms and Wiles 1986; Bottoms and Wiles 1988; Bottoms, Mawby and Xanthos 1989; Bottoms, Claytor and Wiles 1992). They ascribe crime problems on public housing estates partly to public housing allocation policy but maintain that the criminogenic effects of such policy go beyond the mere allocation of crime-prone individuals to public housing. The discussion by Bottoms, Claytor and Wiles (1992) provides the most convenient reference point for such an argument. It must be said at the outset, however, that, while Bottoms, Claytor and Wiles explicitly reject the argument that public housing exerts its effects on the spatial distribution of crime simply by determining the distribution of individuals prone to involvement in crime (Bottoms, Claytor and Wiles 1992: 120), they do not paint an entirely clear picture of the alternative ways in which public housing policy influences crime rates. They point out, for instance, that public housing policies have long-term effects on such things as 'within-area relationships', 'responses by outsiders' and 'leaving decisions by residents' but they do not clearly explicate the mechanisms by which these processes and conditions influence crime.

Perhaps the clearest statement of these mechanisms is to be found in their claim that:

> in order to understand and explain offending behaviour by residents in particular areas it is vital to consider who lives in these areas; how they came to live there in the first place; what kind of social life the residents have created; how outsiders (including official agencies) react to them; and why they remain in the area and have not moved (Bottoms, Claytor and Wiles 1992: 122).

These points are illustrated through a detailed analysis of two public housing estates known, respectively, as Gardenia and Stonewall (located in Sheffield, England). Both these estates were the subject of detailed observational studies by Bottoms and his colleagues in 1975 and again in 1988. In 1975 the two estates were found to differ dramatically in terms of both their offender (i.e. criminal participation) and offence (i.e. recorded crime) rates. Offence and offender rates in Gardenia were about three times higher than they were in Stonewall and these differences were confirmed through victim surveys. Despite this, the two estates did not differ significantly on any of the dimensions normally thought to differentiate high crime areas from low crime areas (e.g. social class, sex composition, age composition, percentage married, percentage unemployed, length of stay in current dwelling). At the time of the second survey, in 1988, however, this picture had changed significantly. Although, according to Bottoms, Claytor and Wiles, there had not been very much demographic change in the intervening years, by 1987 the offence rates of Gardenia and Stonewall appeared to have converged.

Bottoms, Claytor and Wiles highlighted six aspects of the public housing market which they maintained were required to understand the differences between Gardenia and Stonewall in 1975. First, Stonewall was a 'select' estate and was much sought after. Gardenia, on the other hand, was one of the least desirable low-rise housing developments in Sheffield. Second, despite a similar demographic starting point, Gardenia had 'tipped' (quotes in original) in the 1940s, apparently after the allocation to that estate of a couple of 'problem' families. Third, once Gardenia had 'tipped' the Sheffield housing allocation system operated in a way which maintained Gardenia's poor reputation. Incoming tenants, were mostly those who were either desperate for housing or those with family links in the area. Fourth, Gardenia allegedly had a stronger criminal subculture than Stonewall. Fifth, there was a stronger tendency for children and adolescents in Gardenia to play outside their homes and for criminal norms to be transmitted during the context of that play. Sixth, the fact that portions of Gardenia were cut off from other parts of the city by geographical features seemed to help maintain its 'inward-looking' character. The convergence of Gardenia and Stonewall's crime rates by 1987 was attributed to two main factors. First, during the 1970s Stonewall apparently received a high proportion of slum clearance tenants and this was said to have reduced the desirability of the estate. By contrast, Gardenia over the same period received a larger influx of people 'less desperate for housing' (Bottoms, Claytor and Wiles: 141).

It is interesting to note that, while this analysis might appear to suggest that public housing allocation policy exerts more subtle effects on crime than we have supposed, in fact many of the observations made about Gardenia and Stonewall are easily interpreted in terms of the epidemic model. In discussing the selective nature of Stonewall, for example, Bottoms, Claytor and Wiles point out that most of the families which lived in Stonewall showed a greater tendency to supervise their children's leisure time (p. 130). The observation that Gardenia 'tipped' in the 1940s after a number of problem families moved in is suggestive of the possibility that some threshold level of susceptible juveniles was reached which then set off a growth in the offender population. So too is the suggestion that crime rates were higher in Gardenia because there was a stronger tendency on that estate for criminal norms to be transmitted in the context of adolescent play.

The convergence of crime rates between Gardenia and Stonewall is equally explicable in terms of the epidemic model. As Bottoms, Claytor and Wiles point out (p. 136), between 1975 and 1986 there was a significant reduction in the average size of households and therefore the number of children. This change affected both estates but would have benefited Gardenia more because it began with a larger number of children. The fact that Gardenia began to attract a larger number of 'less desperate' families also suggests that the level of economic stress fell in the community. Over time this would have reduced the number of juveniles susceptible to delinquent peer influence and ultimately the size of the resident offender population. Indirect evidence that this in fact occurred may be read into the observation that 'there was a break-up in the old criminal subculture in south-east Gardenia' (Bottoms, Claytor and Wiles 1992: 141).

Some of the inferences which Bottoms, Claytor and Wiles draw from their observations of Gardenia and Stonewall are nevertheless inconsistent with the epidemic model. The suggestion, for example, that the reputation of Gardenia was such that only 'desperate' families tended to move there could only be understood in terms of the epidemic model by supposing that the size of the population of active offenders on a housing estate affected the supply of new *susceptibles* into it. Even if we accept the claim that *some* locations acquire a reputation which in some way or other reinforces their crime problems, we have no warrant for treating 'area reputation' as one of the key determinants of spatial variation in crime. To justify such a conclusion one would want clearer evidence that the spatial distribution of crime or temporal trends in crime cannot be adequately explained without some reference to public perceptions of neighbourhood crime problems (i.e. neighbourhood 'reputations'). Bottoms, Claytor and Wiles may be right in their account of the importance of Gardenia's reputation in maintaining its crime problems but they fail to show the importance of criminal reputation to a general understanding of the spatial distribution of crime.

There is evidence, on the other hand, which suggests that we can account for a very large percentage of the variation in aggregate crime rates by reference to the social and economic factors and that, once these factors have been controlled, the percentage of public housing in an area exerts little effect on crime. Matka (1997) examined the influence which public housing exerted on recorded rates of assault, robbery, malicious damage to property, motor vehicle theft and break and enter in NSW across 234 postcodes in the Sydney metropolitan area. Two features of Matka's study make it particularly instructive for our purposes. The first is that, rather than simply confine her analysis to an examination of the relationship between recorded rates of the above-mentioned offences in a postcode and the percentage of public housing in the postcode, she also examined the influence which the degree of dispersal of public housing had on recorded rates of crime. The second is that, in examining the criminogenic effects of public housing, Matka controlled for a range of important factors which might be expected to affect area crime rates without necessarily encouraging greater interaction between *susceptibles* and *delinquents.* These factors included the percentage of low-income families, the percentage unemployed, the rate of population turnover and the percentage of single-parent families.

Her analysis showed that *before* controls were introduced for these factors, the percentage of public renters in a postcode accounted for between 19.3 per cent (in the case of break and enter dwelling) and 37.9 per cent (in the case of assault) of the variation in recorded crime in a postcode. *After* the introduction of controls, however, the percentage of recorded crime explained rose no higher than 3.25 per cent (in the case of robbery) and fell as low as 0.80 per cent (in the case of break and enter dwelling). The residual effect in both cases was significant but it is equally clear that the quantity of public housing in a postcode exerts little effect on rates of most major offences once controls have been introduced for social and economic factors known to produce higher crime rates. In summary, then, on current evidence there is little reason to believe that the association between public housing and crime reflects much more than the familiar tendency for areas suffering higher levels of economic and social stress to exhibit higher crime rates. Viewed from the perspective of the epidemic model the influence of housing markets on area variation in offender rates is mostly attributable to allocative effects, by which we mean it is not attributable to the effects of public housing *per se* but to the character-istics of the residents who are allocated to public housing. If the dynamics of such a market push low-income families with dependent children into areas which already contain large populations of offenders, the housing market can be expected to increase crime rates. If, on the other hand, the housing market tends to disperse low-income families with dependent children across neigh-bourhoods where parental supervision of children is strong and/or the level of participation in crime is low, the opposite will occur. The only circumstance in which we would expect public housing to exert effects on crime which are not predictable from a knowledge of the socioeconomic profile of a housing estate is where, by reason of its structure, it produces greater interaction between susceptible and delinquent juveniles.

Criminal opportunity theory and aggregate crime rate variation

We turn now to the last significant branch of theory relevant to the spatial distribution of crime, namely, criminal opportunity theory. Several variants of criminal opportunity theory have been formulated, including rational choice theory (Clarke 1983; Clarke and Cornish 1985) routine activity theory (Cohen and Felson 1979) and lifestyle theory (Hindelang, Gottfredson and Garafolo

1978). In addition there have been substantial contributions from Cook (1986), Brantingham and Brantingham (1995), Eck (1995) and Sherman (1995). All these theories seek to explain criminal behaviour in terms of the supply of criminal opportunities and incentives. Few, however, are directly concerned with explaining neighbourhood-level variation in the aggregate rate of crime. Some are concerned to explain the offender decision-making process rather than the spatial distribution of crime. Others are concerned with the spatial distribution of crime but only at what might be called a 'microspatial' level, that is, they are interested in explaining variation in crime among locations within a neighbourhood rather than between neighbourhoods. These intra-neighbourhood analyses of the distribution of crime are better known as 'hotspot' studies.

Most contemporary criminal opportunity theorists are probably more interested in explaining crime 'hotspots' and other microspatial crime phenomena (e.g. repeat victimisation) than in explaining macrospatial variations in crime (i.e. variations in crime across neighbourhoods or larger units of spatial aggregation). Before we begin our discussion of the role of criminal opportunity theory in explaining macrospatial variation in crime some comments about microspatial crime phenomena are in order. Crime hotspots and the factors which generate and sustain them are both an important feature of the spatial distribution of crime and an important challenge to criminological theory. Their significance for a general understanding of crime has been illustrated by Sherman, Gartin and Buerger (1989). They analysed the origin of 323,000 calls to the Minneapolis police in 1986 and found that just 3 per cent of addresses accounted for 50 per cent of the calls received by police.

For the most part, however, crime hotspots and associated phenomena (e.g. repeat victimisation) probably lie outside the perimeter of phenomena able to be explained by reference to the spatial distribution of motivated offenders. It could hardly be said that spatial variation in rates of offending across different addresses within a street, or across different streets within a neighbourhood, has much to do with where offenders reside in a neighbourhood. Instead, phenomena such as crime hotspots or repeat victimisation appear to arise either because they involve locations which attract offenders, bring victims and offenders into close proximity or in some way or other stimulate offending behaviour. It has been found, for example, that (hotel) bars and high schools are often hotspots of personal crime, certain patterns of commercial development are often hotspots of commercial burglary while locations with active drug markets are often hotspots for predatory crime (Eck and Weisburd 1995). All these observations suggest that an adequate explanation of phenomena such as crime hotspots requires an account of the offender decision-making process rather than an account of the process which controls the supply of motivated offenders. Since criminal opportunity theory is pre-eminently concerned with the offender decision-making process, it is far more relevant to an understanding of the microspatial distribution of crime than theories concerned solely with the supply of motivated offenders.

The pre-eminent contribution of criminal opportunity theory to our understanding of macrospatial variation in crime has come from routine activity theory (Cohen and Felson 1979). The cornerstone of routine activity theory is the idea that crime rates are shaped by the convergence in space and time of motivated offenders, suitable targets and capable guardians. According to the theory, changes in any one of these variables could affect crime rates without changes in any of the others. Thus, if the supply of motivated offenders were to remain stable, for instance, a growth in crime would occur if changes in the routine activities of individuals increased the range of circumstances in which motivated offenders and suitable targets converged in the absence of capable guardians. Although Cohen and Felson spoke about the importance of a *convergence* between the supply of motivated offenders, suitable targets and the absence of capable guardians, thereby implying that all three factors were important in shaping spatial and temporal trends in crime, both they and their followers tended to act as if the supply of motivated offenders exerts no effect on the aggregate crime rate. Indeed, for a time, the idea that a supply of motivated offenders may be taken as a given seemed to have acquired something approximating the status of a dictum among criminal opportunity theorists.

Routine activity theory was stimulated, at least in part, by the problem of accounting for the fact that aggregate crime rates in the United States rose sharply during a period (1960 to 1975) in which overall American living standards were rising sharply. Just as Keynes had been prompted to reject classical economic theory by the sustained increase in unemployment rates which occurred during the Great Depression, so Cohen and Felson were prompted to reject classical offender motivation theory (i.e. ESIOM) by the sustained rise in crime which occurred between 1960 and 1975. They began by pointing out that the proportion of blacks who completed high school rose from 43 per cent in 1960 to 61 per cent in 1968, unemployment rates dropped significantly between 1959 and 1967 and the median income of blacks in cities increased from 61 per cent to 68 per cent of median white income. This combination of rising living standards and rising crime rates seemed to them to contradict traditional offender-based theories of crime. On the other hand, during the period over which average living standards in the United States were rising, a number of demographic changes were occurring which, according to Cohen and Felson, increased the supply of suitable but unguarded targets. The supply of portable consumer goods increased. Americans spent an increasing proportion of time away from their homes and, most importantly, the number of single parent households increased.

Cohen and Felson attached particular significance to this last observation. They pointed out, for example, that, in the six years between 1970 and 1975, the proportion of 'non-husband–wife' households rose by 25 per cent. According to Cohen and Felson, this particular trend greatly increased both the vulnerability of individuals to personal crime and the vulnerability of houses to property crime. Neighbourhoods with pronounced family disruption, they reasoned, are less able to provide an effective network of informal social controls. Disrupted households are more frequently unoccupied during the day, less likely to monitor the activity of and challenge strangers, less likely to assume responsibility for youth activity and less capable of intervening in local disturbances. Cohen and Felson therefore attributed the rise in crime rates in the United States during the period 1960–68 to the fact that changes in the routine activity patterns of individuals weakened the capacity of households to protect their belongings and exposed individuals to greater risk of personal victimisation.

With the benefit of hindsight it is now clear that Cohen and Felson were wrong in their assumption that the period 1960–75 witnessed a general rise in living standards and a general decline in racial inequality in the United States. They were also wrong in their assumption that that the concurrence of rising crime and rising numbers of single parent families could only be reconciled by appeal to factors other than a rise in the supply of motivated offenders. Wilson (1987) has shown that most of the rise in black income and employment over the period in question principally benefited middle-class educated blacks (Wilson 1987: 109). He points out that between 1966 and 1981 the percentage of total black income attributable to the lowest two-fifths of black families declined from 15.8 per cent to 13.4 per cent (p. 110). During this period a progressive geographical concentration of the poor (p. 46) occurred along with a change in its profile. Whereas before 1960 a large proportion of those living in poverty were intact families, after 1960 a growing proportion of American families living in poverty were single parent families with dependent children (p. 71). Between 1959 and 1977, for example, the proportion of poor black families headed by women rose from less than 30 per cent to more than 70 per cent (p. 71). The studies we have reviewed all give reason to expect a rise in the proportion of single parent families living in poverty to be accompanied by a growth in the supply of motivated offenders. Thus, although there may have been a general rise in prosperity in the United States through the 1960s, 1970s and 1980s, there was also a rapid growth in economic stress amongst those families whose children, we would argue, are most prone to delinquent activity.

Cohen and Felson also applied routine activity theory to explain cross-sectional variation in crime. At first sight their account of cross-sectional variation in crime might seem to fare little better than their account of the growth in crime in the United States between 1960 and 1975. Criminal opportunity theory would lead one to expect that wealthier households and employed individuals would make more attractive targets for property crime than poorer households and individuals. And yet the preponderance of cross-sectional studies find a positive correlation between measures of economic stress and crime. This suggests that routine activity theory at best provides only a supplementary hypothesis of use in dealing with the one or two recalcitrant findings concerning the correlation between economic stress and crime.

The situation, however, is more complicated than this argument would seem to suggest. Areas with high rates of unemployment are also often areas with large proportions of single parent families and high levels of geographical mobility. Because these last two factors affect the numbers of capable guardians, according to routine activity theorists, they would generate higher crime rates in areas of high unemployment even if unemployment exerted no influence on the supply of motivated offenders. In the case of household crime it could also be argued that wealth reduces the risk of victimisation because high-income earners are better able to afford effective security devices or services (Cohen, Kluegel and Land 1981: 511). Thus, there is, or could be, a systematic confounding of variables relevant to the supply of criminal opportunities and variables relevant to the supply of motivated offenders. It follows that, although the balance of cross-sectional evidence shows a positive relationship between economic stress and crime, we cannot on this account alone rule out explanations for the spatial distribution of crime based on criminal opportunity.

The only way to resolve the apparent confounding of factors which affect an individual's exposure to victimisation risk and factors which affect the supply of motivated offenders is to see whether income is related to the risk of criminal victimisation, when the effects of other factors relevant to victimisation risk have been partialled out. The results of studies which have pursued this line of enquiry have been mixed. Studies examining property offences have found that high-income individuals are more at risk of crime than low-income individuals (Cohen and Cantor 1980; Cohen, Kluegel and

Land 1981) but studies examining violent crimes observe the reverse (Miethe, Stafford and Long 1987). To make matters more complicated, the pattern of results appears to depend upon whether individuals or geographical areas are the unit of observation. While individual-level studies examining the influence of income on exposure to risk of criminal victimisation have found a positive association, most studies which control for areal differences in levels of routine activity and household guardianship find that high-income areas have lower rates of both property and personal crime victimisation than low-income areas (Messner and Blau 1987; Stahura and Sloan 1988; Smith and Jarjoura 1989).

It is possible to explain these findings in terms of routine activity theory but, paradoxically, not without recourse to the assumption that the supply of motivated offenders plays an important role in shaping the macrospatial distribution of victimisation risk. The discrepancy among individual-level studies in the direction of the relationship between income and crime, for example, can be explained by supposing that poorer individuals are more likely to suffer violent offences because they live closer to violent offenders. This would also explain why the relationship between income and violent crime victimisation is the same whether individuals or areas are the unit of observation. The apparent discrepancy between individual and area-based studies on the relationship between income and property crime can be explained by supposing that property offenders are more likely to target wealthier individuals than poorer ones but are still less likely to target individuals (regardless of income) at distances remote from their residential address than at distances proximate to their residential address. Thus, at the individual level there is a positive association between income and property crime victimisation whereas at the neighbourhood level there is a negative relationship.

There is independent evidence to support each of these arguments. The observation that offenders generally offend at points closer to their residence than at points distant from it has been confirmed in a number of studies (Capone and Nichols 1976; Phillips 1980; Rhodes and Conley 1981). The relationship between proximity to motivated offenders and violent crime victimisation risk has been demonstrated by Sampson and Lauritsen (1990), who also show that one of the reasons for the relationship lies in the fact that motivated offenders are themselves at heightened risk of becoming victims of violent crime. Meanwhile Smith and Jarjoura (1989) have confirmed the putative interaction between individual and area economic status in determining victimisation risk. They obtained data on burglary rates from a sample of 9,006 households in fifty-seven residential neighbourhoods scattered across three Standard Metropolitan Statistical Areas in the United States. Their results indicated that, when controls were introduced for neighbourhood economic stress, there was a positive relationship between household income and victimisation risk. Burglary rates, however, were higher in neighbourhoods with low median incomes than in neighbourhoods with medium or high median incomes.

These arguments and observations salvage a role for routine activity. However, they succeed in this endeavour only because they lean on the assumption that spatial proximity to motivated offenders plays an important role in shaping victimisation risk. If we wish to argue that crime rates are higher in poorer areas because the victims of those areas live close to motivated offenders some explanation must be given for the fact that motivated offenders are more prevalent in low-income areas. Such a task clearly lies outside the scope of either routine activity theory or any other criminal opportunity theory. We can only make sense of macrospatial variation in crime in terms of criminal opportunity theory, therefore, if we are prepared to drop the dictum that the supply of motivated offenders can be taken as a given and acknowledge that macrospatial patterns of criminal victimisation are strongly influenced by the supply of motivated offenders.

Integrating offender supply and criminal opportunity theories

It is perhaps not surprising in the circumstances to discover that criminal opportunity theorists have tended to move away from the view that aggregate crime rate variation can be explained by taking the supply of motivated offenders as a given. Several attempts have been made to integrate theories dealing with the supply of motivated offenders with theories dealing with the supply of criminal opportunities (e.g. Clarke and Cornish 1985; Farrington 1995; Felson 1995). In his most recent reformulation of routine activity theory, for example, Felson replaces Hirschi's notion of a 'social bond' with that of a 'handle' and reconstrues parents (the primary source of the social bond in Hirschi's theory) as 'intimate handlers'. His other key concepts are 'target guardians' (i.e. persons capable of protecting potential targets of violence or property crime from offenders, such as bank security staff) and 'place managers' (i.e. persons capable of restricting access to areas affording criminal opportunities, such as janitors, doormen, bus drivers, close neighbours, etc.). The central hypothesis of the theory is that crime rates will be higher whenever there is a shortage of intimate handlers, capable guardians and (effective) place managers.

There is no doubt that, in the final analysis, some form of integration will be required between theories dealing with the supply of criminal opportunities and incentives and theories dealing with the supply of motivated offenders. Some valuable early work in this direction has already been carried out. Rengert (1980), for example, has put forward a model of spatial variation in criminal victimisation in which the supply of opportunities, the density of offenders and the proximity of offenders to opportunities multiplicatively determine its aggregate victimisation rate. The notion that, in choosing an offence location, offenders are sensitive only to the distance involved is, of course, a gross oversimplification. But it does suggest that the relative importance of criminal opportunity and criminal motivation as predictors of spatial variation in crime should depend upon the offence, the geography of an area and the level of spatial aggregation. Offences which typically entail planning and which offer substantial material reward might be expected to be committed at distances more remote from an offender's residence than offences, such as assault, which are often committed without any planning and which offer (if anything) only psychic reward. If offenders are generally loathe to travel further than they must to commit even premeditated offences, however, as a general rule we should expect them to choose the most proximate and attractive target. These expectations, as we have seen, are borne out by empirical evidence.

There have been other more recent attempts to integrate criminal opportunity and criminal motivation theories (Farrington 1995; Felson 1995). There is also no doubt that integrated models, such as those put forward by Farrington and Felson, more faithfully mirror the spectrum of research evidence on the determinants of aggregate crime rate variation. They also offer a more useful heuristic framework for thinking about crime prevention. However, at this stage of their development they remain far too schematic to generate detailed and testable predictions about the spatial distribution of crime or the effect of economic stress on aggregate crime rates. The principal substantive contribution of criminal opportunity theory to our understanding of the spatial distribution of crime is to be found in its treatment of microspatial phenomena. Neither the epidemic model nor any other offender-based theory has much to offer by way of explanation of such phenomena. By contrast, theories dealing with the spatial distribution of criminal opportunities and incentives have much to offer.

Summary and conclusion

We have now reviewed a number of alternative theories concerned, either directly or indirectly, with the spatial distribution of crime. Our purpose in so doing was, first, to identify the points at which the epidemic model contradicted other accounts of the spatial distribution of crime and, second, to assess to what extent the evidence mustered in support of those theories was consistent with the epidemic model.

The epidemic model and social disorganisation theory contradict one another in the mechanisms they posit to explain the effect of poverty, geographical mobility and ethnic heterogeneity on neighbourhood crime rates. Unlike social disorganisation theory (at least on certain interpretations) the epidemic model assigns a causal role to economic stress. More importantly, we are inclined to regard the factors traditionally thought of as producers of social disorganisation (geographical mobility, ethnic heterogeneity, family dissolution) as criminogenic not because of their impact on the level of informal social control in a neighbourhood but because of their impact on the parenting process. The public disorder which is typically found in so-called socially disorganised areas we regard as just another by-product of the forces which produce juveniles disposed to involvement in crime.

The epidemic model also differs at key points from accounts of the spatial distribution of crime put forward by Skogan (1986); Bottoms, Claytor and Wiles (1992); Kelling and Coles (1996). Like the epidemic model these accounts all posit the existence of a positive feedback loop between the level of crime at one point in time in a neighbourhood and the level of crime at a later point in time in the same neighbourhood. The mechanism driving that positive feedback in the epidemic model, however, differs from that in other accounts of crime-prone neighbourhoods. In the epidemic model the positive feedback loop is created by the fact that each increase in the prevalence of involvement in crime expands the scope for further contact between delinquents and susceptibles, thereby fuelling further increases in the level of participation in crime. By contrast, in the accounts provided by Skogan, by Bottoms, Claytor and Wiles and by Kelling and Coles, positive feedback is created either by the impact which crime has on the out-migration of law-abiding residents in a neighbourhood (Skogan), by the impact which the criminal reputation of a neighbourhood has on the distribution of public renters (Bottoms, Claytor and Wiles), or by the impact which tolerance of minor crime has on the emergence of serious crime (Kelling and Coles).

A number of criminal opportunity theories have been put forward which have an actual or potential bearing on the spatial distribution of crime. Generally speaking they fall into two distinct categories. Macrospatial criminal opportunity theories seek to give an account of the spatial distribution of crime in terms of variations in the supply of opportunities and incentives across neighbourhoods. Microspatial criminal opportunity theories seek to give an account of the spatial distribution of crime in terms of the variations in the supply of criminal opportunities and incentives within neighbourhoods. Neither the epidemic model nor any other offender-based theory of crime can provide an adequate account of phenomena associated with microspatial distribution of crime (e.g. crime hotspots, patterns of repeat victimisation). The explanation of such phenomena, moreover, would not appear to call for any special assumptions about the supply of motivated offenders. Most macrospatial criminal opportunity theories, however, lean implicitly on the notion that variations in criminal victimisation rates are shaped in large measure by variations in the supply of motivated offenders. Unlike the epidemic model, criminal opportunity theories give no account of this supply and the factors which affect it.

A complete account of the spatial distribution of crime (at both macro-spatial and microspatial levels) will clearly require an integrated account of the way in which the supply of criminal opportunities and incentives and the supply of motivated offenders combine to shape aggregate crime rates. At this stage, however, efforts to develop such an integrated account remain too schematic to generate detailed and testable predictions. In our view, the best way forward is to develop an adequate account of how aggregate crime rates are influenced by the supply of motivated offenders and then seek to integrate this account with a theory about how these offenders are affected by the supply of opportunities and incentives for crime. Our preoccupation has been with the former task.

Prevention

Preliminary issues

We come, then, to the final issue to be dealt with in this book, that concerning the relevance of the foregoing theory and research for crime prevention policy. Even without any consideration of theory the salience of our empirical analysis for crime prevention policy is obvious. As we noted in the overview to this book, increases in reported child abuse and neglect have been recorded in Britain and Australia while the estimated risk of child abuse and neglect in the United States was one and one-half times higher in 1993 than it was in 1986. Much of this risk is concentrated, as might be expected, among families exposed to economic or social stress. The 1993 national incidence study on child abuse and neglect in the US (NIS-3 1999) indicated that the children of single parent families faced a 77 per cent greater risk of being harmed by physical abuse and an 87 per cent greater risk of being harmed by physical neglect than children living with both parents. It also showed that children from families with annual incomes below $15,000 as compared with children from families with annual incomes above $30,000 per year were over twenty-two times more likely to experience some form of maltreatment.

The potential significance of these changes for future participation in crime is best seen by using the results from the path analysis, together with population data for the urban postcodes, to determine the impact on juvenile participation in crime of an increase in reported neglect or an increase in poverty. Assuming the level of reported child abuse and the levels of poverty, single parent families and crowded dwellings all remain constant, an increase of 1,000 additional neglected children would result in an additional 256 juveniles involved in crime. Similarly, assuming the levels of poverty, single parent families and crowded dwellings remain constant, an increase of 1,000 additional families with incomes less than \$16,000 per annum would result in an additional 141 juveniles involved in crime.[1]

We can take this a step further to determine a lower bound for the additional amount of crime which would result from these increases in neglect or poverty. Coumarelos (1994) estimated that during a (juvenile) criminal career each juvenile offender has 1.82 court appearances. An additional 1,000 neglected children would therefore result in an additional 466 Children's Court appearances and an additional 1,000 poor families would result in an additional 257 Children's Court appearances. As only a small proportion of crimes committed result in a court appearance and many juveniles continue to commit offences in adulthood, the additional number of criminal offences committed is likely to be substantially greater than these estimates. Of course, whether the growth in child maltreatment recorded in countries such as the US translates over time into a growth in crime will be heavily dependent upon other factors, such as trends in drug (particularly cocaine and heroin) use. Nevertheless, the analyses we have conducted provide ample justification for attempting to forestall a growth in crime through policies designed to ameliorate the social and economic conditions which foster child neglect and abuse.

The question we address in this final chapter, then, is how should Governments go about the business of reducing the prevalence of child maltreatment. It is obvious from the preceding discussion that there are essentially three aspects to this problem. The first concerns the question of how macroeconomic policy might be used to reduce the level of economic stress on individuals and neighbourhoods. The second concerns how macrosocial policy might be used to reduce the level of social stress on individuals and neighbourhoods. The third concerns the question of how we go about reducing the risk of delinquency amongst those whose families are exposed to economic and social stress. Debate about the first two of these issues is often mired in philosophic disagreement about the proper role of Government and the duties and responsibilities of citizens. This is hardly surprising. Those who believe Governments should, so far as possible, stay out of the lives of individual citizens are unlikely ever to feel comfortable with policies explicitly designed to alter individual or social behaviour. On the other hand, those who see Government as having a moral responsibility to reduce economic and social inequality are unlikely ever to feel comfortable with policies explicitly designed to minimise the size and influence of Government.

There is no space here to enter into a general philosophic discussion about the role and responsibilities of Government or the rights and duties of citizens.

Nor do we think it necessary to do so. If it is accepted that economic and social stress are inherently criminogenic, Governments must perforce grapple with the question of how best to deal with these problems. If the options for dealing with them are deemed philosophically or politically unacceptable, then other ways of dealing with crime must be found or a higher level of crime itself must be accepted as the price we pay for avoiding policies which are effective in reducing crime but which, for one reason or another, we choose not to pursue.

In discussing options for reducing crime we have limited our attention to those directly raised by the epidemic model. Readers should hardly need to be reminded that there are many other ways of seeking to reduce the incidence of crime than those implied by the epidemic model. As we have already acknowledged it is not a general theory of crime. It makes no assumptions about the factors which control the period of involvement in crime or the frequency with which individuals offend. Yet both these components of offending clearly influence aggregate crime rates. Both therefore offer alternative points of leverage on crime. As an alternative to the options canvassed here, for example, one might seek to reduce the period of involvement in crime with strategies designed to improve employment prospects for parolees or seek to reduce offending frequency with strategies designed to reduce the opportunities and incentives for offending. Our failure to discuss such options should not be construed as signalling any lack of faith in their efficacy. Any comprehensive approach to reducing aggregate crime rates should include strategies designed to reduce the rate of initiation into crime, the period of involvement in it and the frequency of offending. Our discussion of prevention is not intended to be comprehensive.

This said, we would argue that the most fundamental task confronting Government is that of finding a way to reduce the supply of motivated offenders. The evidence from prospective cohort studies has now firmly established the fact that a small group of offenders is disproportionately responsible for most offences. Tracey, Wolfgang and Figlio (1990) examined 13,160 boys born in 1958 and found that although those with five or more juvenile court system contacts constituted only 7.5 per cent of the cohort, between them they accounted for 61 per cent of all recorded offences. Similar results have been found by Shannon (1978), Farrington (1987) and Coumarelos (1994). Small reductions in the supply of persistent offenders therefore stand to produce large crime reduction benefits.

It bears emphasis that strategies designed to reduce the rate of initiation into crime, even if successful, are likely to take a long time to exert any measurable effect on aggregate crime rates. This is because changes in criminal participation rates generally lag behind changes in the rate at which individuals become involved in crime by an amount which increases with the average period of involvement in crime (Collins and Weatherburn 1995). It is impossible to be precise about the size of this lag. But if the period of involvement in crime is measured in years, one would also expect several years to elapse before aggregate crime rates respond fully to a drop in the supply of juveniles involved in crime.

In practice it is likely that other factors will further prolong the period between efforts to reduce the rate of initiation into crime and lower aggregate crime rates. Even the most determined efforts to reduce the level of economic and social stress on families with dependent children will take time to put in place and exert improvements in the quality of parenting. The effects of improved parenting on the rate of juvenile initiation into crime will be still further delayed because their effects will not be felt until the children who benefit from such parenting reach their crime-prone years. These considerations ought not to discourage policy makers from making a determined effort to address the structural conditions which foster crime-prone communities. But they counsel against the expectation that worthwhile investments in crime prevention will necessarily produce quick dividends.

The general role of Government in reducing economic stress

Since poverty and unemployment are the principal manifestations of economic stress we start with these two problems. The notion that we can reduce crime by programs designed to reduce poverty and unemployment hardly needs introduction or, one might have thought, much defence. Insofar as the provision of income support undoubtedly reduces the level of economic stress it seems obvious that it is also an effective long-term crime prevention strategy. In some quarters, however, there is a view that direct Government efforts to reduce poverty and unemployment are doomed to failure. This view probably owes its origin in the main to the alleged failure of the so-called War on Poverty mounted by the Kennedy and Johnson Administrations in the United States in the 1960s. The War on Poverty involved, among other things, expanded eligibility for income transfer programs, increased aid to families with dependent children (AFDC), new or expanded programs such as Medicaid and food-stamps, compensatory job training and compensatory schooling. American expenditure on such programs nearly doubled in real terms between 1950 and 1980 but, despite this, from the early 1970s onwards poverty levels in the United States began to rise.

Debate about why the War on Poverty failed to produce a sustained reduction in US poverty levels has been vigorous to say the least. Charles Murray (1984) has been the most influential among those who argue that US Government efforts to reduce poverty by providing income support to the unemployed and single parent families encouraged it by creating structural disincentives for work and making it easier for women to have children out of wedlock and without the benefit of financial support from a partner. In support of this thesis Murray advanced three key arguments. He pointed out that the upward trend in single parent families closely mirrored both the growth in US poverty rates and Government expenditure on welfare. He cited evidence from a national experiment in income maintenance (known as the Negative Income Tax Experiment; see Murray 1984: 148) which appeared to indicate that income maintenance reduced the amount of time low-paid workers spent in work. Finally, he also endeavoured to show that, during the period of the War on Poverty when welfare benefits were at their most generous, single parents with dependent children were economically better off on welfare than they were in paid employment.

Considerations such as these led Murray to the view that the best way to combat poverty was, paradoxically, to withdraw virtually all Government support for the poor and unemployed. Although few European social policy analysts have been prepared to go so far his views struck a highly receptive chord in the United States. Even at its inception the War on Poverty had to endure criticism. Lewis (1968), for example, argued that Government welfare created a culture of dependence in which 'slum children . . . [absorb] . . . the basic values and attitudes of their subculture and are not psychologically geared to take full advantage of changing conditions or increased opportunities which occur in their lifetime' (Lewis 1968). These doubts were reinforced after Murray's views became widely known by continued growth in the level of American dependence on welfare. While the Clinton Administration has not acceded to Murray's view that welfare ought to be abolished, the reforms to welfare it is engaged in implementing are a measure of his influence on American social policy (*The Economist*, June 1994).

Murray's analysis of the effects of the War on Poverty, has not passed without serious criticism. Summarising the various arguments which have been levelled against the thesis, Wilson (1987) contended, amongst other things, that subsequent research revealed the growth in poverty to be a direct consequence of a downturn in economic conditions during the 1970s. According to Wilson, the fall in labour market participation rates attributed by Murray to a growth in welfare was largely due to structural changes in the American economy which reduced the demand for unskilled labour (Wilson

1987: 39). He also pointed out that the real value of AFDC payments declined after 1972 and that real wages stopped growing at the same time. Furthermore, he identified several weaknesses in Murray's argument that more generous social security payments increased the rate of family dissolution. For his part Wilson cited evidence suggesting that the rise in unemployment among young black men in the United States over the period in question was the principal cause of the concomitant rise in single parent families (Wilson 1987: 82). Without the War on Poverty, he argued, poverty levels in the United States would have risen by far more than they did. Wilson also took issue with the culture of poverty thesis, arguing that the absence of a strong work ethic amongst those living on welfare is a reflection rather than a cause of chronic joblessness. In support of this view he cited evidence from the Michigan Panel Study of Income Dynamics which provided little support for the view that poverty was transmitted across generations (Wilson 1987: 175).

Wilson provides cogent reasons for rejecting the thesis that Government intervention to reduce poverty only succeeds in exacerbating it. However, he was far from uncritical about the assumptions underpinning the War on Poverty. He maintained that its effects were limited because, although joblessness was correctly recognised as a major cause of poverty, Governments misunderstood the cause of joblessness. Rather than viewing it as a failure of American economic organisation it was mistakenly seen as a consequence of racial discrimination and a failure on the part of Government to provide the unemployed with the requisite income and skills needed to function in a free market (Wilson 1987: 130). The provision of unemployment compensation and job training in the absence of appropriate jobs could not be expected to deal with this problem. Public employment programs, he argued, are prone to inefficiency and corruption. Welfare may not exacerbate the situation but it is not enough on its own to resolve it. Accordingly, he maintained that Governments should concentrate on fashioning a macroeconomic policy designed to promote both economic growth and a tight labour market since this will reduce unemployment and raise wages (Wilson 1987: 151).

Wilson's emphasis on the creation of employment opportunities rather than the provision of welfare as the principal means of combating poverty seems entirely reasonable. Apart from the difficulty of sustaining political support for a welfare system which is seen as 'easy' to exploit, dependence on welfare may foster a sense of social isolation which is inimical to effective parenting (see, for example, Weston 1993a: 154). Employment on the whole provides a much more satisfactory means of reducing economic stress than welfare. Even if the provision of welfare does not create a 'culture of poverty' there can be little doubt that the longer the period of unemployment the smaller the proclivity of individuals to seek work (Piggott and Chapman 1995). It therefore makes no sense to increase the level of social security transfer payments to the point where they constitute a positive inducement to leave the labour market.

Those persuaded by these arguments, however, might be tempted to conclude that the role of Government in eliminating poverty is simply to stimulate economic growth while minimising the level of and entitlement to Government income support. It is worth observing, therefore, that there are at least five reasons for rejecting this conclusion.

First, although it makes sense to prevent transfer payments reaching the point where they are commensurate with income obtainable from employment, it does not follow that every decrement in such payments acts as a further stimulus to job-hunting. As Murray himself acknowledges (Murray 1984: 113), for those already involved in crime the lack of an adequate income (even in the presence of job opportunities) may simply produce an increase in income-generating property crime. For those not involved it may only produce an increase in depression and despair, with all their attendant adverse consequences for parental relationships and child-rearing practices.

Second, it is possible to have a rapidly growing economy in which demand for labour is tight but unemployment remains stubbornly high. There are several ways in which this state of affairs could come about. Those without jobs may lack the skills to obtain the jobs available (i.e. structural unemployment). There may be a spatial mismatch between the demand for and supply of labour. Alternatively there may be inadequate access to information networks about available jobs. A good example of the first of these problems is the current decline in manufacturing jobs in Australia and their replacement with jobs in the service sector (Gregory and Hunter 1995). The second has been documented as a factor underpinning unemployment in Sydney by Hunter (1995). The importance of the third factor is hard to quantify but its significance is underlined by research findings showing that the most successful method utilised by unemployed males to find a job is through friends and contacts (Montgomery 1991; Mortensen and Vishwanath 1994). As Gregory and Hunter point out, if the unemployed live together the number of their friends, contacts and relatives who are employed is also likely to fall (Gregory and Hunter 1995: 11). Simply stimulating economic growth, then, even in conjunction with restricted access to welfare benefits, will not necessarily stimulate employment growth.

Third, it is possible to have low unemployment rates yet high levels of poverty because some groups within the community do not participate or give up participating in the workforce. The effect of long-term unemployment on the motivation to seek work is one obvious manifestation of this problem. But single parents provide another and more vivid manifestation. In the absence of access to suitable and affordable childcare many sole parents with dependent children will find themselves confronting what amounts to a choice between poverty and child neglect (see Weston 1993a: 146–150). Given the generally meagre income available to unskilled women employed in part-time work it is hardly surprising that many choose to resolve this dilemma by refusing to seek work. Without Government assistance in providing adequate childcare (and/or tax credits for women with dependent children in low-paid jobs) efforts to reduce poverty by stimulating employment are likely to be far less effective than they could be.

Fourth, from the vantage-point of crime prevention, the spatial distribution of unemployment and poverty is at least as important as its overall prevalence. Growing up in an economically depressed neighbourhood exerts a range of socially deleterious effects above and beyond those to be expected from a consideration of the characteristics of individuals who reside in such neighbourhoods. These effects include increased risk of teenage child-bearing, a lower level of educational attainment and reduced prospects of employment, as well as increased involvement in crime (Jencks and Mayer 1990). Insofar as economic growth produces a general decrease in unemployment levels but no change in the spatial concentration of unemployment it fails to serve the interests of long-term crime prevention.

Fifth, whereas from an economic point of view there is little or nothing to choose between programs which exert equal effects on the unemployment (or participation rate) but which target different groups of people, from a crime prevention point of view the choice is very important. Reductions in the short-term unemployed may reduce offending but the evidence we have examined suggests that the supply of motivated offenders is best reduced through policies which reduce long-term unemployment amongst those either with or likely to acquire dependent children. Classical economic theory might suggest that economic growth, over the long haul, will reduce long-term unemployment. The long haul, however, can be a very long time indeed. By the time economic growth starts to reduce the number of long-term unemployed their number may already have boosted the supply of juveniles susceptible to involvement in crime above the epidemic threshold. The effect of this will persist long after economic growth brings about a reduction in the number of long-term unemployed. Economic growth which fails to stimulate employment growth among the correct population sub-groups will therefore also fail to serve the interests of crime prevention.

Granting, then, the need and scope for Government intervention to reduce economic stress in the interests of crime prevention, the question arises as to which forms of intervention are most desirable. Four forms of intervention stand out as particularly important. The first involves the access of low-income families (particularly those exposed to social stress) to subsidised childcare. The second involves the creation of an efficient system for ensuring the payment of child maintenance. The third involves active labour market programs targeted at the long-term unemployed. The fourth involves strategies for reducing the spatial concentration of economic disadvantage. We will deal with each of these in turn.

The role of childcare

Because the time and energy of individuals are finite resources there is an intrinsic tension between the demands of employment and those of effective parenting. For many households this tension is barely noticeable. Where one parent is no longer present to provide parenting support or where both parents must work full-time to support the family the tension between work and parenting becomes more palpable. Family dissolution, in particular, often results in a substantial drop in income and increased social isolation for the primary caregiver (Harrison and Tucker 1986; Harrison 1993). Of course, neither poverty nor sole parent family status lead automatically to maltreatment or delinquency. Risk factors for child maltreatment and delinquency tend to be cumulative in their effect (Belsky 1984; Yoshikawa 1994; National Crime Prevention 1999). The tension between employment and competent parenting is most likely to prove corrosive of parenting and therefore criminogenic when a parent's ability to cope with the pressures of child rearing is already compromised by problems such as poor education, poor mental health, drug dependence, a large family and/or an unsupportive partner or other problems which compromise parental patience and understanding.

If economic growth and the creation of employment opportunities are to be made the means by which we combat poverty, access to childcare would seem, *prima facie*, a valuable means by which to limit the risk that economic and/or social stress will lead to child neglect and abuse. Recognition of the importance of parenting and the intrusions of modern life upon it, however, has prompted some to urge a return to 'the traditional family' (see Sullivan 1997), with tax concessions being proposed to encourage carers to stay at home for child-rearing purposes. If tax concessions for 'stay-at-home' parents increase the number of families where one parent (of either gender) is able to remain more fully occupied in child-rearing activity during the early years of a child's life, they are a positive contribution to better parenting. But it would be naive to imagine that tax concessions compensate adequately for the loss of income, social worth or social contact attendant upon giving up paid employment. It would also be naive to suppose that the phenomenal growth in the number of working women which has occurred over the last twenty years is simply a response to household economic imperatives. Thus, while it might be prudent to offer a choice between access to subsidised childcare and tax concessions for 'stay-at-home' parents on low incomes, the former is bound to offer a more important line of defence against child maltreatment than the latter.

A more sophisticated argument against subsidised access to childcare, however, has been put by Steuerle (1998). He points out that the problem with many credits and allowances in the US is that they subsidise childcare outside the home even when it might be provided more efficiently by grandparents, other relatives, cooperative arrangements, or neighbours. He suggests that, rather than providing childcare subsidies, a better alternative would be to try to determine what overall level of help is going to be provided on condition of work, but then retain flexibility about what forms that help might take. Thus, for example, in some cases one might provide additional transportation subsidies while, in others additional educational support may be more appropriate.

The flexibility of Steuerle's approach has obvious attractions but from our point of view the question of how best to provide support to families with a view to maximising the quality of parenting is ultimately an empirical one. In the present state of knowledge, high quality childcare has the advantage that it is known to reduce the incidence of child behaviour problems and improve children's language and cognitive development (NICHD 1999). Since early behaviour problems and poor school performance are among the strongest predictors of delinquency, the fact that quality childcare produces improvements in these areas is a powerful, albeit indirect, endorsement of its potential value as a crime prevention tool. The emphasis on quality childcare is important, however, because childcare should not be seen simply as a means of warehousing children while their parents work. If childcare is to prove of assistance in reducing crime, those who deliver it should aim to reduce the major risk factors associated with later juvenile involvement in crime. In other words, they should aim to improve the child's cognitive and reasoning skills, discourage disruptive and aggressive behaviour, and increase the ability of parents to manage their children.

The importance of an effective child maintenance scheme

Notwithstanding the value of access to childcare, many sole parents with dependent children find it difficult to obtain part-time employment which provides an adequate income. Their difficulties are further compounded by the fact that the level of Government income support available to sole parents with dependent children often drops off sharply even at very low levels of earned income. The provision of affordable childcare may alleviate this state of affairs by making it possible for sole parents to engage in full-time employment. Yet full-time employment for sole parents is not necessarily the most desirable of outcomes from the standpoint of child-rearing, particularly if the income obtained from such employment is very low. The result of this state of affairs for many parents is a 'poverty trap' (Brownlee 1985). Whether caregivers choose to remain on welfare or seek employment they seemed condemned to remain in poverty.

Increasing the level of welfare benefits for sole parents is not the most satisfactory means of eliminating this trap. Even if such benefits do not encourage people to leave paid employment there is a limit to the extent to which Governments can afford to cushion individuals from the financial burdens of child-rearing. For these reasons child maintenance emerges as a highly desirable means of reducing the level of economic stress on sole parents with dependent children while taking the strain off them to engage in full-time employment. But there are also two other reasons for ensuring the existence of an effective and vigorously enforced system of child maintenance: one symbolic and the other practical. The practical reason is that the more child support obtained through maintenance, the smaller a Government's outlays in social security payments. The symbolic reason for active pursuit of child maintenance stems from the fact that it is universally agreed that the decision to have children is not one to be taken lightly and, once taken, carries responsibilities which endure regardless of whether the relationship between parents remains intact or dissolves. Those responsibilities include ensuring that, to the extent possible, both parents contribute to the welfare of their child or children. The adoption by the State of a laissez faire attitude toward the payment of child maintenance can be seen as potentially corrosive of social norms in relation to the execution of these responsibilities.

It is hard to obtain comparative data on the extent to which sole parents with dependent children are paid child maintenance by the non-resident parent, but if the Australian experience is any guide there is certainly room for improvement. In their longitudinal analysis of parental income in the wake of family dissolution, Harrison and Tucker (1986: 261) found that, for young mothers separated from the fathers of their children, the percentage of fathers paying any form of maintenance declined from 23 per cent at the time of separation to 7 per cent two years later. Amongst those who did receive some maintenance payments the level of maintenance payment was generally quite small and declined sharply in the two years following separation (Harrison and Tucker 1986: 263).

Of course, there are many reasons why maintenance might not be paid. Separated parents usually repartner and such repartnering may greatly improve the economic well-being of the custodial parent. It should also be observed that payment of maintenance as well as non-payment can be a source of economic stress. Harrison and Tucker examined the perceived effects of maintenance on parental well-being but, unfortunately, did not distinguish between hardship caused by the payment of maintenance and hardship caused by the non-payment of maintenance. It is noteworthy, however, that three years after separation 20 per cent of men but 43 per cent of women surveyed said that some or great hardship was being caused by the payment or non-payment of maintenance. Given that women are much more likely than men to end up with custody of the children (and therefore to be receiving rather than giving maintenance) these data are consistent with the assumption that non-payment of maintenance is a more enduring source of hardship for custodial parents than its payment is for non-custodial parents.

These observations reinforce the importance of schemes which compel non-resident parents to make adequate contributions to the financial support of their children. It may be objected that such schemes are only likely to be beneficial where the non-custodial parent is in paid employment. Where both parents are unemployed or subsisting on very low wages the scope for increasing maintenance payments without producing other undesirable social effects is limited or non-existent. It should not be assumed, however, that efforts to improve the level of maintenance payment inevitably push a large proportion of those responsible for paying maintenance into poverty. In her assessment of the potential impact of proposed reforms to Australian child maintenance law designed to increase the level of child maintenance payments, Weston (1993b: 161–162) found that substantial increases in the level of maintenance payments could be effected without significantly increasing the percentage of those paying maintenance who fell beneath the Australian poverty line. Since the introduction of those reforms the proportion of eligible sole parent families receiving maintenance payments has increased from 26 per cent to 42 per cent, and the annual savings in social security outlays as a result of maintenance payment have increased from $35.5 million in 1989–90 to $146.1 million in 1996 (Department of Social Security 1996).

Even more encouraging findings have been obtained in the US. Sorensen and Halpern (1999) have shown that both never-married and previously married mothers experienced significant improvements over the last twenty years in their child support receipt rate. In the case of never-married mothers the child support receipt rate increased fourfold between 1976 and 1997, from 4 per cent to 18 per cent. In the case of previously married mothers the child support rate increased more moderately over the same period, from 36 per cent to 42 per cent. Sorensen and Halpern estimate that 56 per cent of the rise in child support receipt rates for never-married mothers and 33 per cent of the rise in child support rates for previously married mothers can be attributed to enforcement actions on the part of Federal and State Governments.

The role of labour market programs

Most criminological attention to labour market issues has been directed at programs designed to increase employment rates amongst those already involved in crime or those at immediate risk of such involvement. These programs have recently been reviewed by Bushway and Reuter (1997) with fairly disappointing results. The only program whose effectiveness they found well supported by evidence involved the provision of short-term vocational training for older male ex-offenders no longer involved in the criminal justice system (Bushway and Reuter 1997: 6–37). These results may be disappointing but they should not be discouraging. If the epidemic model is correct, the sorts of employment programs which are most likely to reduce crime in the long run are not those which target offenders but those which target chronic economic stress among families with dependent children. Since chronic economic stress is most produced by chronic unemployment this means that, for crime prevention purposes, most interest should centre on the problem of reducing long-term unemployment among those who either support or are likely soon to acquire responsibility for supporting dependent children.[2]

Labour market programs come in two forms: programs in which public employment is geared toward the unemployed and programs in which the private sector firms are subsidised to offer jobs to the unemployed. Kenyon (1994) has recently reviewed the efficacy of both types of program. There is no evidence that countries which spend a larger proportion of gross domestic product (GDP) on active labour market programs (ALMPs) enjoy lower rates of unemployment but, as Kenyon points out, there are many factors, other than expenditure on ALMPs, which affect the rate of unemployment. Micro-economic analyses present more encouraging results. They suggest that job-search assistance and case management by Public Employment Services is effective for targeted groups with poor labour market characteristics when the overall rate of unemployment is high.

Although microeconomic analyses indicate that job-search assistance and case management result in positive net employment generation they can also produce offsetting and negative effects. Two particular offsetting and negative effects highlighted by Kenyon are known as 'deadweight' and 'displacement'. 'Deadweight' refers to the fact that some proportion of persons targeted in any employment program would have been employed without the program. 'Displacement' refers to the fact that, when individuals are employed under a labour market program, to some extent they displace other workers who would have been employed but for the introduction of the program. Kenyon argues that many of the studies which purport to have found positive benefits for labour market programs have failed to account for deadweight and displacement effects (Kenyon 1994: 287).

More encouraging evidence on the effectiveness of labour markets programs comes from Piggott and Chapman (1995). They set out to assess the cost of the Australian Job Compact, a comprehensive labour market program which included many of the features which Kenyon found to have been effective in microeconomic analyses of ALMPs, such as counselling and job-search assistance, training and training wage subsidies, wage subsidies and some public sector job creation schemes. The distinctive feature of Piggott and Chapman's analysis is that in their assessment of the Job Compact they took into account the impact of the program on deadweight and displacement. Their work confirms the importance of these parameters as determinants of program cost-effectiveness but they found that for plausible estimates of their value and the effectiveness of the Compact in generating employment (the latter being determined from earlier Australian studies of the effectiveness of labour market programs), the opportunity cost of the Compact was modest and may even have been negative. In other words the savings from increased tax receipts (as a result of increased employment) and reduced outlays on unemployment benefits were close to the budgetary cost of the program. This analysis suggests that Government labour market programs, properly run, can be an extremely cost-effective way of reducing the level of economic stress.

Approaches to neighbourhood poverty

This brings us to the vexed question of how Governments should go about the task of reducing the spatial concentration of economic disadvantage. We have already argued that concentrated disadvantage acts to increase the rate of offending because it increases the level of contact between juveniles already involved in crime and juveniles susceptible to such involvement. At this juncture it is worth pointing out that concentrated disadvantage may affect crime in other ways as well. Hagan (1993) has argued (and provided evidence supporting the thesis) that youths embedded in criminal contexts can become isolated from the likelihood of legitimate adult employment through loss of contact with employed persons. This occurs for several reasons. Juveniles embedded in a criminal subculture lack access to information about legitimate job opportunities. They are, on the other hand, provided with a wealth of information about illegitimate income-generating activities and rarely come into contact with legitimately employed people who might serve as a role model. The result is an intergenerational bias away from involvement in legitimate income-earning activity and toward illegitimate income-earning activities. The spatial concentration of disadvantage, then, tends to become self-entrenching.

Three main strategies have been put forward to reduce the spatial concentration of disadvantage. Following Hughes (1987) we will refer to them, respectively, as *development, dispersal* and *mobility* strategies.

Development strategies are sometimes referred to as 'ghetto gilding', a term coined initially by Kain and Persky (1969) who wished to distinguish it from their preferred strategy of *dispersal*. Generally speaking, *development* strategies involve attempts to improve the structure of depressed neighbourhoods through job creation schemes, improved housing or increased educational opportunities. More recent efforts to improve employment opportunities in highly disadvantaged areas have concentrated on the creation of 'enterprise zones' (Erickson and Friedman 1991). Such zones are generally created by offering tax incentives, tax credits for job creation or investment funds accessible to firms who locate in particular areas.

Dispersal strategies, as the term suggests, are designed to encourage dis-advantaged people to leave impoverished neighbourhoods. There are three main ways in which this can be accomplished. One option involves creating employment opportunities in areas surrounding a ghetto in the hope that this will prompt its residents to move into such areas. The second option involves providing rent subsidies for people resident in ghettos who are willing to move into other neighbourhoods. The third option involves ensuring that public housing is dispersed through areas which are not highly disadvantaged. Needless to say, these options are not mutually exclusive.

Mobility strategies, which have received the most attention of late, are those designed to provide the residents of ghettos with access to suburban employ-ment opportunities (Hughes 1987: 514). Amongst the various initiatives which might be included in a mobility strategy, Hughes has suggested providing job training to prepare would-be workers for suburban labour markets, providing job information systems to match city workers to suburban employers, restructuring transportation systems to facilitate journeys to work, providing day-care facilities and subsidies for parents of young children, and supplementing the wages of entry-level jobs with a tax credit which provides a mechanism for supporting low-income workers while delivering that support through employment.

One difficulty in evaluating these strategies is that their efficacy is almost certainly context-dependent. In the United States, where most research on ghetto amelioration has been carried out, the putative effectiveness of each strategy depends upon how large a role one assigns to race discrimination in limiting the job prospects and earnings of ghetto residents. As Hughes (1987) points out, it also depends upon the particular spatial configuration of jobs, housing and public transport. In Australia, for example, the only manifestly race-based areas of extreme poverty are those associated with Aboriginal settlements in rural areas or small urban enclaves. While discriminatory employment policies are almost certainly a factor in the reproduction of poverty in these areas, the small size of the Aboriginal population makes racial segregation far less relevant to an understanding of urban ghettos and their amelioration in Australia than in the United States.

These caveats aside, each of the options for reducing the spatial concentration of economic stress has some general strengths and weaknesses. Many of Kain and Persky's early criticisms of *development* strategies seem pertinent today (Kain and Persky 1969). They argued, for instance, that efforts to improve the quality of life in suburban American ghettos only succeed in encouraging residents to remain in the 'ghetto', therefore making it more difficult to solve ghetto-related problems. The spatial concentration of poverty, they hypothesised, limits access to information about job opportunities, restricts the tax base on which municipal authorities can draw to improve services and institutionalises social pathologies such as crime, drug usage and family dissolution.

Hunter (1995) has also advanced a number of criticisms of *development* strategies. Subsidies for firms to locate in particular areas (as a means of stimulating employment) would be inefficient. Furthermore, locating firms in highly disadvantaged areas would only reduce their levels of unemployment if groups who have a low risk of long-term unemployment (and who may live relatively close to a ghetto) can somehow be prevented from taking the created jobs. Restrictions in the supply of jobs may mean that *development* strategies may only affect commuting patterns rather than employment in low-status neighbourhoods. Finally, given the existence of neighbourhood effects on employment prospects, supplying jobs to depressed neighbourhoods may not be the most efficient means by which to increase employment in low status neighbourhoods.

The limited evaluation work done on enterprise zones appears to support at least some of Hunter's concerns. In their review of the relevant literature Bushway and Reuter (1997) found that in some locations the creation of enterprise zones only succeeded in relocating jobs from neighbouring communities while in others it seemed to produce a net increase in employment. All the same, they cite the enterprise zones as one of the more promising of the *development* strategies. It is worth noting, moreover, that there are circumstances in which *development* strategies may constitute the only viable option for reducing economic stress. *Dispersal* and *mobility* may make sense where the geography of poverty is such that the poor are concentrated in the inner city while the jobs are dispersed through the suburbs. But in countries such as Australia and Canada, there are extremely high levels of crime, poverty and family dissolution amongst indigenous people resident in remote rural areas. These problems have been exacerbated by the increasingly mechanised and capital-intensive nature of the rural economy and the consequent loss of employment opportunities for unskilled and semi-skilled labour.

Attempts to deal with these problems by encouraging greater mobility or geographical dispersal of those who are disadvantaged are likely to prove impractical and could do further damage to local kinship and family structures, thereby exacerbating rather than alleviating rural crime problems. There is little risk, moreover, that competition for employment in remote rural areas will cause employers in rural areas to prefer the less disadvantaged segments of the population. In many rural towns in Australia, for example, Aboriginal people make up almost all of the unemployed population. Thus, while *development* policies may provide a less than ideal way of reducing poverty and unemployment, for some communities they also may confer social benefits which are worth the economic costs involved.

In urban areas *dispersal* might appear a more attractive way of dealing with the problems created by concentrated social and economic disadvantage. Yet *dispersal* presents its own unique set of problems. One can, of course, offer financial inducements to the residents of ghettos to encourage them to move out, and on the one occasion in which such a strategy was implemented and evaluated it seemed to produce beneficial effects (Bushway and Reuter 1997: 6–23). As Bushway and Reuter point out, however, attempts to disperse whole neighbourhoods of disadvantaged people are likely to meet either with resistance from residents being relocated or with opposition from residents of the neighbourhoods into which they are being dispersed.

Public housing policy probably offers the most viable means through which effectively to implement a policy of dispersal. For short-term economic reasons Governments have traditionally tended to locate public housing in areas where land is inexpensive to purchase. In Australia public housing policy has also been geared increasingly to those who are very poor (Gregory and Hunter 1995: 30). Both these trends have led to a spatial concentration of economic and social disadvantage. This concentration has been further exacerbated by a tendency on the part of Government public housing authorities to prefer forms of public housing (e.g. estates, high-rise apartments) which are less expensive to build but which result in even higher population densities of economically stressed individuals and families. The short-term economic benefits of these practices are almost certainly outweighed by their long-term social costs. A policy of progressive dispersal of public renters, say through 'spot' purchases of existing dwellings in less disadvantaged neighbour-hoods, offers one way in which these costs may be reduced.

Overall, *mobility* strategies probably offer the most practical avenue through which to prevent the spatial concentration of disadvantage. We have already discussed the key role which childcare plays in determining the rate at which single parents with dependent children participate in the workforce. The issue of job training is one we deal with in detail below. But the other points Hughes makes also have obvious merit. Tax credits for entry-level jobs ought to be effective in increasing the attractiveness of paid employment over Government income support especially where entry-level jobs are poorly paid. If, as the evidence suggests, the spatial concentration of unemployment weakens the effectiveness of informal information networks for obtaining information about jobs, it makes sense to create a formal system for matching job vacancies with potential employees.

It goes without saying, of course, that employment information and public transportation systems are neither easy or inexpensive to establish and run. This makes them easy targets for public or political criticism. The budgetary cost of such systems, however, is not the relevant criterion against which they should be assessed. If they succeed in creating employment the budgetary cost will be offset by the benefits they produce in terms of reduced outlays in unemployment benefits and increased tax receipts. If they succeed, as well, in reducing crime, the budgetary cost will be further offset through reduced outlays on law and order.

Social capital and the role of Government in reducing social stress

At first blush the problem of reducing social stress might appear to be reducible to the task of finding programs which tackle each of the risk factors which increase the level of social stress. These factors, it will be recalled, include sole parent family status, large family size, depression or drug use disorder, responsibility for a disabled or behaviourally maladjusted child, deficiencies in maternal problem-solving skills, family conflict, and residency in a neighbourhood with high rates of geographical mobility and/or ethnic heterogeneity.

For a variety of reasons this way of looking at the problem is unsatisfactory. To begin with it is neither easy nor always desirable to alter conditions such as the level of geographical mobility, ethnic heterogeneity or family dissolution. While Governments might be well advised to avoid taking actions which increase neighbourhood instability, as we saw in the previous section, in modern free-market economies a mobile workforce is essential to ensuring an efficient match between job vacancies and job seekers. Ethnic heterogeneity may impede the formation of social networks but ethnic diversity is inevitable in countries which have had a history of ethnic diversity in their immigrant intake or where the importation of labour (whether skilled or unskilled) is essential to their future economic growth. Many would argue, moreover, that the benefits which ethnic diversity brings to a country far outweigh any costs associated with it.

Even family dissolution, which most people would regard as undesirable, is not something easily influenced by Governments. To be sure, from time to time it is suggested that rates of family dissolution might be reduced if Governments reduced or eliminated income support for single parent families, or if we reverted to a situation where women were economically dependent on their spouses instead of being in paid employment, or if divorce were made more difficult to obtain. As Wilson (1987) argues, however, there is little evidence to support the view that income support for single parent families actually increases the rate of family dissolution. And while there are undoubtedly social costs associated with the increase in marital dissolution there would be few who would support a reversal of the hard-won gains in equal employment opportunity for women or a return to more restrictive divorce laws as a means of trying to reduce these costs. On the other side of the ledger, there are substantial benefits associated with the entry of women into the paid workforce and with less restrictive access to divorce. The former greatly increases the productive potential of an economy. The latter facilitates the termination of personal relationships marked by chronic and severe marital conflict. This reduces the risk of domestic violence and the number of children exposed to intense or prolonged marital conflict. Family conflict, as we have seen, is one of the risk factors associated with child neglect.

The question which must be addressed, then, is how best to go about the task of reducing social stress in circumstances where geographical mobility, ethnic heterogeneity and family dissolution must to a greater or lesser extent be taken as a given. In answering this question the important point to bear in mind is that the prevalence of conditions such as depression, drug-dependence, deficiencies in maternal problem-solving skills, or family conflict is strongly influenced by the social conditions in which individuals and families live. An individual's capacity to cope with the pressures of poverty or child-rearing is not just a function of their own personal characteristics but depends to a significant extent on the level of support, encouragement, advice and guidance available from local institutions, relatives, friends and neighbours. Individuals resident in neighbourhoods with high levels of geographical mobility and/or ethnic heterogeneity are less likely to establish friends or be able to call upon them for support when it is needed. For low-income parents without supportive partners this deficiency will combine with the stresses of parenting to increase the risk of family conflict, depression or drug abuse. It will also limit a parent's exposure to the 'collective wisdom' associated with child-rearing which plays an important role in facilitating the acquisition of parental problem-solving skills. In considering ways in which to reduce problems such as child maltreatment, then, it is important to begin with a consideration of the social conditions which foster weaknesses in the quality of parenting.

Social capital theory

In a seminal discussion of ways in which sociological and economic conceptions of social behaviour might be integrated, Coleman (1988) introduced the notion of 'social capital', arguing that it is no less important to creating a more productive society than the creation of physical and human capital. Whereas the accumulation of physical capital facilitates production by changing raw materials to form tools and machines, and human capital achieves the same result through changes in individual skills and capabilities, social capital, according to Coleman, facilitates productive activity by fostering certain kinds of relationships between individuals.

Three forms of social capital are identified by Coleman (1988: 101). The first involves the creation of reciprocal obligations and expectations between people. The second involves the creation of information channels. The third involves the creation of social norms and effective sanctions for violating them. Each of these forms of social capital allows certain valuable activities to occur which could not occur (or could not easily occur) in its absence. Thus, for example, neighbours who share responsibility for purchasing food can buy it more cheaply than those who do not. Scientists who share information about research findings are more productive than those who work in isolation from one another's work. Communities with strong social norms concerning offensive behaviour make it possible for elderly people to walk freely at night without fear for their safety.

While Coleman was concerned primarily to highlight the value of social capital to productive activity, the creation of social capital can also be thought of as central to the prevention of social stress. As Belsky (1993) points out, strong personal relationships and social networks permit the sharing of responsibility for childcare and supervision (mutual obligation), the exchange of information about child-rearing, employment and other forms of household assistance (information channels) and an opportunity for informal social sanctions to be imposed for inappropriate parental behaviour (reinforcement of social norms and expectations).

One virtue of thinking about the task of reducing social stress as a problem in social capital formation is that it highlights the potential importance to crime prevention of the vast array of social services provided by different agencies within Government (and different levels of Government) for reasons other than crime prevention. Such services include language courses for newly arrived immigrants, marriage guidance, substitute care, adoption, home school liaison, home care, child protection, childcare, disability support services, family support programs, neighbourhood drop-in centres, emergency accommodation and parent training, to name just a few. Public and political support for these services is often eroded by a widespread belief that they involve the expenditure of large sums of money for no measurable social return. Looked at through the lens of long-term crime prevention this is clearly a mistake. While one should not automatically assume that each of these services is equally effective in building social capital, to the extent to which they are, they make a significant contribution to long-term crime prevention policy.

Another useful aspect of the notion of social capital is that it facilitates an assessment of the relative merits of various programs from the vantage-point of long-term crime prevention. The more strongly a particular program can be regarded as fostering social capital formation, particularly among poor families with dependent children, the more important it may be judged to be to long-term crime prevention. Most child protection agencies, for example, concentrate a substantial proportion of their budget on detecting and responding to alleged cases of child neglect and abuse, and only a small proportion of their budget on providing poor single parent families with access to adequate childcare or programs designed to foster mutually suppor-tive relationships between families exposed to economic and/or social stress. This fact reflects the widespread but erroneous view that socially destructive behaviour is best discouraged through the criminal justice system. Investments in childcare and parental support programs, however, are almost certainly of greater value than investments in systems for detecting and responding to parents who maltreat or neglect their children.

As with the problem of reducing economic stress, the problem of promoting social capital formation is best seen in geographic rather than individual terms. The sources of social capital lie in the networks of family and social relationships which permeate settled stable communities but which remain so obviously vestigial in localities of high population turnover, ethnic heterogeneity, cultural disintegration and/or poverty. Efforts to reduce crime by reducing social stress are therefore best pursued by targeting whole neighbourhoods or localities where the level of social stress is most acute and mounting a comprehensive effort to improve the social capital of the neighbourhood. Sampson (1995) has recently suggested a number of ways in which this might be achieved. For example, neighbourhood social interactions are often limited by fear of crime, incivility and low-level manifestations of public disorder (e.g. public drinking and rowdy behaviour by young males). Whatever their putative impact on the level of informal social control in a neighbourhood it seems highly likely that these problems inhibit the formation of social networks and supports which help attenuate the effects of economic stress on parenting. Encouraging local authorities to clean up graffiti, trash, needles etc. and impose strict controls on the sources of public disorder (e.g. liquor outlets) is therefore not only desirable as an end in itself, it is also one way in which local authorities can act to foster the creation of social capital.

Another valuable contribution to social capital creation highlighted by Sampson involves maintaining the municipal service base. In countries such as Australia (and probably Canada as well) where a large segment of the population lives in urban areas, Governments are under constant pressure to withdraw services from rural areas or consolidate them in major rural towns. The withdrawal or contraction of police, court, medical, educational, employment or social services, however, can have a devastating impact on the level of social cohesion in rural communities especially where businesses (such as banks) are engaged in similar activity. As with the decision to locate public housing in areas where real estate is cheap, the decision to rationalise or centralise Government services may offer short-term economic benefits which are outweighed by the long-run social costs.

Other strategies canvassed by Sampson for building neighbourhood social capital include the avoidance of urban renewal and development programs which result in the dislocation of entire communities, encouraging public tenants to purchase the properties they rent, integrating community with child development and health policy (so that child development and health care are seen to be fostered by local institutions), maintaining the municipal service base and empowering local communities by increasing their involvement in decisions which affect the quality of neighbourhood life. Admittedly the efficacy of these strategies has not been demonstrated through research. Given the manifest importance of neighbourhoods to the creation of social capital, however, each of them would seem sensible ways in which to foster the growth of social capital in a neighbourhood, thereby enhancing the capacity of families to cope with economic and social stress.

One of the most significant impediments to the creation of social capital, as Latham (1996) points out, is that most of the Government programs which are useful to this end have been organised around professional groupings or guilds. To use his words 'Government has been laid out like a series of silos, with the public moving between each guild-based function to access services' (Latham 1996: 9). The result is that efforts to maximise the beneficial effect of Government intervention in the locations where it is most needed are hampered by conflicting views among Government agencies about where their activities should be focused and how they should be coordinated. Shifting the focus of Government action to reduce social stress from individuals or groups to localities is an important step in improving its effectiveness in reducing the flow of juveniles susceptible to involvement in crime.

Developmental intervention programs

So far we have discussed ways of reducing criminal participation rates by reducing economic and/or social stress. One of the more providential aspects of crime prevention is that it is possible to ignore them and yet forestall many of their criminogenic effects. The possibility arises because a number of developmental intervention programs have been developed which are generally agreed to be effective either in improving the quality of parenting or ameliorating problem behaviour amongst children at risk of involvement in crime. As the studies evaluating these programs have recently been reviewed by a number of authors (Yoshikawa 1994; Tremblay and Craig 1995; Sherman et al. 1997) there is little point in recapitulating the details of each study here. Instead, we will briefly describe some of the more successful programs with a view to highlighting what appear to be their common elements and then move on to a general discussion of the most appropriate policy framework within which to administer early intervention programs.

Perhaps the most salient point to emerge from reviews of research on developmental intervention programs is that the earlier the intervention the greater its prospects for success. Interventions with children in the first few years of life consistently show strong positive effects while interventions with juveniles already involved in crime show the smallest prospects of success. In some ways this is not so surprising. One would expect behavioural patterns established and reinforced over many years to be difficult to change. The failure of correctional programs to affect adult recidivism is well known (Lipton, Martinson and Wilks 1975). However, the dismal results obtained from programs designed to reduce involvement in crime amongst adolescents or teenagers are not confined to those delivered within a correctional setting. Failures have also been reported with programs targeting teaching practices, the school curriculum, teenage moral reasoning and association with delinquent peers (Tremblay and Craig 1995).

In his review of the early intervention literature Yoshikawa (1994) cited four programs as having been shown in experiments using randomised controls to produce long-term reductions in antisocial behaviour, delinquency or chronic delinquency. These were the Perry Pre-School Project, the Houston Parent Child Development Project, the Syracuse Family Development Research Project and the Yale Child Welfare Project. All four of these programs targeted multiple risk factors for delinquency rather than just one. Each, however, included measures designed to improve child cognitive development and weekly home visits by a professional, designed to allow systematic assessment of a child's needs and interests, and/or teach parents how to manage problem behaviours among children and/or provide them with social support.

One of the distinctive features of these interventions is that they produce benefits other than reduced delinquency or adult criminality. As Yoshikawa (1994) points out, the Perry project produced improved family economic outcomes, improved child cognitive development and reduced adult criminality. The Houston project produced improved child cognitive development and reduced antisocial school behaviour in late childhood. The Syracuse project produced improved cognitive ability and earlier juvenile socioemotional competence. The Yale project produced improved family economic outcomes, improved cognitive ability and reduced antisocial school behaviour.

The results of interventions with school children, while somewhat less encouraging, still offer some basis for optimism. Reported failures include efforts to reduce delinquency among adolescents, either through cognitive-behavioural therapy intended to reduce aggressive behaviour, or through psychological counselling for juveniles deemed at risk of involvement in crime. Reported successes include several multi-modal interventions, such as one intervention which combined parent and social skills training, another which combined parent and (adolescent) cognitive skills training and a third which combined classroom, cognitive skills and parent training with a view to promoting stronger family and school bonds (Tremblay and Craig 1995). Sherman et al. (1997: 4–19), however, has questioned even the positive results among these studies, pointing out that many of them involve small samples, short (or no) follow-up periods and other methodological weaknesses. By contrast a more recent very strong test of a very expensive program designed to link schools and families of high risk youth has apparently failed to provide any evidence of a reduction in delinquency (Sherman et al. 1997: 4–21). In her review Gottfredson (1997) takes a more optimistic view of school-based interventions, particularly where the intervention is designed not to prevent future delinquency so much as to control its current manifestations.

Despite the fact that it is now easy to identify early intervention programs which are effective in preventing delinquency, there is still a persistent tendency on the part of policy makers to underestimate their importance to crime prevention policy. There are several reasons for this. One is that the crime reduction benefits of early intervention take several years to be felt while the costs are incurred immediately. This reduces their political appeal. Another is a tendency to see the prevention of child maltreatment as requiring coercive forms of intervention designed to separate children from their abusers or deter abusers from engaging in further maltreatment. The third is a tendency on the part of some of the Government agencies best placed to assist in delivering early intervention programs to reduce delinquency (e.g. Public Health and School Education) to view such programs as lying outside their 'core' business.

The problem of arousing political interest in policies which produce immediate costs but delayed benefits is endemic to democracies. In the context of crime prevention it can probably only be dealt with by harnessing public concern about crime to improve public understanding of what works in dealing with it. Researchers at the Rand Corporation have recently carried out some highly imaginative work in this regard. Greenwood et al. (1997) compared the cost-effectiveness of four early interventions against California's three-strikes law, a punitive sentencing regime designed to reduce crime by incapacitating repeat offenders. The early intervention strategies examined were home visits and day care, parent training, graduation incentives and delinquent supervision. Of the five forms of intervention to reduce crime, home visits and day care directed at families whose children were at risk of delinquency emerged as the most cost-effective way of reducing crime.

The other impediments to greater use of early intervention strategies are progressively being overcome with greater realisation of the need for a 'whole of Government' response to crime prevention. Progress from research to policy in this area, however, is not likely to prove easy, even for well-intentioned policy makers. It makes economic sense, for example, to provide early intervention programs only to those families whose children are at significant risk of persistent involvement in crime. Yet targeting single parent families in poverty or families from minority ethnic groups runs the risk of further stigmatising these groups, an outcome which at the very least might reduce the number of parents willing to take advantage of the program.

It may be, as Yoshikawa (1994) suggests, that early intervention programs can be targeted at the right groups on the understanding that they are designed to ameliorate social disadvantage rather than prevent crime. On the other hand Sherman et al. (1997) might be right in supposing that universal access to early intervention programs is the only reliable way of dealing with the problem of social stigma and attracting the requisite level of Government support necessary to ensure that early intervention programs are effective in preventing crime. This is not a question which can be resolved in a general way. The correct approach will depend upon contextual factors which vary from country to country or even from place to place within a country. What is important is that Governments make a serious effort to ensure that early intervention programs are accorded a priority within crime control policy which is commensurate with their proven cost-effectiveness in reducing crime.

Summary and conclusion

Strategies designed to reduce the incidence of child neglect and abuse are of central importance to long-term crime prevention. There are several means by which to reduce the scale of these problems. Macroeconomic policy offers perhaps the most important avenue because rates of child neglect and abuse are so closely linked to levels of poverty. Sustained economic growth, however, can occur without significantly alleviating levels of economic stress among families most at risk of neglecting or abusing their children (i.e. those exposed to social stressors, such as lack of a supportive partner, social isolation, depression, etc.). To be maximally effective in reducing neglect and abuse, therefore, macroeconomic policy must aim at more than just sustained economic growth.

A social welfare safety net for parents who cannot work is obviously imperative. However, the economic keys to improve parenting are not to be found in ever more generous social security systems. They are to be found in policies which increase rates of employment among families exposed to social stress without at the same time reducing the quality of care provided to their children. Policies – such as labour market programs designed to reduce the level of long-term unemployment and tax credits for entry-level jobs – need to be combined with an effective child maintenance scheme and subsidized access to high-quality childcare for low income families. Moreover, because there are concentration effects of poverty on the development of delinquent-prone communities, general economic and labour market policies need to be buttressed with measures designed to reduce the spatial concentration of poverty and social disadvantage.

In most instances the economic measures best suited to this end are probably 'mobility' strategies, that is, strategies which seek to reduce or overcome the obstacles to employment *outside* of an impoverished neighbour-hood (e.g. lack of information about job opportunities, a spatial mismatch between unemployment and the supply of employment opportunities). In some circumstances (e.g. remote rural communities), however, enhancing the mobility of the unemployed does not overcome the problem of chronic unemployment. In such circumstances it may be necessary to pursue what have sometimes been unfairly dismissed as 'ghetto guilding' strategies, that is, measures which seek to create improved employment opportunities *within* impoverished neighbourhoods.

Since social support can buffer the effects of economic stress, efforts to combat neighbourhood poverty need to be combined with measures designed to strengthen social capital in poor neighbourhoods. The most valuable of these measures are those which seek to strengthen and maintain the municipal service base in areas of disadvantage. The plethora of servies provided by Government under the general heading of 'social service' (e.g. language courses for newly arrived immigrants, disability support service, home school liaison) may sometimes be seen as a wasteful drain on public funds but, to the extent that such services foster neighbourhood integration, they help forstall the corrosive effects of poverty on parenting and crime.

Fortunately, even where we cannot create an economic and social climate fully conducive to caring and effecting parenting, it is possible to provide support to individual families in ways which reduce both the risk of neglect and abuse and the chance of juvenile involvement in crime. It is now well known that programs designed to provide parental support and advice in the first few years of a child's life can substantially reduce the risk of later criminality. The significance of this discovery is only now becoming fully appreciated by Government. The challenge which lies ahead is to find ways of bringing these programs within easy reach of those who stand to benefit most from them.

Notes

1 THE ESIOM PARADIGM AND ITS PROBLEMS

1. It is interesting to note at this juncture that nothing in Hirschi's control theory actually contradicts the hypothesis that economic stress and crime are causally linked. Had he observed a relationship between social status or family income and self-reported delinquency, it would have been open to him to argue that economic stress weakens the bond or level of involvement between children and their parents. In later theoretical work he considered this possibility (Gottfredson and Hirschi 1990, p. 104).

2. These observations may have reduced concerns about the association between economic stress and crime. However, concern about the fact that white-collar crime is less easily detected and recorded and less frequently prosecuted than blue-collar crime remains a common source of criticism amongst those who reject the claim that economic stress and crime are linked. Yet the existence of white-collar crime is hardly proof that crime and economic stress are unrelated. Opportunities for committing white-collar crime are mostly confined to those who are fairly affluent. It is simply not open to most citizens to commit insider trading or engage in transfer pricing. We should therefore expect to find that cases of white-collar crime predominate among the more affluent sections of the community. Opportunities for committing the more commonly recorded forms of crime (e.g. assault, robbery, car theft, burglary), however, are distributed almost universally through the population. The fact that economically disadvantaged groups appear to exploit these opportunities more frequently than more affluent groups therefore warrants some further explanation.

3. It might be countered that many individuals do not commence their involvement in crime until quite late. This point must be conceded. Longitudinal studies show, however, that those who begin their period of involvement in crime early account for a disproportionate share of total recorded offending. This suggests that those who begin their criminal careers early probably also exert a disproportionate influence on aggregate crime rate variation. Of course economic factors may

influence adult offending behaviour without necessarily influencing the onset of involvement in crime. But the mere fact that involvement in crime is predictable from early childhood tends to undermine (even if it does not refute) the claim that involvement in crime is driven principally by the effect of economic stress on the motivation to offend.

4. The theory of reintegrative shaming subsequently proposed by Braithwaite is not discussed here because, although it differs in some key respects from the variant of social opportunity theory explored by Braithwaite in 1979, it does not offer a substantially different account of the relationship between economic stress and crime.

3 PARENTING, PEERS AND DELINQUENCY

1. According to Loeber and Stouthamer-Loeber the *neglect paradigm* encompasses studies examining the effects of parenting patterns where 'parents spend insufficient time positively interacting with their children', the *conflict paradigm* encompasses studies which examine family patterns 'in which parents and children become enmeshed in escalations of conflict', the *deviant behaviours and attitudes paradigm* encompasses studies which examine either genetic transmission of criminality or the effect of deviant parental behaviour on children, and the *disruption paradigm* encompasses studies examining the effects of parental separation or family break-down.

2. Loeber and Stouthamer-Loeber define a normal sample as one in which the sample was 'not selected on the basis of the absence or presence of delinquency or conduct problems but that contain a cross-section of children on either dimension'.

3. The statistic d is calculated as the standardised difference between two group means (i.e. the difference between two group means divided by the pooled within-group variation).

4 DELINQUENCY GENERATION AT THE INDIVIDUAL LEVEL

1. Parenting style was classified by the Western Australian researchers (Silburn et al., 1996) as *encouraging* (high use of rewards and reinforcements, low frequency of coercive methods of discipline), *inconsistent* (high use of rewards and reinforcements, high frequency of coercive methods of discipline), *neutral* (low use of rewards and reinforcements, low frequency of coercive methods of discipline) or *coercive* (low use of rewards and reinforcements, high frequency of coercive methods of discipline). We combined *encouraging* or *neutral* parenting into one category and *inconsistent* or *coercive* parenting into another.

2. All of the data analysis reported in this chapter was performed under contract by the Australian Bureau of Statistics at our direction, because they would not release unit record data from the survey. The specific correlation structure of the Western Australian Child Health Survey data was modelled by the Australian Bureau of Statistics; they had developed a SAS algorithm for this purpose for their own data analysis.

3. Although the neighbourhood type variable was found to be significant in the regression in the presence of other factors, these two percentages are not signifi-

cantly different: their confidence intervals are quite large and overlap each other. This is probably the result of poor statistical power as there were very few poorly supervised juveniles in the total sample.

5 DELINQUENCY GENERATION AT THE AGGREGATE LEVEL

1. The neighbourhood measure was calculated as follows. Each postcode in NSW (New South Wales) is an administrative area for the purpose of addressing and delivering mail. The boundaries of postcodes do not align with the boundaries of other defined regional units. For example, each postcode may fall partly within a number of Local Government Areas and each Local Government Area may contain part or all of several postcodes. For each postcode we first determined all the Local Government Areas which contained part (or all) of the specified postcode; then we determined which *other* postcodes fell wholly or partly within these Local Government Areas. The resulting set of postcodes was defined to be the *neighbourhood* of the originally specified postcode. The value of the relevant response variable was determined for the entire area encompassed by this *neighbourhood*. In this manner a neighbourhood measure was calculated for each postcode.

2. The rates of participation in crime, being based on court appearance rates, are effectively censored at zero. The five postcodes with zero court appearances may have differed in their real level of juvenile participation in violent crime, despite having equal court appearance rates. We chose to exclude these records rather than use analytical techniques for dealing with censored data because there were so few postcodes affected and because the analysis of participation in violent crime was a subsidiary analysis.

3. To produce Figure 5.2, the postcodes were first sorted according to their rates of neglect and then grouped into 20 groups, each containing either 13 or 14 postcodes (18 groups with 13 postcodes, 2 groups with 14 postcodes). The average rates of juvenile participation in crime were then plotted against the average rates of neglect for the 20 groups of postcodes.

4. Because there is no unique identifier included in court appearance records in New South Wales we were limited to using data from a pilot project to establish a re-offending database. Using probability matching techniques this project had established a database of unique individuals with at least one Local Court appearance in New South Wales over the four-year period from January 1990 to December 1993.

5. One postcode with missing data for adult participation in crime was excluded from the data set used for the correlation calculation.

6 AN EPIDEMIC MODEL OF OFFENDER POPULATION GROWTH

1. National crime victim surveys carried out in Australia in 1983 and 1993 confirm significant increases in victimisation rates for break and enter, robbery and assault, even if the size of these rate increases is generally less than that found for trends in police recorded crime. It is therefore difficult to argue that the increase in recorded crime just reflects an increase in public willingness to report or police capacity to record offences.

7 THEORIES OF CRIME AND PLACE

1. To an Australian scholarly audience both of these theories, but particularly Skogan's, might seem almost melodramatic. While phenomena such as an out-migration of residents in response to crime or fear of crime are not unheard of in Australia, they are generally highly localised (e.g. affecting a block or housing estate rather than an entire neighbourhood) and, one suspects, fairly rare compared with either the United States or Britain. This is probably because racial stereotypes and assumptions are an important contributing factor to residential movement patterns in the United States and other Western countries (e.g. Britain) which have large and highly disadvantaged black populations (see Bursik 1986, p. 50), whose members are overrepresented among crime victims and offenders. Australians no doubt possess the same stereotypes and assumptions about race as are held in the United States and Britain and indigenous Australians are probably just as overrepresented among offenders as the black population is in the United States. However, the Aboriginal population in Australia is very small by comparison with black populations in other Western countries and the scope for inward migration of Aboriginal people into white neighbourhoods to trigger an outward migration of non-Aboriginal people is therefore very much smaller. This should not distract us from the task of weighing the evidence adduced by both theorists to support their claims. But it is important to keep in mind the large differences between countries in the size and composition of their ethnic minorities when assessing research evidence on the role of ethnicity in shaping spatial variation in crime.

2. To be fair, many of these points have been conceded by Skogan. As he points out (Skogan 1986, p. 204), the dynamic aspects of his theory are largely hypothetical because there is no research on trends in fear of crime and actual crime which links people to their neighbourhood environment.

8 PREVENTION

1. In the area covered by the urban postcodes there were 1,284,749 families, 851,786 children aged 0–15 and 432,973 juveniles aged 10–17 at the 1991 census. The path coefficients indicate that, with other variables held constant, (1) a unit increase in *neglect* results in a 0.50 unit increase in juvenile participation in crime, and (2) a unit increase in *poverty* results in a 0.42 unit increase in juvenile participation in crime (0.20 directly plus $0.39 \times 0.50 + 0.27 \times 0.10$ indirectly via neglect and abuse). Hence 1,000 additional children reported for neglect would be equivalent to a 1.17 ($= 1,000 \ / \ 851.786$) unit increase in the neglect rate per thousand children, which would result in a 0.59 ($= 1.17 \times 0.50$) unit increase in the rate of juvenile participation in crime or an additional 256 ($= 0.59 \times 432.973$) juveniles appearing before the Children's Courts. The impact of an increase in the number of poor families is calculated similarly.

2. The issue of long-term unemployment is particularly salient for countries such as Australia, which has had persistent problems of unemployment during several years of sustained economic growth. Much of the unemployment appears to be structural, with about 250,000 people (i.e. approximately a quarter of the unemployed population) who have been actively and unsuccessfully searching for employment

for twelve months or longer (Chapman 1997). In fact, although the size of the population of long-term unemployed in Australia has tended to rise and fall with each recession, the number of long-term unemployed has trebled since 1978 (Chapman 1997: 2).

References

Agnew, R., 1985, 'A revised strain theory of delinquency', *Social Forces*, vol. 64, pp. 151–167.

Agnew, R., 1991a, 'The interactive effects of peer variables on delinquency', *Criminology*, vol. 29, pp. 47–71.

Agnew, R., 1991b, 'A longitudinal test of social control theory and delinquency', *Journal of Research in Crime and Delinquency*, vol. 28, no. 2, pp. 126–156.

Agnew, R., 1993, 'Why do they do it? An examination of the intervening mechanisms between "social control" variables and delinquency', *Journal of Research in Crime and Delinquency*, vol. 30, no. 3, pp. 245–266.

Agnew, R. and White, H. R., 1992, 'An empirical test of general strain theory', *Criminology*, vol. 30, pp. 475–499.

Allan, E. A. and Steffensmeier, D. J., 1989, 'Youth, underemployment, and property crime: Differential effects of job availability and job quality on juvenile and young adult arrest rates', *American Sociological Review*, vol. 54, pp. 107–123.

Allen, R. C., 1996, 'Socioeconomic conditions and property crime: A comprehensive review and test of the professional literature', *American Journal of Economics and Sociology*, vol. 55, pp. 293–308.

Andrew Brion Research 1995, 'The family quiz (family circle): national survey, comparisons with family circle core readers and segmentation', unpublished report for Murdoch Magazines, North Sydney.

Australian Institute of Health and Welfare 1998, 'Child protection Australia 1996–97', AIHW cat. no. CWS 5, Canberra, Child Welfare Series, no. 21.

Barnes, G. M. and Farrell, M. P., 1992, 'Parental support and control as predictors of adolescent drinking, delinquency, and related problem behaviors', *Journal of Marriage and the Family*, vol. 54, pp. 763–776.

Baumrind, D., 1994, 'The social context of child maltreatment', *Family Relations*, vol. 43, pp. 360–368.

Becker, G. S., 1968, 'Crime and punishment: An economic approach', *Journal of Political Economy*, vol. 76, pp. 169–217.

Belknap, J., 1989, 'The economics–crime link', *Criminal Justice Abstracts*, March, pp. 140–157.

Belsky, J., 1984, 'The determinants of parenting: A process model', *Child Development*, vol. 55, pp. 83–96.

Belsky, J., 1993, 'Etiology of child maltreatment: A developmental-ecological analysis', *Psychological Bulletin*, vol. 114, no. 3, pp. 413–434.

Berk, R. A., Lenihan, K. J. and Rossi, P. H., 1980, 'Crime and poverty: Some experimental evidence from ex-offenders', *American Sociological Review*, vol. 45, pp. 766–786.

Blackson, T. C., Tarter, R. E., Loeber, R., Ammerman, R. T. and Windle, M., 1996, 'The influence of paternal substance abuse and difficult temperament in fathers and sons' disengagement from family to deviant peers', *Journal of Youth and Adolescence*, vol. 25, pp. 389–411.

Block, M. K. and Heineke, J. M., 1975, 'A labour theoretic analysis of the criminal choice', *American Economic Review*, vol. 65, pp. 314–325.

Blumstein, A., Cohen, J., Roth, J. A. and Visher, C. A. (eds) 1986, *Criminal Careers and Career Criminals*, vol. 1, National Academy Press, Washington DC.

Bottomley, K. and Coleman, C., 1981, *Understanding Crime Rates*, Gower Publishing, Westmead.

Bottoms, A. E., 1994, 'Environmental criminology', in *The Oxford Handbook of Criminology*, eds M. Maguire, R. Morgan and R. Reiner, Oxford University Press, Oxford.

Bottoms, A. E., Claytor, A. and Wiles, P., 1992, 'Housing markets and residential community crime careers: A case study from Sheffield', in *Crime, Policing and Place: Essays in Environmental Criminology*, eds D. J. Evans, N. R. Fyfe and D. T. Herbert, Routledge, London, pp. 118–144.

Bottoms, A. E., Mawby, R. I. and Xanthos, P., 1989, 'A tale of two estates', in *Crime and the City*, ed. D. Downes, Macmillan, London.

Bottoms, A. E. and Wiles, P., 1986, 'Housing tenure and residential community crime careers in Britain', in *Communities and Crime*, eds A. J. Reiss Jr and M. Tonry, *Crime and Justice: A Review of Research*, vol. 8, eds M. Tonry and N. Morris, University of Chicago Press, Chicago, IL.

Box, S., 1987, *Recession, Crime and Punishment*, Macmillan, London, pp. 68–229.

Braithwaite, J., 1978, 'Unemployment and adult crime: An interpretation of the international evidence', in *Unemployment and Crime: Proceedings of the Institute of Criminology*, no. 36, Sydney University, pp. 54–71.

Braithwaite, J., 1979, *Inequality, Crime and Public Policy*, Routledge and Kegan Paul, London.

Braithwaite, J., 1988, *Crime, Shame and Reintegration*, Cambridge University Press, Cambridge.

Brantingham, P. and Brantingham, P., 1995, 'Criminality of place: Crime generators and crime attractors', *European Journal on Criminal Policy and Research*, Crime, Environments and Situational Prevention, vol. 3, no. 3, pp. 5–26.

Brennan, P. A., Mednick, S. A. and Volava, J., 1995, 'Biomedical factors in crime', in *Crime*, eds J. Q. Wilson and J. Petersilia, ICS Press, San Francisco, CA, pp. 65–90.

Brownfield, D. and Thompson, K., 1991, 'Attachment to peers and delinquent behaviour', *Canadian Journal of Criminology*, January, pp. 45–60.

Brownlee, H., 1985, 'Poverty traps', *Australian Tax Forum*, vol. 2, pp. 161–172.

Bruinsma, G. J. N., 1992, 'Differential association theory reconsidered: An extension and its empirical test', *Journal of Quantitative Criminology*, vol. 8, no. 9, pp. 29–49.

Buchanan, C. and Hartley, P. R., 1992, *Criminal Choice: The Economic Theory of Crime and Its Implications for Crime Control*, The Centre for Independent Studies, Sydney.

Burgess, R. L. and Akers, R. L., 1968, 'A differential association-reinforcement theory of criminal behavior', *Social Problems*, vol. 14, pp. 128–147.

Burnell, J. D., 1988, 'Crime and racial composition in contiguous communities as negative externalities', *American Journal of Economics and Sociology*, vol. 47, pp. 177–193.

Bursik, R. J. Jr, 1986, 'Ecological stability and the dynamics of delinquency', in *Communities and Crime*, eds A. J. Reiss Jr and M. Tonry, *Crime and Justice: A Review of Research*, vol. 8, eds M. Tonry and N. Morris, University of Chicago Press, Chicago, IL.

Bursik, R. J. Jr, 1988, 'Social disorganisation and theories of crime and delinquency: Problems and prospects', *Criminology*, vol. 26, no. 4. pp. 519–551.

Bursik, R. J. Jr and Grasmick, H. G., 1993, *Neighborhoods and Crime: The Dimensions of Effective Community Control*, Lexington, New York.

Burton, V. S. Jr, Cullen, F. T., Evans, T. D., Dunaway, R. G., Kethineni, S. R. and Payne, G. L., 1995, 'The impact of parental controls on delinquency', *Journal of Criminal Justice*, vol. 23, no. 2, pp. 111–126.

Bushway, S. and Reuter, P., 1997, 'Labor markets and crime risk factors', in Sherman et al. (1997).

Byrne, J. M. and Sampson, R. J., 1986, 'Key issues in the social ecology of crime', in *The Social Ecology of Crime*, eds J. M. Byrne and R. J. Sampson, Springer-Verlag, New York, pp. 1–19.

Caliso, J. A. and Milner, J. S., 1994, 'Childhood physical abuse, childhood social support, and adult child abuse potential', *Journal of Interpersonal Violence*, vol. 9, no. 1, pp. 27–44.

Cantor, D. and Land, K. C., 1985, 'Unemployment and crime rates in the post-World War II United States: A theoretical and empirical analysis', *American Sociological Review*, vol. 50, June, pp. 317–332.

Capone, D. L. and Nichols, W. W. Jr, 1976, 'Urban structure and criminal mobility', *American Behavioral Scientist*, vol. 20, no. 2, pp. 1199–1212.

Chaffin, M., Kelleher, K. and Hollenberg, J., 1996, 'Onset of physical abuse and neglect: Psychiatric, substance abuse, and social risk factors from prospective community data', *Child Abuse and Neglect*, vol. 20, no. 3, pp. 191–203.

Chaiken, J. M. and Chaiken, M., 1982, *Varieties of Criminal Behavior*, Rand Report R-2814–NIJ, Rand Corporation, Santa Monica, CA.

Chapman, B., 1997, 'Long term unemployment and labour market programs', paper prepared for the Industry Commission Workshop, *Changing Labour Markets: Prospects for Productivity Growth*, Melbourne, 20–21 February.

Chiricos, T., 1987, 'Rates of crime and unemployment: An analysis of aggregate research evidence', *Social Problems*, vol. 34, no. 2, pp. 187–212.

Clarke, R. V., 1983, 'Situational crime prevention: Its theoretical basis and practical scope', in *Crime and Justice: An Annual Review of Research*, vol. 4, eds M. Tonry and N. Morris University of Chicago Press, Chicago, IL. pp. 225–256.

Clarke, R. V., 1995, 'Situational crime prevention', in *Building a Safer Society: Strategic Approaches to Crime Prevention*, eds M. Tonry and D. P. Farrington, *Crime and Justice: A Review of Research*, vol., 19, ed. M. Tonry, University of Chicago Press, Chicago, IL.

Clarke, R. V. and Cornish, D. B., 1985, 'Modelling offenders' decisions: A framework for research and policy', in *Crime and Justice: An Annual Review of Research*, vol. 6, eds M. Tonry and N. Morris, University of Chicago Press, Chicago, IL.

Cloward, R. A. and Ohlin, L. E., 1960, *Delinquency and Opportunity: A Theory of Delinquent Gangs*, The Free Press, New York.

Cohen, A. K., 1955, *Delinquent Boys: the Culture of the Gang*, The Free Press, New York.

Cohen, L. E. and Cantor, D., 1980, 'The determinants of larceny: An empirical and theoretical study', *Journal of Research in Crime and Delinquency*, vol. 17, pp. 140–159.

Cohen, L. E. and Felson, M., 1979, 'Social change and crime rate trends: A routine activity approach', *American Sociological Review*, vol. 44, pp. 588–608.

Cohen, L. E., Kluegel, J. R. and Land, K. C., 1981, 'Social inequality and predatory criminal victimization: An exposition and test of a formal theory', *American Sociological Review*, vol. 46, October, pp. 505–524.

Coleman, J. S., 1988, 'Social capital in the creation of human capital', *American Journal of Sociology*, vol. 94, no. 1, Supplement pp. S95–S121.

Collins, M. F. and Weatherburn, D., 1995, 'Unemployment and the dynamics of offender populations', *Journal of Quantitative Criminology*, vol. 11, no. 3, pp. 231–245.

Conger, R. D., Conger, K. J., Elder, G. H., Lorenz, F. O., Simons, R. L. and Whitbeck, L. B., 1992, 'A family process model of economic hardship and adjustment of early adolescent boys', *Child Development*, vol. 63, pp. 526–541.

Coohey, C., 1995, 'Neglectful mothers, their mothers, and partners: The significance of mutual aid', *Child Abuse and Neglect*, vol., 19, no. 8, pp. 885–895.

Coohey, C., 1996, 'Child maltreatment: Testing the social isolation hypothesis', *Child Abuse and Neglect*, vol. 20, no. 3, pp. 241–254.

Cook, P. J., 1986, 'The demand and supply of criminal opportunities', in *Crime and Justice: An Annual Review of Research*, vol. 7, eds M. Tonry and N. Morris, University of Chicago Press, Chicago, IL, pp. 1–28.

Cotterell, J. L., 1986, 'Work and community influences on the quality of child rearing', *Child Development*, vol. 57, pp. 362–374.

Coulton, C. J. and Pandey, S., 1992, 'Geographic concentration of poverty and risk to children in urban neighborhoods', *American Behavioral Scientist*, vol. 35, no. 3, pp. 238–257.

Coulton, C. J., Korbin, J. E., Su, M. and Chow, J., 1995, 'Community level factors and child maltreatment rates', *Child Development*, vol. 66, pp. 1262–1276.

Coumarelos, C., 1994, *Predicting Persistence and Determining the Cost-Effectiveness of Interventions*, NSW Bureau of Crime Statistics and Research, Sydney.

Cowell, F. A., Jenkins, S. P. and Litchfield, J. A., 1996. '*The changing shape of the UK income distribution: Kernel density estimates'*, in *New Inequalities: The Changing Distribution of Income and Wealth in the United Kingdom*, ed. John Hills, Cambridge, Cambridge University Press.

Crane, J., 1991. 'The epidemic theory of ghettos and neighborhood effects on dropping out and teenage childbearing', *American Journal of Sociology*, vol. 96, no. 5, pp. 1226–1259.

Creighton, S. and Noyes, P., 1989, *Child Abuse Trends in England and Wales 1983–1987*, NSPCC, London.

Davis, S. K., 1990, 'Chemical dependency in women: A description of its effects and outcome on adequate parenting', *Journal of Substance Abuse Treatment*, vol. 7, pp. 225–232.

De Fleur, M. D. and Quinney, R., 1966, 'A reformulation of Sutherland's differential association theory and a strategy of empirical verification', *Journal of Research in Crime and Delinquency*, vol. 3, no. 1, pp. 1–22.

Department of Social Security 1996, Annual Report 1995–96, Department of Social Security, Canberra.

Deutsch, J., Spiegel, U. and Templeman, J., 1992, 'Crime and income inequality: An economic approach', *Atlantic Economic Journal*, vol. 20, no. 4, pp. 46–54.

Devery, C., 1991, *Disadvantage and Crime*, NSW Bureau of Crime Statistics and Research, Sydney.

Devery, C., 1992, *Domestic Violence in NSW: A Regional Analysis*, NSW Bureau of Crime Statistics and Research, Sydney.

Dore, M. M., 1993, 'Family preservation and poor families: When "homebuilding" is not enough', *Families in Society: The Journal of Contemporary Human Services*, November, pp. 545–556.

Dore, M. M., Doris, J. M. and Wright, P., 1995, 'Identifying substance abuse in maltreating families: A child welfare challenge', *Child Abuse and Neglect*, vol. 19, no. 5, pp. 531–543.

Durkin, M. S., Davidson, L. L., Kuhn, L., O'Connor, P. and Barlow, B., 1994, 'Low-income neighbourhoods and the risk of severe pediatric injury: A small-area analysis in northern Manhattan', *American Journal of Public Health*, vol. 84, no. 4, pp. 587–592.

Eck, J. E., 1995, 'A general model of the geography of illicit retail marketplaces', in *Crime Prevention Studies*, ed. R. V. Clarke, Criminal Justice Press, Monsey, New York and The Police Executive Research Forum, Washington DC.

Eck, J. E. and Weisburd, D., 1995, 'Crime places in crime theory', in *Crime and Place*, eds J. E. Eck, and D. Weisburd, Crime Prevention Studies, vol. 4, Criminal Justice Press, Monsey, New York, and The Police Executive Research Forum, Washington DC.

The Economist, June 1994, 'Welfare reform in America', pp. 19–21, London.

Ehrlich, I., 1973 'Participation in illegitimate activities: A theoretical and empirical investigation', *Journal of Political Economy*, vol. 81, no. 3, pp. 521–565.

Elder, G. H. Jr, Van Nguyen, T. and Caspi, A., 1985, 'Linking family hardship to children's lives', *Child Development*, vol. 56, pp. 361–375.

Elliott, D. S. and Huizinga, D., 1983, 'Social class and delinquent behavior in a national youth panel: 1976–1980', *Criminology*, vol. 21, pp. 149–177.

Elliott, D. S., Huizinga, D. and Ageton, S. S., 1985, *Explaining Delinquency and Drug Use*, Sage, Newbury Park, CA.

Elliott, D. S., Wilson, W. J., Huizinga, D., Sampson, R. J., Elliott, A. and Rankin, B., 1996, 'The effects of neighborhood disadvantage on adolescent development', *Journal of Research in Crime and Delinquency*, vol. 33, no. 4, pp. 389–426.

Erickson, R. A. and Friedman, S. W., 1991, 'Comparative dimensions of state enterprise zone policies', in *Enterprise Zones: New Dimensions in Economic Development*, ed. R. E. Green, Sage Focus Edition, Newbury Park, CA.

Farrell, G., 1995, 'Preventing repeat victimization', in *Building a Safer Society: Strategic Approaches to Crime Prevention*, eds M. Tonry and D. P. Farrington, *Crime and Justice: A Review of Research*, vol., 19, ed. M. Tonry, University of Chicago Press, Chicago, IL.

Farrington, D. P., 1987, 'Early precursors of frequent offending', in *From children to citizens: Families, Schools and Delinquent Prevention*, eds J. Q. Wilson and G. C. Loury, Springer-Verlag, New York.

Farrington, D. P., 1995, 'Key issues in the integration of motivational and opportunity-reducing crime preventing strategies', in *Integrating Crime Prevention Strategies: Propensity and Opportunity*, eds P.-O. H. Wikstrom, R. V. Clarke, J. McCord, National Council for Crime Prevention, Stockholm.

Farrington, D. P., Gallagher, B., Morley, L., St. Ledger, R. J. and West, D. J., 1986, 'Unemployment, school leaving, and crime', *British Journal of Criminology*, vol. 26, no. 4, pp. 335–356.

Farrington, D. P., Gundry, G. and West, D. J., 1971, 'A comparison between early delinquents and young aggressives', *British Journal of Criminology*, vol. 11, pp. 341–358.

Farrington, D. P and Hawkins, J. D., 1990, 'Predicting participation, early onset, and later persistence in officially recorded offending', *Criminal Behavior and Mental Health*, vol. 1, pp. 1–33.

Farrington, D. P., Loeber, R., Elliott, D. S., Hawkins, J. D., Kandel, D. B., Klein, M. W., McCord, J., Rowe, D. C. and Tremblay, R. E., 1990, 'Advancing knowledge about the onset of delinquency and crime', in *Advances in Clinical Child Psychology*, vol. 13, eds B. B. Lahey and A. E. Kazdin, Plenum Press, New York.

Felson, M., 1995, 'Those who discourage crime', in *Crime and Place*, eds J. E. Eck and D. Weisburd, Crime Prevention Studies, vol. 4, Criminal Justice Press, Monsey, New York, and The Police Executive Research Forum, Washington DC.

Field, S., 1990, 'Trends in crime and their interpretation: A study of recorded crime in post-war England and Wales', *Home Office Research Study*, no. 119, HMSO, London.

Fine, D., 1993, 'Herd immunity: History, theory, practice', *Epidemiologic Reviews*, vol. 15, no. 2, pp. 265–302.

Fowles, R. and Merva, M., 1996, 'Wage inequality and criminal activity: An extreme bounds analysis for the United States, 1975–1990', *Criminology*, vol. 34, no. 2, pp. 163–182.

Freeman, R. B., 1995, 'The labour market', in *Crime*, eds J. Q. Wilson and J. Petersilia, ICS, San Francisco, CA.

Garbarino, J. and Kostelny, K., 1992, 'Child maltreatment as a community problem', *Child Abuse and Neglect*, vol. 16, pp. 455–464.

Garbarino, J. and Sherman, D., 1980, 'High-risk neighbourhoods and high-risk families: The human ecology of child maltreatment', *Child Development*, vol. 51, pp. 188–198.

Gaudin, J. M. Jr, Polansky, N. A. Kilpatrick, A. C. and Shilton, P., 1993, 'Loneliness, depression, stress, and social supports in neglectful families', *Americal Journal of Orthopsychiatry*, vol. 63, no. 4, pp. 597–605.

Gaudin, J. M. Jr, Polansky, N. A., Kilpatrick, A. C. and Shilton, P., 1996, 'Family functioning in neglectful families', *Child Abuse and Neglect*, vol. 20, no. 4, pp. 363–377.

Gill, O., 1977, *Luke Street: Housing Policy, Conflict and the Creation of the Delinquent Area*, Macmillan, London.

Gillespie, R. W., 1978, 'Economic factors in crime and delinquency: A critical review of the empirical evidence', *Unemployment and Crime: Hearings Before the Subcommittee on Crime of the Committee on the Judiciary, House of Representatives*, US Government Printing Office, Washington DC, pp. 601–626.

Giovannoni, J. M., 1971, 'Parental mistreatment: Perpetrators and victims', *Journal of Marriage and Family*, vol. 33, pp. 649–657.

Giovannoni, J. M and Billingsley, A., 1970, 'Child neglect among the poor: A study of parental adequacy in families of three ethnic groups', *Child Welfare*, vol. 49, pp. 196–206.

Gladwell, M., 1996, 'The tipping point', *The New Yorker*, 3 June, pp. 32–38.

Glueck, S. and Glueck, E. T., 1950, *Unraveling Juvenile Delinquency*, Harvard University Press, Cambridge, MA.

Gottfredson, D. C., 1997, 'School-based crime prevention', in Sherman, L. W., Gottfredson, D., MacKenzie, D., Eck, J., Reuter, P. and Bushway, S., 1997, *Preventing Crime: What Works, What Doesn't, What's Promising*, A Report to the United States Congress, prepared for the National Institute of Justice, Washington DC.

Gottfredson, D. C., McNeil, R. J. and Gottfredson, G. D., 1991, 'Social area influences on delinquency: A multilevel analysis', *Journal of Research in Crime and Delinquency*, vol. 28, no. 2, pp. 197–226.

Gottfredson, M. R., 1986, 'Substantive Contributions of Victimization Surveys', in *Crime and Justice: An Annual Review of Research*, eds M. Tonry and N. Morris, University of Chicago Press, Chicago, IL, vol. 7, pp. 251–287.

Gottfredson, M. R. and Hindelang, M., 1979, 'A study of the behavior of the law', *American Sociological Review*, vol. 44, pp. 3–18.

Gottfredson, M. R. and Hirschi, T., 1986, 'The true value of Lambda would appear to be zero: An essay on career criminals, criminal careers, selective incapacitation, cohort studies, and related topics', *Criminology*, vol. 24, pp. 213–233.

Gottfredson, M. R. and Hirschi, T., 1990, *A General Theory of Crime*, Stanford University Press, Stanford, CA.

Granovetter, M., 1978, 'Threshold models of collective behaviour', *American Journal of Sociology*, vol. 83, no. 6, pp. 1420–1443.

Granovetter, M. and Soong, R., 1983, 'Threshold models of diffusion and collective behaviour', *Journal of Mathematical Sociology*, vol. 9, pp. 165–179.

Green, A. E., 1994, *The Geography of Poverty and Wealth*, Institute for Employment Research, University of Warwick, Coventry.

Greenberg, D. F., 1979, *Mathematical Criminology*, Rutgers University Press, New Brunswick, NJ.

Greenberg, S. W., Rohe, W. M. and Williams, J. R., 1993, *Informal Citizen Action and Crime Prevention at the Neighborhood Level*, National Institute of Justice, Washington DC, cited in Bursik and Grasmick (1993).

Greenwood, P. W., Model, K. E., Rydell, C. P. and Chiesa, J., 1997, *Diverting Children from a Life of Crime: Measuring Costs and Benefits*, Rand, Santa Monica, CA.

Gregory, R. and Hunter, B., 1995, 'The macro economy and the growth of ghettos and urban poverty in Australia', unpublished discussion paper no. 325, Centre for Economic Policy Research, Australian National University.

Hagan, J., 1993, 'The social embeddedness of crime and unemployment', *Criminology*, vol. 31, no. 4, pp. 461–491.

Hale, C., 1991, 'Unemployment and crime: Differencing is no substitute for modeling', *Journal of Research in Crime and Delinquency*, vol. 28, no. 4, pp. 426–429.

Hale, C. and Sabbagh, D., 1991, 'Testing the relationship between unemployment and crime: A methodological comment and empirical analysis using time series data from England and Wales', *Journal of Research in Crime and Delinquency*, vol. 28, no. 4, pp. 400–417.

Hampton, R. and Newberger E., 1985, 'Child abuse incidence and reporting by hospitals: Significance of severity, class, and race', *American Journal of Public Health*, vol. 75, pp. 56–60.

Harrington, D., Dubowitz, H., Black, M. M. and Binder, A., 1995, 'Maternal substance use and neglectful parenting: Relations with children's development', *Journal of Clinical Child Psychology*, vol. 24, no. 3, pp. 258–263.

Harris, K. M. and Marmer, J. K., 1996, 'Poverty, paternal involvement, and adolescent well-being', *Journal of Family Issues*, vol. 17, no. 5, pp. 614–640.

Harrison, M., 1993, 'Patterns of maintenance payment over time', in *Settling Down: Pathways of Parents After Divorce*, eds K. Junder, M. Harrison and R. Weston, Australian Institute of Family Studies, Commonwealth of Australia, Canberra, pp. 116–134.

Harrison, M. and Tucker, T., 1986, 'Maintenance, custody and access', in *Settling Up: Property and Income Distribution on Divorce in Australia*, ed. P. McDonald, compiled by the Australian Institute of Family Studies, Prentice-Hall, Sydney.

Herbert, D. T., 1980, 'Urban crime and spacial perspectives: The British experience', in *Crime: A Spacial Perspective*, eds D. E. Georges-Abeyie and K. D. Harries, Columbia University Press, New York.

Herbert, D. T. and Hyde, S. W., 1984, 'Residential crime and the urban environment', Unpublished Report to the Economic and Social Research Council, Department of Geography, University College of Wales, Swansea.

Hindelang, M. J., Gottfredson, M. R. and Garafolo, J., 1978, *Victims of Personal Crime*, Ballinger, Cambridge, MA.

Hindelang, M. J., Hirschi, T. and Weis, J. G., 1979, 'Correlates of delinquency: The illusion of discrepancy between self-report and official measures', *American Sociological Review*, vol. 44, pp. 995–1014.

Hirschi, T., 1969, *Causes of Delinquency*, University of California Press, Berkeley, CA.

Hubbs-Tait, L., Osofsky, J. D. Hann, D. M. and Culp, A., 1994, 'Predicting behavior problems and social competence in children of adolescent mothers', *Family Relations*, vol. 43, pp. 439–446.

Hughes, M. A., 1987, 'Moving up and moving out: Confusing ends and means about ghetto dispersal', *Urban Studies*, vol. 24, pp. 503–517.

Huizinga, D., Esbensen, F. and Weiher, A. W., 1991, 'Are there multiple paths to delinquency?', *The Journal of Criminal Law and Criminology*, vol. 82, no. 1, pp. 83–117.

Human Rights and Equal Opportunity Commission 1997, *Bringing Them Home*, Report of the National Inquiry into the Separation of Aboriginal and Torres Strait Islander Children from their Families, Human Rights and Equal Opportunity Commission, Sydney.

Hunter, B., 1995, 'Changes in the geographic dispersion of urban employment in Australia: 1976–1991', unpublished PhD thesis, Australian National University.

Jarjoura, G. R. and Triplett, R., 1997, *Journal of Criminal Justice*, vol. 35, no. 2, pp. 125–139.

Jaudes, P. K., Ekwo, E. and Van Voorhis, J., 1995, 'Association of drug abuse and child abuse', *Child Abuse and Neglect*, vol. 19, no. 9, pp. 1065–1075.

Jencks, C. and Mayer, S. E., 1990, 'The social consequences of growing up in a poor neighborhood', in *Inner-City Poverty in the United States*, eds L. E. Lynn Jr and M. G. H. McGeary, National Academy Press, Washington DC.

Johnson, R. A., Su, S. S., Gerstein, D. R., Shin, H. C. and Hoffmann, J. P., 1995, 'Parental influences on deviant behavior in early adolescence: A logistic response analysis of age and gender-differentiated effects', *Journal of Quantitative Criminology*, vol. 11, no. 2, pp. 167–193.

Johnstone, J. W. C., 1978, 'Social class, social areas and delinquency', *Sociology and Social Research*, vol. 63, pp. 49–77.

Jones, E. D. and McCurdy, K., 1992, 'The links between types of maltreatment and demographic characteristics of children', *Child Abuse and Neglect*, vol. 16, pp. 201–215.

Junankar, P. N. and Kapuscinski, C. A., 1992, *The Costs of Unemployment*, Public Policy Program, Australian National University, Background Paper No. 24, Australian Government Publishing Service, Canberra.

Kain, J. F. and Persky, J. J., 1969, 'Alternatives to the gilded ghetto', *The Public Interest*, Winter no. 14, pp. 74–87.

Kang, K. M. and Seneta, E., 1980, 'Path analysis: An exposition', in *Developments in Statistics, Vol. 3*, ed. P. R. Krishnaiah, Academic Press, New York.

Kapsis, R. E., 1978, 'Residential succession and delinquency: A test of Shaw and McKay's theory of cultural transmission', *Criminology*, vol. 15, no. 4, pp. 459–486.

Katzman, M. T., 1980, 'The contribution of crime to urban decline', *Urban Studies*, vol. 17, pp. 277–286.

Keenan, K., Loeber, R., Zhang, Q., Stouthamer-Loeber, M. and van Kammen, W., 1995, 'The influence of deviant peers on the development of boys' disruptive and delinquent behavior: A temporal analysis', *Development and Psychopathology*, vol. 7, pp. 715–726.

Kelley, S. J., 1992, 'Parenting, stress and child maltreatment in drug-exposed children', *Child Abuse and Neglect*, vol. 16, pp. 317–328.

Kelling, G. L. and Coles, C. M., 1996, *Fixing Broken Windows: Restoring Order and Reducing Crime in Our Communities*, Martin Kessler Books, The Free Press, New York.

Kenyon, P., 1994, 'The job compact: What does the international evidence on active labour market policies suggest about the likelihood of its success?', *Australian Bulletin of Labour*, vol. 20, no. 4, pp. 272–297.

Kornhauser, R. R., 1978, *Social Sources of Delinquency*, University of Chicago Press, Chicago, IL, pp. 139–180.

Kotch, J. B., Browne, D. C., Ringwalt, C. L., Stewart, P. W., Ruina, E., Holt, K., Lowman, B. and Jung, J., 1995, 'Risk of child abuse or neglect in a cohort of low-income children', *Child Abuse and Neglect*, vol. 19, no. 9, pp. 1115–1130.

Kotch, J. B. and Thomas, L. P., 1986, 'Family and social factors associated with substantiation of child abuse and neglect reports', *Journal of Family Violence*, vol. 1, no. 2, pp. 167–179.

Krishnan, V. and Morrison, K. B., 1995, 'An ecological model of child maltreatment in a Canadian province', *Child Abuse and Neglect*, vol. 19, no. 1, pp. 101–113.

Lacharité, C., Ethier, L. and Couture, G., 1996, 'The influence of partners on parental stress of neglectful mothers', *Child Abuse Review*, vol. 5, pp. 18–33.

Lahey, B. B., Conger, B. M., Atkeson, B. M. and Treiber, F. A., 1984, 'Parenting behavior and emotional status of physically abusive mothers', *Journal of Consulting and Clinical Psychology*, vol. 52, no. 6, pp. 1062–1071.

Land, K. C., Cantor, D. and Russell, S. T., 1995, 'Unemployment and crime rate fluctuations in post-World War II United States: Statistical time-series properties and alternative models', in *Crime and Inequality*, eds J. Hagan and R. D. Peterson, Stanford University Press, Stanford, CA.

Larzelere, R. E. and Patterson, G. R., 1990, 'Parental management: Mediator of the effect of socioeconomic status on early delinquency', *Criminology*, vol. 28, no. 2, pp. 301–323.

Latham, M., 1996, *Making Welfare Work*, Centre for Independent Studies, Melbourne.

Lavrakas, P. J., Herz, L. and Salem, G., 1981, 'Community organization, citizen participation, and neighborhood crime prevention', Paper presented at the annual meeting of the American Psychological Association.

Lawrence, R., 1991, 'School performance, peers and delinquency: Implications for juvenile justice', *Juvenile and Family Court Journal*, pp. 59–69.

Lempers, J., Clark-Lempers, D. and Simons, R., 1989, 'Economic hardship, parenting and distress in adolescence', *Child Development*, vol. 60, pp. 25–49.

Levy, F. and Murnane, R., 1992, 'US Earnings levels and earnings inequality: A review of recent trends and proposed explanations', *Journal of Economic Literature*, September, pp. 1333–1381.

Lewis, O., 1968, 'The Culture of Poverty', in *On Understanding Poverty: Perspectives from the Social Sciences*, ed. D. P. Moynihan, Basic Books, New York, pp. 187–200.

Liang, K.-Y. and Zeger, S. L., 1993, 'Regression analysis for correlated data', *Annual Review of Public Health*, vol. 14, pp. 43–68.

Lipton, D., Martinson, R. and Wilks, J., 1975, *The Effectiveness of Correctional Treatment: A Survey of Treatment Evaluation Studies*, Praeger, New York.

Loeber, R. and Stouthamer-Loeber, M., 1986, 'Family factors as correlates and predictors of juvenile conduct problems and delinquency', in *Crime and Justice: An Annual Review of Research*, vol. 7, eds M. Tonry and N. Morris, University of Chicago Press, Chicago, IL, pp. 29–149.

Loeber, R., Stouthamer-Loeber, M., van Kammen, W. and Farrington, D. P., 1991, 'Initiation, escalation and desistance in juvenile offending and their correlates: Pittsburgh Youth Study', *The Journal of Criminal Law and Criminology*, vol. 82, no. 1, pp. 36–82.

Long, S. K. and Witte, A. D., 1981, 'Current economic trends: Implications for crime and criminal justice', in *Crime and Criminal Justice in a Declining Economy*, ed. K. N. Wright, Oelgeschlager, Gunn and Hain, Cambridge, MA.

Mak, A. S., 1994, 'Parental neglect and overprotection as risk factors in delinquency', *Australian Journal of Psychology*, vol. 46, no. 2, pp. 107–111.

Martens, P., 1992, *Family, Environment and Delinquency*, National Council for Crime Prevention, Stockholm, Sweden.

Martin, E. P. and Martin, J. M., 1978, *The Black Extended Family*, University of Chicago Press, Chicago, IL.

Martin, M. J. and Walters, J., 1982, 'Familial correlates of selected types of child abuse and neglect', *Journal of Marriage and the Family*, May, pp. 267–276.

Massey, D. and Denton, N., 1993, *American Apartheid: Segregation and the Making of the Underclass*, Harvard University Press, Cambridge, MA.

Matka, E., 1997, *Public Housing and Crime in Sydney*, NSW Bureau of Crime Statistics and Research, Sydney.

Matsueda, R. L. and Heimer, K., 1987, 'Race, family structure, and delinquency: A test of differential association and social control theories', *American Sociological Review,* vol. 52, December, pp. 826–840.

Matsumoto, Y., 1970, 'The distribution of juvenile delinquency in the social class structure: A comparative analysis of delinquency rate between Tokyo and Nashville', *Japanese Sociological Review,* vol. 20, pp. 2–18.

McCarthy, B., 1996, 'The attitudes and actions of others: Tutelage and Sutherland's theory of differential association', *British Journal of Criminology,* vol. 36, no. 1, pp. 135–147.

McCord, J., 1979, 'Some child-rearing antecedents of criminal behaviour in adult men', *Journal of Personality and Social Psychology,* vol. 37, pp. 1477–1486.

McCord, J., 1980, 'Patterns of deviance', in *Human Functioning in Longitudinal Perspective,* eds S. B. Sells, R. Crandall, M. Roff, J. S. Strauss and W. Pollin, Williams and Wilkins, Baltimore, pp. 157–162.

McCord, J., 1983, 'A forty year perspective on effects of child abuse and neglect', *Child Abuse and Neglect,* vol. 7, pp. 265–270.

McCord, J., 1991, 'Family relationships, juvenile delinquency, and adult criminality', *Criminology,* vol. 29, no. 3, pp. 397–417.

McGahey, R. M., 1986, 'Economic conditions, neighbourhood organization and urban crime', in *Communities and Crime,* eds A. J. Reiss Jr and M. Tonry, *Crime and Justice: A Review of Research,* vol. 8, eds M. Tonry and N. Morris, University of Chicago Press, Chicago, IL.

McLoyd, V. C. and Wilson, L., 1990, 'Maternal behavior, social support, and economic conditions as predictors of distress in children', in *Economic Stress: Effects on Family Life and Child Development, New Directions for Child Development,* no. 46, eds V. C. McLoyd and C. A. Flanagan, Jossey-Bass, San Francisco, CA, pp. 49–70.

Merton, R. K., 1968, *Social Theory and Social Structure,* The Free Press, Glencoe, IL.

Messner, S. F. and Blau, J. R., 1987, 'Routine leisure activities and rates of crime: A macro-level analysis', *Social Forces,* vol. 65, no. 4, pp. 1035–1052.

Miethe, T. D., Stafford, M. C. and Long, J. S., 1987, 'Social differentiation in criminal victimization: A test of routine activities/lifestyle theories', *American Sociological Review,* vol. 52, April, pp. 184–194.

Montgomery, J. D., 1991, 'Social networks and labor-market outcomes: Toward an economic analysis', *American Economic Review,* vol. 81, no. 5, pp. 1408–1418.

Morris, T., 1957, *The Criminal Area,* Routledge and Kegan Paul, New York, pp. 42–53, reprinted in eds H. L. Voss and D. M. Petersen, 1971, *Ecology, Crime and Delinquency,* Appleton-Century-Crofts, New York, pp. 47–64.

Mortensen, D. T. and Vishwanath, T., 1994, 'Personal contacts and earnings: It is who you know!', *Labour Economics,* vol. 1, pp. 187–201.

Mukherjee, S. K. and Dagger, D., 1990, *The Size of the Crime Problem in Australia,* 2nd edn, Australian Institute of Criminology, Canberra, p. 24.

Murray, C., 1984, *Losing Ground: American Social Policy, 1950–1980,* Basic Books, New York.

Nagin, D. S. and Smith, D. A., 1990, 'Participation in and frequency of delinquent behavior: A test for structural differences', *Journal of Quantitative Criminology,* vol. 6, no. 4, pp. 335–356.

National Research Council, 1993, *Understanding Child Abuse and Neglect,* National Academy Press, Washington DC.

Nelson, K. E., Saunders, E. J. and Landsman, M. J., 1993, 'Chronic child neglect in perspective', *Social Work*, vol. 38, no. 6, pp. 661–671.

Nettler, G., 1978, *Explaining Crime*, 2nd edn, McGraw Hill, New York.

Ney, P. G., Fung, T. and Wickett, A. R., 1994, 'The worst combinations of child abuse and neglect', *Child Abuse and Neglect*, vol. 18, no. 9, pp. 705–714.

NICHD 1999, *The NICHD Study of Early Child Care*, National Institute of Child Health and Development, US Department of Health and Human Services, NIH Pub. no. 98–4318, Washington DC.

NIS-3 1999, Third national incidence study of child abuse and neglect, http://www.calib.com/nccanch/services/stats/htm

Norstrum, T., 1988, 'Theft, criminality and economic growth', *Social Science Research*, vol. 17, pp. 48–65.

Orsagh, T. and Witte, A. D., 1980, *Economic Status and Crime: Implications for Offender Rehabilitation*, University of North Carolina, Charlotte, NC.

Pabon, E., Rodriguez, O. and Gurin, G., 1992, 'Clarifying peer relations and delinquency', *Youth and Society*, vol. 24, no. 2, pp. 149–165.

Paternoster, R. and Brame, R., 1997, 'Multiple routes to delinquency?: A test of developmental and general theories of crime', *Criminology*, vol. 35, no. 1, pp. 49–84.

Paternoster, R. and Mazerolle, P., 1994, 'General strain theory and delinquency: A replication and extension', *Journal of Research in Crime and Delinquency*, vol. 31, no. 3, pp. 235–263.

Paternoster, R. and Triplett, R., 1988, 'Disaggregating self-reported delinquency and its implications for theory', *Criminology*, vol. 26, no. 4, pp. 591–625.

Patterson, E. B., 1991, 'Poverty, income inequality, and community crime rates', *Criminology*, vol. 29, no. 4, pp. 755–776.

Patterson, G. R., Capaldi, D. and Bank, L., 1991, 'An early starter model for predicting delinquency', in *The Development and Treatment of Childhood Aggression*, eds D. J. Pepler and K. H. Rubin, Erlbaum, Hillsdale, NJ.

Patterson, G. R. and Dishion, T. J., 1985, 'Contributions of families and peers to delinquency', *Criminology*, vol. 23, no. 1, pp. 63–79.

Pett, M. A., Vaughan-Cole, B. and Wampold, B. E., 1994, 'Maternal employment and perceived stress: Their impact on children's adjustment and mother–child interaction in young divorced and married families', *Family Relations*, vol. 43, pp. 151–158.

Phillips, P. D., 1980, 'Characteristics and typology of the journey to crime', in *Crime: A Spacial Perspective*, eds D. E. Georges-Abeyie and K. D. Harries, Columbia University Press, New York.

Piggott, J. and Chapman, B., 1995, 'Costing the Job Compact', *The Economic Record*, vol. 71, no. 215, pp. 313–328.

Rankin, J. H. and Kern, R., 1994, 'Parental attachments and delinquency', *Criminology*, vol. 32, no. 4, pp. 495–515.

Reiss, A. J. Jr, 1986a, 'Co-offender influences on criminal careers', in *Criminal Careers and 'Career Criminals'*, vol. 2, eds A. Blumstein, J. Cohen, J. A. Roth and C. A. Visher, National Academy Press, Washington DC, pp. 121–160.

Reiss, A. J. Jr, 1986b, 'Why are communities important in understanding crime?', in *Communities and Crime*, eds A. J. Reiss Jr and M. Tonry, *Crime and Justice: A Review of Research*, vol. 8, eds M. Tonry and N. Morris, University of Chicago Press, Chicago, IL.

Reiss, A. J. and Rhodes, A. L., 1961, 'The distribution of juvenile delinquency in the social class structure', *American Sociological Review*, vol. 26, pp. 720–732, cited in Braithwaite (1979: 119).

Rengert, G., 1980, 'Spacial aspects of criminal behavior', in *Crime: A Spacial Perspective*, eds D. E. Georges-Abeyie and K. D. Harries, Columbia University Press, New York.

Reserve Bank of Australia 1991, *Reserve Bank of Australia Bulletin September 1991*, Reserve Bank of Australia, Sydney.

Rhodes, W. and Conley, C., 1981, 'Crime and mobility: An empirical study', in *Environmental Criminology*, eds P. J. Brantingham and P. L. Brantingham, Sage, Beverley Hills, CA.

Robins, L. and Regier, D. (eds) 1991, *Psychiatric Disorders in America: The Epidemiological Catchment Area Study*, Free Press, New York.

Rossi, P. H., Berk, R. A. and Lenihan, K. J., 1980, *Money, Work, and Crime: Some Experimental Results*, Academic Press, New York.

Rowe, D. C. and Farrington, D. P., 1997, 'The familial transmission of criminal convictions', *Criminology*, vol. 35, no. 1, pp. 177–201.

Salmelainen, P., 1995, *The Correlates of Offending Frequency: A Study of Juvenile Theft Offenders in Detention*, NSW Bureau of Crime Statistics and Research, Sydney.

Salmelainen, P., 1996, *Child Neglect: Its Causes and its Role in Delinquency*, Crime and Justice Bulletin No. 33, NSW Bureau of Crime Statistics and Research, Sydney.

Sampson, R. J., 1985, 'Neighborhood and crime: The structural determinants of personal victimization', *Journal of Research in Crime and Delinquency*, vol. 22, no. 1, pp. 7–40.

Sampson, R. J., 1986, 'Effects of socioeconomic context on official reaction to juvenile delinquency', *American Sociological Review*, vol. 51, pp. 876–885.

Sampson, R. J., 1995, 'The community', in *Crime*, eds J. Q. Wilson and J. Petersilia, ICS Press, San Francisco, CA.

Sampson, R. J. and Groves, W. B., 1989, 'Community structure and crime: Testing social-disorganization theory', *American Journal of Sociology*, vol. 94, no. 4, pp. 774–802.

Sampson, R. J. and Laub, J. H., 1990, 'Crime and deviance over the life course: The salience of adult social bonds', *American Sociological Review*, vol. 55, pp. 609–627.

Sampson, R. J. and Laub, J. H., 1993, *Crime in the Making: Pathways and Turning Points Through Life*, Harvard University Press, Cambridge, MA.

Sampson, R. J. and Laub, J. H., 1994, 'Urban poverty and the family context of delinquency: A new look at structure and process in a classic study', *Child Development*, vol. 65, pp. 523–540.

Sampson, R. J. and Lauritsen, J. L., 1990, 'Deviant lifestyles, proximity to crime, and the offender-victim link in personal violence', *Journal of Research in Crime and Delinquency*, vol. 27, no. 2, pp. 110–139.

Sampson, R. J. and Lauritsen, J. L., 1994, 'Violent victimization and offending: Individual-, situational-, and community-level risk factors, in *Understanding and Preventing Violence*, vol. 3, *Social Influences*, eds A. J. Reiss Jr and J. A. Roth, National Academy Press, Washington DC, pp. 1–114.

Sampson, R. J., Raudenbusch, S. W. and Earls, F., 1997, 'Neighborhoods and violent crime: A multilevel study of collective efficacy', *Science*, vol. 277, August, pp. 918–924.

Sampson, R. J. and Wilson, W. J., 1995, 'Toward a theory of race, crime, and urban inequality', in *Crime and Inequality*, eds J. Hagan and R. D. Peterson, Stanford University Press, Stanford, CA.

Saunders, P., 1993, 'Economic adjustment and distributional change: Income inequality in Australia in the eighties', Social Policy Research Centre Discussion Paper no. 47, November. University of New South Wales, Sydney.

Saunders, P., Stott, H. and Hobbes, G., 1991, 'Income inequality in Australia and New Zealand: International comparisons and recent trends', *Review of Income and Wealth*, series 37, no. 1, March, pp. 63–79.

Schuerman, L. and Kobrin, S., 1986, 'Community Careers in Crime', in *Communities and Crime*, eds A. J. Reiss Jr and M. Tonry, *Crime and Justice: A Review of Research*, vol. 8, eds M. Tonry and N. Morris, University of Chicago Press, Chicago, IL, pp. 67–100.

Shannon, L. W., 1978, 'A longitudinal study of delinquency and crime', in *Quantitative Studies in Criminology*, ed. C. Welford, Sage, Beverly Hills, CA, pp. 121–146.

Shaw, C. R. and McKay, H. D., 1969, *Juvenile Delinquency and Urban Areas*, University of Chicago Press, Chicago, IL, p. 51.

Sherman, L. W., 1995, 'Hot spots of crime and criminal careers of places', in *Crime and Place*, eds J. E. Eck and D. Weisburd, Crime Prevention Studies, vol. 4, Criminal Justice Press, Monsey, New York and The Police Executive Research Forum, Washington DC.

Sherman, L. W., Gartin, P. R. and Buerger, M. E., 1989, 'Hot spots of predatory crime: Routine activities and the criminology of place', *Criminology*, vol. 27, no. 1, pp. 27–55.

Sherman, L. W., Gottfredson, D., MacKenzie, D., Eck, J., Reuter, P. and Bushway, S., 1997, *Preventing Crime: What Works, What Doesn't, What's Promising*, A Report to the United States Congress, prepared for the National Institute of Justice, Washington DC.

Silbereisen, R. K., Walper, S. and Albrecht, H., 1990, 'Family income loss and economic hardship: Antecedents of adolescents' problem behaviour', in *Economic Stress: Effects on Family Life and Child Development*, New Directions for Child Development, no. 46, eds V. C. McLoyd and C. A. Flanagan, Jossey-Bass, San Francisco, CA, pp. 27–47.

Silburn, S. R., Zubrick, S. R., Garton, A., Gurrin, L., Burton, P., Dalby, R., Carlton, J., Shepherd, C. and Lawrence, D., 1996, *Western Australian Child Health Survey: Family and Community Health*, Australian Bureau of Statistics and the TVW Telethon Institute for Child Health Research, Perth.

Simcha-Fagan, O. and Schwartz, J. E., 1986, 'Neighborhood and delinquency: An assessment of contextual effects', *Criminology*, vol. 24, no. 4, pp. 667–703.

Simons, R. L., Conger, R. D. and Whitbeck, L. B., 1988, 'A multistage social learning model of the influences of family and peers upon adolescent substance abuse', *The Journal of Drug Issues*, vol. 18, no. 3, pp. 293–315.

Simons, R. L. and Robertson, J. F., 1989, 'The impact of parenting factors, deviant peers, and coping style upon adolescent drug use', *Family Relations*, vol. 38, pp. 273–281.

Simons, R. L., Robertson, J. F. and Downs, W. R., 1989, 'The nature of the association between parental rejection and delinquent behavior', *Journal of Youth and Adolescence*, vol. 18, no. 3, pp. 297–310.

Simons, R. L., Whitbeck, L. B., Conger, R. D. and Conger, K. J., 1991, 'Parenting factors, social skills, and value commitments as precursors to school failure, involvement with delinquent peers and delinquent behaviour', *Journal of Youth and Adolescence*, vol. 20, no. 6, pp. 645–664.

Simons, R. L., Wu, C., Conger, R. D. and Lorenz, F. O., 1994, 'Two routes to delinquency: Differences between early and late starters in the impact of parenting and deviant peers', *Criminology*, vol. 32, no. 2, pp. 247–276.

Skogan, W., 1986, 'Fear of crime and neighborhood change', in *Communities and Crime*, eds A. J. Reiss, Jr and M. Tonry, *Crime and Justice: A Review of Research*, vol. 8, eds M. Tonry and N. Morris, University of Chicago Press, Chicago, IL.

Skogan, W. G., 1990, *Disorder and Decline: Crime and the Spiral of Decay in American Neighborhoods*, The Free Press, New York.

Smith, C. and Thornberry, T. P., 1995, 'The relationship between childhood maltreatment and adolescent involvement in delinquency', *Criminology*, vol. 33, no. 4, pp. 451–481.

Smith, D. A. and Brame, R., 1994, 'On the initiation and continuation of delinquency', *Criminology*, vol. 32, no. 4, pp. 607–629.

Smith, D. A., and Jarjoura, G. R., 1988, 'Social structure and criminal victimization', *Journal of Research in Crime and Delinquency*, vol. 25, pp. 27–52.

Smith, D. A. and Jarjoura, G. R., 1989, 'Household characteristics, neighborhood composition and victimization risk', *Social Forces*, vol. 68, no. 2, pp. 621–640.

Smith, D. A., Visher, C. A. and Jarjoura, G. R., 1991, 'Dimensions of delinquency: Exploring the correlates of participation, frequency, and persistence of delinquent behavior', *Journal of Research in Crime and Delinquency*, vol. 28, no. 1, pp. 6–32.

Snyder, J. and Patterson, G., 1987, 'Family interaction and delinquent behavior', in *Handbook of Juvenile Delinquency*, ed. H. C. Quay, John Wiley and Sons, New York, pp. 216–243.

Sorensen, E. and Halpern, A., 1999, *Child Support Enforcement is Working Better Than We Think*, the Urban Institute, http://newfederalism.urban.org/html/anf_31.html

Sorenson, A. M. and Brownfield, D., 1995, 'Adolescent drug use and a general theory of crime: An analysis of a theoretical integration', *Canadian Journal of Criminology*, January, pp. 19–37.

Spearly, J. L. and Lauderdale, M., 1983, 'Community characteristics and ethnicity in the prediction of child maltreatment rates', *Child Abuse and Neglect*, vol. 7, pp. 91–105.

Stahura, J. M. and Sloan, J. J., 1988, 'Urban stratification of places, routine activities and suburban crime rates', *Social Forces*, vol. 66, pp. 1102–1118.

Steinberg, L., 1987, 'Single parents, stepparents, and the susceptibility of adolescents to antisocial peer pressure', *Child Development*, vol. 58, pp. 269–275.

Steuerle, C.E., 1998, *Systematic Thinking About Subsidies for Child Care. Part Three: Applications of Principles*, the Urban Institute, http://www.urban.org/tax/tax21c.html

Sullivan, L., 1997, *Rising Crime in Australia*, Centre for Independent Studies, Policy Monograph 39, Sydney.

The Sun-Herald, 4 Feb. 1996, 'Bored and lodging', p. 29.

Sutherland, E. H. and Cressey, D. R., 1978, *Criminology*, 10th edn, Lippincott, PA.

Sutton, A. and Hazlehurst, K. M., 1996, 'Crime prevention', in *Crime and Justice: An Australian Textbook in Criminology*, ed. K. M. Hazlehurst, LBC Information Services, Sydney.

The Sydney Morning Herald, 21 Nov. 1995, 'The suburb living in fear', p. 11, Sydney.

The Sydney Morning Herald, 16 Dec. 1995, 'Public housing is a foundation of society', Spectrum, p. 2, Sydney.

Tarling, R., 1982, 'Unemployment and Crime', *Home Office Research Bulletin*, no. 14, HMSO, London.

Tarling, R., 1993, *Analyzing Offending: Data, Models and Interpretations*, HMSO, London.

Thornberry, T. P., Lizotte, A. J., Krohn, M. D., Farnworth, M. and Jang, S. J., 1991, 'Testing interactional theory: An examination of reciprocal causal relationships among family, school, and delinquency', Rochester Youth Development Study, *The Journal of Criminal Law and Criminology*, vol. 82, no. 1, pp. 3–33.

Thornberry, T. P., Lizotte, A. J., Krohn, M. D., Farnworth, M. and Jang, S. J., 1994, 'Delinquent peers, beliefs, and delinquent behavior: A longitudinal test of interactional theory', *Criminology*, vol. 34, no. 1, pp. 47–83.

Thorsell, B. and Klemke, L., 1976, 'The labelling process: Reinforcement or deterrent', in *Back on the Street: The Diversion of Juvenile Offenders*, eds R. Carter and M. Klein, Prentice-Hall, New York.

Tittle, C. R., Villemez, W. J. and Smith, D. A., 1978, 'The myth of social class and criminality', *American Sociological Review*, vol. 43, pp. 643–656.

Tomison, A., 1996a, 'Child maltreatment and family structure', National Child Protection Clearing House Discussion Paper, no. 1, Australian Institute of Family Studies, Melbourne.

Tomison, A., 1996b, 'Child maltreatment and substance abuse', National Child Protection Clearing House Discussion Paper, no. 2, Australian Institute of Family Studies, Melbourne.

Tomison, A., 1996c, 'Intergenerational transmission of maltreatment', National Child Protection Clearing House Discussion Paper, no. 6, Australian Institute of Family Studies, Melbourne.

Tracey, P. E., Wolfgang, M. E. and Figlio, R. M., 1990, *Delinquency Careers in Two Birth Cohorts*, Plenum Press, New York.

Tremblay, R. E. and Craig, W. M., 1995, Developmental crime prevention, in *Building a Safer Society: Strategic Approaches to Crime Prevention*, eds M. Tonry and D. P. Farrington, University of Chicago Press, Chicago, IL.

UK Department of Health 1999, Children on Protection Registers, http://www.doh.-gov.uk/sd/tab1_1.xls

US Department of Health and Human Services, Administration for Children, Youth, and Families, Children's Bureau, National Centre on Child Abuse and Neglect 1988, *Study Findings: Study of National Incidence and Prevalence of Child Abuse and Neglect: 1988*, US Department of Health and Human Services, Washington DC.

Vaughn, M. S., 1991, 'The relationship between unemployment and crime in Japan from 1926 to 1988: Trends during Emperor Hirohito's reign', *International Journal of Comparative and Applied Criminal Justice*, vol. 15, no. 2, pp. 153–173.

Vinson, T., Berreen, R. and McArthur, M., 1989, 'Class, surveillance and child abuse', *Impact*, April/May, pp. 19–21.

Visher, C. A. and Roth, J. A., 1986, 'Participation in criminal careers', in *Criminal Careers and Career Criminals*, vol. 1, eds A. Blumstein, J. Cohen, J. A. Roth and C. A. Visher, National Academy Press, Washington DC, pp. 211–291.

Vold, G. B. and Bernard, T. J., 1986, *Theoretical Criminology*, 3rd edn, Oxford University Press, Oxford.

Vondra, J. I., 1986, 'Socioeconomic stress and family functioning in adolescence', in *Troubled Youth, Troubled Families: Understanding Families At-Risk for Adolescent Maltreatment*, eds J. Garbarino, C. J. Schellenbach, J. M. Sebes, Aldine, New York.

Vondra, J. I., 1990, 'Sociological and ecological factors', in *Children at Risk: An Evaluation of Factors Contributing to Child Abuse and Neglect*, eds R. T. Ammerman and M. Hersen, Plenum Press, New York.

Warr, M., 1993a, 'Parents, peers, and delinquency', *Social Forces*, vol. 72, no. 1, pp. 247–264.

Warr M., 1993b, 'Age, peers, and delinquency', *Criminology*, vol. 31. no. 1, pp. 17–40.

Warr, M., 1996, 'Organization and instigation in delinquent groups', *Criminology*, vol. 34, no. 1, pp. 11–37.

Warr, M. and Stafford, M., 1991, 'The influence of delinquent peers: What they think or what they do?', *Criminology*, vol. 29, no. 4, pp. 851–866.

Watters, J., White, G., Parry, R., Caplan, P. and Bates, R., 1986, 'A comparison of child abuse and child neglect', *Canadian Journal of Behavioral Science*, vol. 18, no. 4, pp. 449–459.

Weatherburn, D., 1992, *Economic Adversity and Crime*, Trends and Issues in Crime and Criminal Justice, no. 40, Australian Institute of Criminology, Canberra.

Weatherburn, D. and Lind, B. L., 1997, *Social and Economic Stress, Child Neglect and Juvenile Delinquency*, NSW Bureau of Crime Statistics and Research, Sydney.

Weeks, P., 1988, *The American Indian Experience – A Profile: 1524 to the Present*, Forum, Arlington Heights, IL.

Weintraub, K. J. and Gold, M., 1991, 'Monitoring and delinquency', *Criminal Behavior and Mental Health*, vol. 1, pp. 268–281.

West, D. and Farrington, D., 1977, *The Delinquent Way of Life*, London, Heinemann.

Weston, R., 1986, 'Changes in household income circumstances', in *Settling Up: Property and Income Distribution on Divorce in Australia*, ed. P. McDonald, compiled by the Australian Institute of Family Studies, Prentice-Hall, Sydney.

Weston, R., 1993a, 'Income circumstances of parents and children: A longitudinal view', in *Settling Down: Pathways of Parents After Divorce*, eds K. Funder, M. Harrison and R. Weston, Australian Institute of Family Studies, Melbourne.

Weston, R., 1993, 'A Model of the Effects of the Child Support Scheme', in *Settling Down: Pathways of Parents After Divorce*, eds K. Funder, M. Harrison and R. Weston, Australian Institute of Family Studies, Melbourne.

White, J. L., Moffit, T. E., Earls, F., Robins, L. and Silva, P. A., 1990, 'How early can we tell? Predictors of childhood conduct disorder and adolescent delinquency', *Criminology*, vol. 28, no. 4, pp. 507–528.

Widom, C. S., 1989, 'Child abuse, neglect, and violent criminal behavior', *Criminology*, vol. 27, no. 2, pp. 251–271.

Wilson, H., 1975, 'Juvenile delinquency, parent criminality and social handicap', *British Journal of Criminology*, vol. 15, pp. 241–250.

Wilson, J. Q. and Herrnstein, R. J., 1985, *Crime and Human Nature*, Simon and Schuster, New York.

Wilson, J. Q. and Kelling, G. L., 1982, 'Broken Windows', *The Atlantic Monthly*, March, pp. 29–38.

Wilson, W. J., 1987, *The Truly Disadvantaged: The Inner City, the Underclass, and Public Policy*, University of Chicago Press, Chicago, IL.

Wolfgang, M. E., Figlio, R. M. and Sellin, T., 1972, *Delinquency in a Birth Cohort*, University of Chicago Press, Chicago, IL.

York, G., 1989, *The Dispossessed: Life and Death in Native Canada*, Vintage Books, London.

Yoshikawa, H., 1994, 'Prevention as cumulative protection: Effects of early family support and education on chronic delinquency and its risks', *Psychological Bulletin*, vol. 115, no. 1, pp. 28–54.

Young, G. and Gately, T., 1988, 'Neighborhood impoverishment and child maltreatment', *Journal of Family Issues*, vol. 9, no. 2, pp. 240–254.

Young, L., Baker, J. and Monnone, T., 1989, *Poverty and Child Abuse in the Sydney Metropolitan Area*, NSW Department of Community Services, pp. 1–19.

Zeisel, H., 1982, 'Disagreement over the evaluation of a controlled experiment', *Australian Journal of Sociology*, vol. 88, no. 2, pp. 378–389.

Zingraff, M. T., Leiter, J., Myers, K. A. and Johnsen, M. C., 1993, 'Child maltreatment and youthful problem behavior', *Criminology* vol. 31, no. 2, pp. 173–201.

Zubrick, S. R., Silburn, S. R., Garton, A., Burton, P., Dalby, R., Carlton, J., Shepherd, C. and Lawrence, D., 1995, *Western Australian Child Health Survey: Developing Health and Well-being in the Nineties*, Australian Bureau of Statistics and the Institute for Child Health Research, Perth.

Zuravin, S., 1986, 'Residential density and urban child maltreatment: An aggregate analysis', *Journal of Family Violence*, vol. 1, no. 4, pp. 307–322.

Zuravin, S. J. and DiBlasio, F. A., 1996, 'The correlates of child physical abuse and neglect by adolescent mothers', *Journal of Family Violence*, vol. 11, no. 2, pp. 149–166.

Index